ATLANTA

In the series

Comparative American Cities

edited by Joe T. Darden

ATLANTA

RACE, CLASS,

AND

URBAN EXPANSION

Larry Keating

 Temple University Press
PHILADELPHIA

Temple University Press, Philadelphia 19122
Copyright © 2001 by Temple University
All rights reserved
Published 2001
Printed in the United States of America

⊗ The paper used in this publication meets the requirements of the
American National Standard for Information Sciences—Permanence
of Paper for Printed Library Materials, ANSI Z39.48-1984

Library of Congress Cataloging-in-Publication Data

Keating, Larry, 1942–
    Atlanta : race, class, and urban expansion / Larry Keating.
        p.   cm. — (Comparative American cities)
    Includes bibliographical references and index.
    ISBN 1-56639-820-7 (cloth : alk. paper) — ISBN 1-56639-821-5
    (pbk. : alk. paper)
        1. Atlanta (Ga.)—Economic conditions.   2. Atlanta (Ga.)—Race
    relations.   3. Atlanta (Ga.)—Politics and government.   4. Elite
    (Social sciences)—Georgia—Atlanta.   5. Afro-Americans—
    Georgia—Atlanta.   I. Title.   II. Series.

    HC108.A75 K42 2001
    305.8'009758'231–dc21   00-039281

To Eleanor, Lauren, and Lisa

Contents

List of Maps and Tables

Maps

Tables

Acknowledgments

Many people contributed to the production of this book, and I thank each of you for your help and patience:

Jon Abercrombie	Janet Greenwood
Michael Ames	Stan Harvey
Ron Bayor	Bill Holt
John Berdine	Cynthia Kay
Brad Calvert	Ed Lowe
Jennifer Carmen	Cam Mathis
Alicia Corral	Ethel Mae Matthews
Kelly Cooney	Michele Murff
Max Creighton	Rachel Prioleau
Bill Durlin	Brian Renner
Mike Elliott	David Sjoquist
Gene Fergeson	Charles Starks
Stan Fitterman	Caitlin Waddick
Larry Frank	Columbus Ward
Jeann Greenway	Dana White

Any errors are, of course, mine.

ATLANTA

Introduction

ortuitously poised as a Sun Belt regional center, Atlanta grew
faster than most metropolitan areas over the past twenty-
five years. But the expansion of the economy and the increase in population exacerbated historical class and racial
separations. Income inequality increased, particularly for
African Americans. The end of legal segregation opened economic doors for segments of the black population, but few
blacks entered the upper classes, and poor blacks' relative
economic position deteriorated. The type of work people do
is still largely determined by race and sex. White women
increased their presence in better jobs, and black women
moved into white-collar jobs (though mostly as clerical or
administrative-support workers), but black men lost ground
in terms of better-paying, more prestigious jobs. Black unemployment declined, but the ratio of black-to-white unemployment increased. National research has documented the
increasing bifurcation of income between rich and poor as an
inherent attribute of the American economy. The analyses
of Atlanta in Chapter One will show that the region's exceptional economic development did not ameliorate previous
inequalities; it deepened them.

Increasing inequality weighs more heavily on the African
American population, whose historically restricted living
conditions provide lower starting points. Increasing class
inequality and persistent racial residential segregation,

1

combined with new forms of edge-city suburban development, exclusionary suburban land-use regulations, enduring discriminatory mortgage lending, institutionally segregated real-estate-brokerage systems, and weak fair-housing enforcement, reinforced class and racial separations. Timid regulation of office, commercial, manufacturing, warehousing, and research-and-development facilities resulted in their being located farther and farther from the city in the largely white northern suburbs, leaving the black population south of the old central business district more distant from jobs and commerce. Chapter Two examines how the housing market, real-estate development practices, and local governance exacerbate the negative effects of economic growth.

Examination of local governance will show that business-driven public policy plays an integral role in augmenting the disadvantages of the economy. Where local policy should attempt to rectify the damaging aspects of the economy, it compounds them. In spite of African American electoral ascension, Atlanta business still dominates local politics. That domination has pursued narrowly defined conceptions of public interests, and the resulting development initiatives have frequently undermined both the larger interests of the region and the pursuit of a fairer society. Governance that is responsible to all its citizens requires a firm basis in inclusively defined public interests. Instead of fostering development that enhances the lives of the people who live in Atlanta, public policy focuses on serving non-Atlantans: conventioneers, tourists, national and international sports fans, and new middle- and upper-class residents. The limited focus of Atlanta's successive governing coalitions has produced a series of heavily subsidized development projects that have damaged both local and regional interests. At the same time, extensive political and financial resources and the participation of the mass media have protected these projects from the scrutiny that informed judgment and responsible public planning require. This anti-public-planning ideology is a major part of the basis of the city and the region's incapacity to translate a robustly expanding economy into closing historic gaps.

Chapters Three through Seven examine the history of development and development politics. From the late 1940s to the early '70s, city government was dominated by wealthy, white downtown business leaders.

Throughout most of this period the government depended on the support of a biracial coalition. In the '50s, while William Hartsfield was mayor, and the '60s, while Ivan Allen Jr. was mayor, the white downtown business elite managed to hold on to city hall by maintaining an informal political alliance with the city's middle-class African American political leadership. The white elite supported elements of desegregation and the civil-rights struggle, and expansion of housing for middle-class blacks. In return, black, middle-class political leaders secured the African American vote for Hartsfield and Allen, providing the electoral margin the white elite needed to stay in power. Cooperation between black and white leaders broke down briefly when blacks took control of city hall in the early '70s. But the partnership was quickly revived in a new form. Even though African Americans now controlled city government, black elected officials often cooperated with white business leaders outside government. For the next two decades, black-run city government was a frequent ally of major business interests.

The pursuit of narrowly defined objectives that were damaging to the interests of the broader community characterized the succession of development projects Atlanta's governing coalition promoted. Urban renewal forcibly removed lower-class white and black residents from many neighborhoods surrounding the core of the city, providing neither sufficient relocation payments nor replacement housing. The stadiums, civic centers, university buildings, and middle- and upper-income housing that replaced these neighborhoods were inaccessible to the former residents and provided only modest benefits to most Atlantans. Construction of a multibillion-dollar rapid-rail system might have helped structure land use in environmentally sustainable ways that would have allowed increased mobility, but an insistence on laissez-faire development inverted the role of the system from "growth shaping" to "growth chasing," with a concomitant reduction in public benefits. Restructuring the bus and rail systems to eliminate transit-passenger-based central-city retail establishments deprived the area of the commercial vitality it once had, and neither the heavily subsidized convention center nor an equally heavily subsidized and now defunct entertainment complex has replaced the lost activity. The redevelopment triggered by the Olympic Games initially promised a broader range of community benefits, but reversion to narrow concepts of the public interest severely hurt the poor, insured that the original expectations would not be realized, and converted the public balance sheet from profit to loss.

Preoccupation with this succession of projects meant far less attention and resources for the basics of urban governance. The combined future bill to repair and upgrade water and sewage systems exceeds $2 billion. Closed bridges dot the city. Atlanta has yet to adopt a comprehensive capital-improvements program and budget. Some of the largest costs for the concentration on glamorous but limited development will be paid by future residents.

This business-dominated political coalition was first described and analyzed by Clarence Stone. The biracial partnership has been such a central force in the city's politics and has endured for so long that it has been accurately characterized by Stone as a regime. His analysis of Atlanta politics built on and extended the work of Floyd Hunter, who described the behavior and internal dynamics of Atlanta's white power structure from the late '40s through the mid-'50s.

Stone dissected Atlanta's political decisions to show that the most influential factor in local governance was the ability of a corporate elite to mobilize political and fiscal resources behind specific projects. Omnipotence in a socially non-cohesive and sometimes chaotic world is not attainable, but the capacity to marshal the political and fiscal capital to pursue particular projects is, and it is this capacity that has maintained business' political leadership.

These resources are of two types: rewards and deprivations for individuals, and institutional abilities to mobilize on particular issues.[1] Rewards and deprivations for individuals are both political and personal. Examples are familiar: campaign fund-raising support; introductions to important people; business opportunities, referrals, contacts, and contracts; and myriad forms of immediate and ongoing assistance. Institutional resources that allow mobilization on particular issues compose an extensive list in Atlanta. Central Atlanta Progress, an advocacy group for the central business district, maintains a professional staff of planners, researchers, and specialists in several areas. CAP has periodically organized funding for special-purpose subsidiaries to promote and implement such projects as Park Central Inc.; the organization that fostered the development of the east-side Bedford Pine Urban Renewal Area; and the Centennial Olympic Park Authority, which performed a similar function on the west side of the central business district (CBD). Likewise, the Atlanta Chamber of Commerce maintains a staff of planners, researchers, and specialists. Corporate support funds Research Atlanta, a respected public-policy research operation that recently affiliated with Georgia State University. Integral to this network of analytical and public-opinion-molding organizations are the *Atlanta Journal* and *Atlanta Constitution*, both owned by Cox Enterprises. The two papers unapologetically promote the perspective of the business elite and ignore or marginalize opposing figures and issues.

Supplementing this formidable array of institutions are corporate-controlled philanthropic organizations, such as the Woodruff (Coca-Cola) family of foundations, the Metropolitan Community Foundation, and the Cousins Foundation. An example of the mobilization of these resources is the Atlanta Neighborhood Development Partnership, a foundation-supported "intermediary" between private financing and Atlanta's fledgling nonprofit community-development corporations. At the behest of the Chamber of Commerce, the ANDP recently agreed to be the lead agency implementing the current phase of the business community's long-standing program of developing middle- and upper-income housing around the CBD. This role distorts the organization's primary purpose of fostering the development of lower-income housing, and will exacerbate the damaging effects on low-income people of publicly supported gentrification of central-city neighborhoods.

These institutions support the public policy and development objectives of the business elite more cohesively and effectively than the city's less-well-endowed planning department or any of the much smaller environmental, homeless, community-development, and social-justice advocacy groups. Development of more broadly based, independent, competitive perspectives of public policy is limited by lack of resources. Advocacy groups and individual researchers occasionally capture attention and catalyze action on specific issues, but these are transitory exceptions.

Part of the reason for the absence of more effective countervailing institutions is that Atlanta has very few labor unions, and most of those that exist are weak. For many years, Atlanta's economic-development strategies—like those of the South in general—were predicated on the supply of nonunion, low-wage labor. The legacy of these policies is an undereducated and weakly organized workforce that can marshal few institutional resources in support of public policies.

Although the formerly hegemonic capacity of the business elite to shape public policies and subsidies is still the dominant force in Atlanta politics, Atlanta is no longer the sole focus of local political activity. The surrounding suburbs, containing more than 80 percent of the regional population, enjoy more new economic development, better-funded governments, and political opportunities. Though still cohesive, the networks of corporate executives of Atlanta companies have weakened as the regional economy has internationalized. Ivan Allen Jr.'s office-supply company, from which he ran successfully for mayor in the 1960s, is now part of a national office-supply chain. Consolidation in the banking industry moved the regional financial capital from Atlanta to North Carolina. Both of Atlanta's major department-store chains are now owned by the same national conglomerate, which is based elsewhere. The electric utility is a subsidiary of a regional holding company. The city is still home to some of the wealthiest corporate executives, but many others live in affluent suburbs, their attachments to Atlanta softened not only by their political separation but by the fact that career advancement requires moves from the region. In the absence of new countervailing political institutions, the intricacies of mutually reinforcing business and political networks maintain the form but not all the substance of the public-policy hegemony of past years.

In addition, the power of business elites has been diminished by the regional nature of problems faced by governments. Within the city, neglect of basic infrastructure now requires amelioration that local businesses are not equipped to oversee or provide. The region has a history of narrowly defined premises for planning, leading to crises in mass transportation, highway construction, air quality, water supply, sewage disposal, environmental degradation, and development regulation; all these now require regional and intergovernmental resolution. Business and corporate perspectives are still potent influences on each of these policy areas, but less dominatingly so.

Race, Class, and the Atlanta Economy

etropolitan Atlanta has grown rapidly since the end of World War II. Up until the 1990s, most of this growth occurred in the city's northern suburbs. Underwritten by subsidies for expressways, owner-occupied housing, and schools, this dramatic shift northward was overtly racial at first. Affluent whites moved to the northern suburbs to live at a distance from the city's blacks, whom segregation had concentrated in the near south side. Eventually this northward shift in the city's white population, though still heavily subsidized, became a self-reinforcing trend.

The expansive growth of residential development in the north metro area brought growth in retail and office space as well. In the '70s and '80s, six large shopping malls were built in this northern region, and there was a boom in office-tower construction, primarily along the interstates. Business parks and strip malls soon followed. After four decades of nonstop expansion, the north metro area has become the epitome of modern urban sprawl—a vast expanse of housing tracts and condominium and apartment complexes, with shopping centers, mini-malls, convenience stores, and office parks scattered chaotically across the landscape. The metropolitan area as defined by the Atlanta Regional Commission is shown in Map 1 (p. 9).

The growth of the north metro region has had a profound effect on the city. One of the main consequences has been the dispersal of employment. The northward shift of the metro region's white population and the rapid office, commercial, and retail development in the north metro area have absorbed most of the new growth over the past three decades (see Map 2, p. 10). One measure of this change is the extent to which the central business district's position in the regional office market has declined. In 1966, more than two-thirds of private office space was located in the CBD. In 1997 that figure was one-sixth. Proportionally, the central area's share had declined by 75 percent.

Atlanta's central business district did not lose office space; it actually gained a small amount. But almost all of the new growth was on the north side. Parallel reductions of the city's share of retail, service, manufacturing, and other jobs have intensified racial and class divisions. Many whites do not have to go to the city to work, shop, or play; they can stay in the racially homogeneous north side. The city's blacks, increasingly isolated on the city's south side, find that jobs and stores are moving farther and farther away. Adequate public transportation does not extend to the northern suburbs, so many poor blacks who do not own cars find it difficult to reach jobs in these outlying districts. This is a significant but indeterminate number of people: According to the 1990 Census, 39.2 percent of all black households in Atlanta did not have access to cars.[1]

After fifty years of increasingly segregated growth, Atlanta has become two largely separate cities: a mostly white north side of town, where economic activity is vigorous and expanding, and a mostly black south side, where the economy lags badly. It is true that many blacks have prospered in Atlanta's growing economy, but blacks as a whole are still far behind whites economically. In fact, according to every measure of economic strength, inequality between the city's blacks and whites has actually increased over the past forty years.

Not only are there a white north Atlanta and a mostly black south Atlanta, there are also two black Atlantas. Not only is there growing economic inequality between blacks and whites, there is also growing economic inequality between middle-class blacks and poor blacks. Like many major American cities, Atlanta has a growing black underclass, and

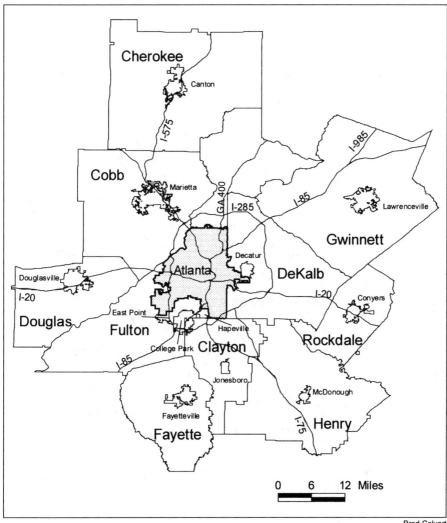

Brad Calvert

Map 1. Atlanta Metropolitan Region

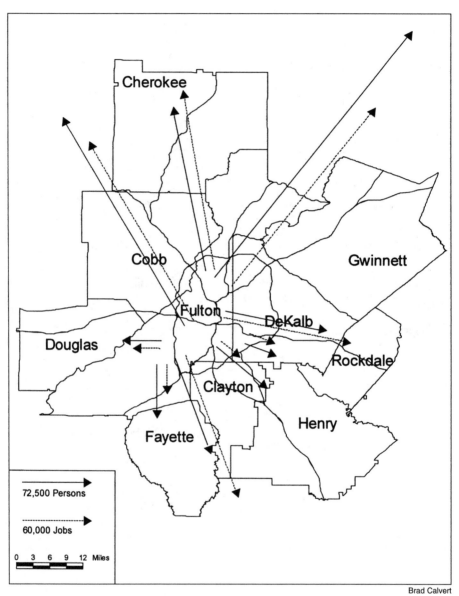

Cherokee

Cobb

Gwinnett

Fulton

DeKalb

Douglas

Rockdale

Clayton

Fayette

Henry

72,500 Persons

60,000 Jobs

0   3   6   9   12 Miles

Map 2.   Directions of Growth, Atlanta Metropolitan Region, 1980–1998

the city suffers from all the problems that attend persistent urban poverty. The standard of living of a sizable minority of the city's blacks is much closer to that of middle-class whites than to that of poor blacks. Race and class fracture the Atlanta community aĩong several different fault lines.

The Regional Economy

Atlanta is the dominant wholesale and retail trade center of the Southeast. The metro area is the regional center for markets in furniture, textiles, and other products, and it is a shipping and distribution center for a wide variety of goods. The metro area has fourteen high-priced regional shopping malls, the most exclusive and expensive of which draw up to 40 percent of their customers from outside the area. Atlanta has also been part of a nationwide expansion in service employment. Service jobs now account for a larger percentage of Atlanta-area jobs than any other employment sector.

Transportation is another major sector of the Atlanta economy. It accounts for a larger proportion of jobs in the Atlanta metro region than in any other metropolitan area in the nation. The city's location makes it a natural transportation hub. Indeed, rail transportation was Atlanta's original raison d'être. After the Cherokee Indians were forced the vacate the northern quarter of Georgia between the 1830s and 1850s, the state built railroads through the Appalachian Mountains to the Tennessee River. Atlanta provided rail connections between the Gulf and Atlantic coastal regions and the Midwest. It remains a substantial rail connection today, and has become a major trucking and air hub as well.

In recent years the Atlanta economy has experienced especially robust growth. Table 1 describes this growth by industry. Between 1980 and 1998, the Atlanta regional economy grew by 906,928 jobs, a rate of increase of 99 percent.[2] Much of this growth occurred in the service sector, which between 1980 and 1998 recorded both the largest absolute increase in jobs of any sector, 283,425, and the second-largest proportional increase, 112 percent (after government employment). In both 1980 and 1998, the service sector was by far the largest sector in the Atlanta economy; in 1998 it accounted for nearly three in ten jobs (29.4 percent).

Table 1.   Number of Jobs by Industry, Atlanta Region,[a] 1980 and 1998

Industry	1980		1998		Number Change 1980–1998	Percentage Change 1980–1998
	Number	Percent	Number	Percent		
Construction	47,108	5.1	88,194	4.8	41,086	87.2
Manufacturing	133,287	14.5	171,732	9.4	38,445	28.8
Transportation and utilities	91,312	10.0	164,725	9.0	73,413	80.4
Wholesale trade	100,739	11.0	165,190	9.1	64,451	64.0
Retail trade	163,092	17.8	329,059	18.0	165,967	101.8
Finance, investment, and real estate	67,734	7.4	128,425	7.0	60,691	89.6
Services	252,990	27.6	536,415	29.4	283,425	112.0
Government[b]	55,092	6.0	225,860	12.4	170,768	310.0
Miscellaneous	5,122	0.6	13,804	0.8	8,682	169.5
Total nongovernment	861,384	94.0	1,597,544	87.6	736,160	85.5
Total	916,476	100.0	1,823,404	100.0	906,928	99.0

[a]Includes Cherokee, Clayton, Cobb, DeKalb, Douglas, Fayette, Fulton, Gwinnett, Henry, and Rockdale counties.
[b]Federal, state, and local.
Source: Georgia Department of Labor, Average Monthly Employment by Year.

Retail employment has grown almost as quickly as service employment, adding 165,967 workers over the eighteen-year period, an increase of 101.8 percent. Retail in 1998 accounted for 18 percent of the jobs in the Atlanta metro region, up slightly from 17.8 percent in 1980.

The transportation and public-utilities sector also showed significant growth during this period. Between 1980 and 1998, it added 73,413 jobs to the area's economy, an 80.4 percent increase. The growth in this sector is due in part to the prominence of the airport—the world's busiest, by some measures—and the area's increasing role as a distribution center for the Southeast.

In 1998, the finance, insurance, and real-estate sector accounted for only 7 percent of the region's employment, down from 7.4 percent in 1980. The total number of jobs in this sector grew by 60,691, an 89.6 percent rate of increase—lower than the 99 percent rate of increase in total jobs. Part of the reason that this sector did not grow at a faster rate is that during this period Atlanta ceased to be the financial capital of the Southeast. National and international consolidation of firms in the finance industry manifested itself in the external acquisition of formerly major local banks, with consequent reductions in employment.

Despite the presence of two automobile plants in the region, manufacturing has never been a major part of Atlanta's economy. In 1980, manufacturing accounted for 14.5 percent of the jobs in the metro area. By 1998 that percentage had dropped considerably, to 9.4 percent. During this period, manufacturing added 38,445 jobs to the regional economy, a growth rate of 28.8 percent. This is by far the lowest growth rate recorded by any sector of the Atlanta economy. The manufacturing sector is relatively small in all Sun Belt cities, partly because in recent years, manufacturing companies throughout the South have been locating new plants outside urban areas to take advantage of lower wage rates. Companies typically locate within fifty to 200 miles of urban centers to retain access to metropolitan markets and distribution networks. In the Atlanta area economy, the manufacturing sector is smaller than it was in other large metropolitan areas in the Sun Belt, such as Los Angeles (20 percent), Dallas–Fort Worth (17 percent), and Houston (17 percent). The smaller size of Atlanta's manufacturing sector is typical of relatively smaller Sun Belt cities such as Tampa–St. Petersburg (10 percent), Phoenix (14 percent), and Miami (8 percent).[3]

By far the largest growth rate experienced by any sector of the Atlanta economy between 1980 and 1998 was that of government. Atlanta is the state capital and one of eight regional headquarters of the federal government, and the surrounding suburban region is home to a plethora of city and county governments. In 1998, government at all levels employed 170,768 people, a 310 percent increase over the 1980 total of 55,092. Government's share of employment over the period more than doubled, from 6 percent in 1980 to 12.4 percent in 1998.[4]

Driven largely by an average annual addition of 50,385 jobs, the region's economy increased by 1,220,159 people over the same period. Table 2 (p. 16) documents the metro area's population growth over the past two decades. As forthcoming sections will show, much of this growth occurred in the northern counties of Gwinnett, Cobb, and Cherokee, and the northern sections of Fulton and DeKalb counties.

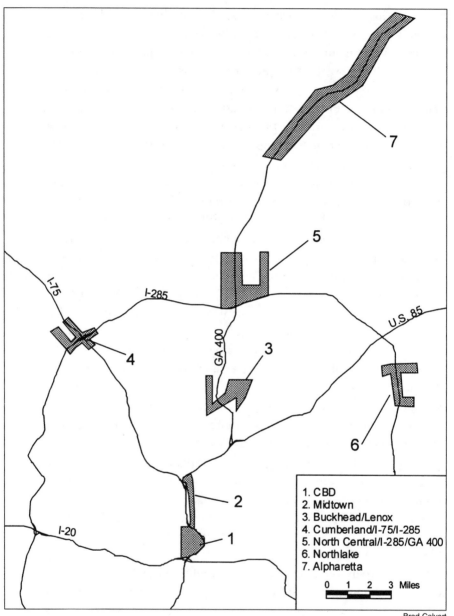

1. CBD
2. Midtown
3. Buckhead/Lenox
4. Cumberland/I-75/I-285
5. North Central/I-285/GA 400
6. Northlake
7. Alpharetta

0 1 2 3 Miles

Brad Calvert

Map 3.   Atlanta Edge Cities

Office and Commercial Development in the North Metro Area

The rapid residential expansion on the city's north side stimulated the subsequent construction of nine large shopping malls throughout this northern region. And this rapid growth of retail space was matched by an equally rapid growth of office space. As the northern suburbs grew, there was extensive, ongoing construction of office buildings throughout the north metro area. Most of this intensive office development occurred around shopping malls; some of it occurred around major highway intersections.

Over the past three decades, the office market in metro Atlanta as a whole has undergone rapid expansion. In 1970 Atlanta had slightly more than 23 million square feet of office space. By the end of 1999 this figure had grown sevenfold, to 161,391,352 square feet.[5] By far the largest portion of this growth has occurred in the city's northern suburbs. Eight of the area's eleven largest office submarkets are in the north metro area: Cumberland, Buckhead/Lenox Square, North Central, Roswell/Alpharetta, Northeast Expressway, I-285/85 Gwinnett, Northlake, and Peachtree Corners. In 1998, these eight major office areas accounted for 72.7 percent of all the Class A and Class B office space in the metro area.[6]

The rapid expansion of economic activity and commercial development in the northern suburbs has cost downtown Atlanta its preeminence as the city's business center. Over the past twenty years, banks, law firms, real-estate developers, stockbrokers, accounting firms, and retail stores have all left the downtown area. The central city's share of retail sales, which includes shopping centers within the city, declined by more than a third between 1982 and 1992, from 20.2 percent to 12.3 percent.[7] In 1966, more than two-thirds of the public, corporate, and private office space in the metro area was located in the CBD; by 1999 less than one-sixth (13.3 percent) was. The higher rents, occupancies, and amounts of higher-quality space commanded by other submarkets are indicative of the diminished esteem in which private businesses hold the CBD. In submarkets with significant amounts of Class A space, the Cumberland, North Central, Buckhead/Lenox, and

Table 2.   Population, Atlanta Region,[a] 1980 and 1998

County	Year 1980	Year 1998	Number Change 1980–1998	Percentage Change 1980–1998
Cherokee	51,699	134,498	82,799	160.2
Clayton	150,357	208,999	58,642	39.0
Cobb	297,718	566,203	268,485	90.2
DeKalb	483,024	593,850	110,826	22.9
Douglas	54,573	89,843	35,270	64.6
Fayette	29,043	88,609	59,566	205.1
Fulton	589,904	739,367	149,463	25.3
Gwinnett	166,903	522,095	355,192	212.8
Henry	36,309	104,667	68,358	188.3
Rockdale	36,747	68,305	31,558	85.9
Total	1,896,277	3,116,436	1,220,159	64.3

[a]Includes Cherokee, Clayton, Cobb, DeKalb, Douglas, Fayette, Fulton, Gwinnett, Henry, and Rockdale counties.
Source: U.S. Census.

Midtown submarkets command both higher Class A rents and occupancies than the central business district. By 1999 the CBD was only the third-largest Class A and Class B office submarket, behind Cumberland and North Central.

The exodus of businesses from the downtown area was marked by two particularly significant departures. One of these was when Rich's Department Stores closed its downtown location on July 13, 1991. To Atlantans, the downtown Rich's was more than just a store; it was a local institution. Although owned by a national department-store conglomerate, the company had been founded by an Atlanta family and had flourished as an integral part of the life of the city. The downtown store had long since ceased to carry the broadest selection of goods, first falling behind the Lenox Square store and eventually trailing all the suburban stores. The closing of the store was a dramatic reminder to Atlantans that the downtown area had lost preeminence as a retail center. Another departure with special meaning came in the same year, when the Citizens and Southern National Bank vacated its downtown office, donating the building to Georgia State University, which is located in the area. It was in this building that Mayor Ivan Allen Jr. had first spoken with Mills Lane, president of the bank, about arranging financing for the city's first major-league baseball stadium. The stadium was pivotal in the attempt to boost the downtown economy, and when the bank that thirty years earlier had tried to reinvigorate the economy departed, Atlantans could not help but recognize the irony.

But the growing dominance of the northern suburbs in private office markets tells only a partial story. To get a complete picture of how the CBD compares with the office districts north of the city, two other categories of property must be considered: owner-occupied space and government-occupied space. Corporate owner-occupied space—primarily Coca-Cola and Georgia Pacific—still has a presence in the CBD. Government is a strong presence in the downtown area, occupying almost 10 million square feet of space. The federal government occupies almost 2.5 million square feet; the state government occupies nearly 4 million; and Fulton County and the City of Atlanta, which have their central offices downtown, occupy approximately 3 million.

When all categories of office space are considered together, the CBD still has the largest concentration in the region—a total of 32.9 million square feet. This is 20.4 percent of regional office space, but only 1.2 million more than in the North Central area, the largest metro-area office center for private leases, and only 9.1 million more than in the Cumberland area, the second-largest. Furthermore, the CBD still has the largest concentration of jobs in the metro region. Due not only to the concentration of multiple kinds of office space but also to the presence of the convention industry, the CBD was the locus of 110,440 jobs in 1998. The northern spine ranked second, third, and fourth, with North Central accounting for 77,494 jobs, Alpharetta/North Point for 66,474, and Buckhead for 60,545.[8]

Even though the CBD is no longer the primary market for higher-quality, privately brokered office leases, it still plays an important role in the economic life of the city. But the trend toward decentralization is clear. Atlanta resembles most large American cities in the growing suburbanization of both its retail and its office space. A common theme in much of the recent literature is that suburban shopping centers and suburban office developments are the centers of new urban forms that have sprung up naturally in response to new living patterns. In the popular press, terms such as "urban villages" and "edge cities" are currently in vogue to describe these autonomous suburban aggregations. Academics have devised more unwieldy terms: "suburban activity centers," "polynucleated cities," "non-monocentric cities."

One of the basic concepts behind these terms is that suburban business districts are physically analogous, or at least comparable, to downtown business districts in being compact nodes, or concentrated centers of interdependent activity. But in Atlanta's north metro area, shopping areas consist of conventional suburban malls separated from surrounding office and commercial areas by a sea of surface parking. Instead of being concentrated centers of activity accessible to pedestrians, the office districts are dispersed and accessible only by automobile. The only one of the eight office developments on the north side that is concentrated and therefore functions something like a true traditional downtown district is the Buckhead/Lenox area. In all the others, office buildings are physically separate, located in long stretches of development along major thoroughfares—expressways, major arterials, or new internal roads. Map 3 (p. 14) illustrates the close proximity of Atlanta's edge cities to major thoroughfares.

The Cumberland district stretches for six miles along two parallel highways, I-75 and U.S. 41. It also includes four and a half miles of development along I-285, the Perimeter Highway, which bisects the other two highways. So the overall district consists of three linear strands of development, with a regional mall surrounded by strip malls off to one side.

The North Central submarket, the largest of these north-metro-area office submarkets, extends a mile and three-quarters along the Perimeter Highway (I-285) and two miles up the Georgia 400 expressway. A few more buildings are scattered along nearby major arterial roads. The area's nearly square shape suggests that it might be a node, an actual community, but it is actually a pattern of linear segments that connect only at their intersections. Automobile traffic is extremely heavy, and there is very little pedestrian traffic between buildings. The regional Perimeter Mall sits at the southwest corner of the square.

The Northeast Expressway district, an 80 percent Class B office submarket, has one of the most pronounced linear forms of all these suburban developments. It stretches for seven and a half miles along both sides of Interstate 85 inside the Perimeter Highway. Composed primarily of office parks and detached single-occupant buildings along expressway frontage roads, this submarket contains only three Class A buildings and 140 Class B structures. Unlike the other suburban office developments, the Northeast Expressway district has attracted very limited office development along intersecting arterial roads. Development remains confined to a long, very narrow strip.

The Northlake district is clustered around Northlake Mall, which lies just inside the Perimeter Highway several miles east of the North Central district. Chaos accurately describes development in this area. It is crisscrossed by four intersecting arterials. Fifty-nine Class B office buildings are interspersed randomly among strip shopping centers, a regional and several subregional malls, discount stores, apartments, jails, and five Class A buildings.

The Roswell/Alpharetta or Georgia 400/North Fulton County submarket is one of the most striking suburban office developments. Built entirely within the past decade, it now totals more than 9 million square feet of space, strung along ten miles of the six-lane Georgia 400 expressway. The expressway splits the residential area, which real-estate professionals refer to as the "favored quarter," the home of "executive housing." Most homes in this area sell for between $440,000 and $760,000.[9]

In spite of its affluent locale, the office buildings reflect cautious capital markets bruised by the late 1980s real-estate recession, during which they were constructed: smaller, cheaper structures, which are less risky than large towers and more likely to attract financing. Buildings are low- to mid-rise, four to seven stories high, and contained within campus-style developments accessed through internal roadways. Bland, windowed exteriors are frequently encircled by landscaped green space.

The North Point regional mall, located two miles from the south end of the submarket, is the largest of the twelve shopping centers scattered throughout the district. The Buckhead/Lenox area is the only aggregation of mixed uses whose form approximates a node. In part because it evolved from the first regional mall located in a previously developed area, but more because the two adjacent malls anchor more than 3.4 million square feet of retail and commercial space[10] serving the most affluent neighborhoods in Georgia, development has attained a density and intensity with some contiguity and centrality. Frequent expansions and rehabilitations of the primary mall have increased its vertical profile to four stories; the constraints of a limited site and the highest demand in the region have dictated decking the parking, one of the consequences of which is that pedestrians can reach the mall from adjacent residential areas.

The affluence of the mall and its market has driven proximate development to include a much broader range of land use than in its more suburban counterparts. Owned and rented high-rise housing is interspersed with increasingly dense street-oriented retail stores, hotels, restaurants, bars, dance clubs, and offices. Stations on two different rail lines and the only bus in the city that operates at six-minute intervals help shoppers who can't or don't want to drive reach the city's largest and most fashionable selection of goods.

In spite of the diversity in land use and patronage, and in spite of the intensity of development immediately around the malls, Buckhead's building density rapidly declines to linear, physically separated, automobile-oriented office buildings interrupted by strip malls and entertainment nodes along the district's multiple arterial roadways. Although Buckhead has the highest concentration of high-rise housing in the city, single-family, detached homes on ample lots predominate.

Given the comparatively low levels of retail and housing units in the old city center, Buckhead has clearly supplanted the CBD as "Atlanta's white downtown." White dominance in Buckhead is obvious; blacks and other racial minorities are present as service workers or patrons, but not as residents. The business of Buckhead is business; there are no government, social, or philanthropic institutions in the area, with the exception of the Atlanta History Center. Regionally, the shift of Atlanta's "center" six miles to the north mirrors the northern expansion of economic and residential activity.[11] One of the most telling points is that the last white mayor of Atlanta, Sam Massell, is known as the (unelected) "mayor" of the relocated and reconstituted white downtown.

With the qualified exception of Buckhead, none of these suburban business districts serves as the center of a true "edge city" or "urban village." Those who use these terms have in mind an urban configuration that promotes interactive living. But the configuration of office districts in the north metro area prevents them from being the centers of coherent communities. Stretched out in long, narrow strips of development along major thoroughfares, they discourage or even prevent walking between buildings. And the heavy traffic filling the thoroughfares makes even short car trips difficult and time-consuming. Workers are largely isolated in their buildings. Two of these office districts, the Northeast Expressway district and the Peachtree Corners district, have no shopping centers. And the basic look of the higher-priced developments does not reflect a spirit of interactive, village-style living. There is a cold, impersonal, almost unfriendly feel to many of them. Many office buildings are sheathed in reflective glass, and hardly any contain street-level shops or restaurants. Most have a forbidding, almost fortress-like appearance.

These outlying office districts could have been the nuclei of coherent, livable communities had they evolved as a planned response to living patterns. Instead, they are the product of unchecked, unregulated, atomistic development. When the exodus of office uses to the suburbs began some thirty years ago, local governments were eager to encourage growth and were therefore unwilling to regulate land use to create the kind of synergy that is essential for livable community spaces. Local governments were also unwilling to regulate development to create the aggregations of uses and densities that would have rationalized a mass-transportation system. Because these outlying office districts comprise office buildings that were designed as autonomous, automobile-dependent structures, they cannot be efficiently served by present forms of mass transit. Buildings are spaced far apart on separate, campus-style developments; having buses stop at each development would result in ridiculously long routes, and since walking between the developments is either dangerous or almost impossible, bus stops at every third or fourth development are no solution.

The metro region's rapid-rail system is an even less effective means of transportation to these districts. In their efforts to make rapid rail acceptable to voters and local governments, business leaders argued that the system would make economic sense if land-use regulations were passed that concentrated high-density development around rail lines and stations. But local governments never passed such regulations, and the result was the opposite: extremely low densities. The Roswell/Alpharetta office submarket spreads less than a fifth as much office space as the CBD over a linear distance seven times as great. Rapid-transit rail lines to the northern suburbs reach out to dispersed strands of development, and stations are miles away from most office buildings.

Northwest and northeast of the city, in Cobb and Gwinnett counties, pro-development, anti-mass-transit, and particularly local governments opposed to the Metropolitan Atlanta Rapid Transit Authority (MARTA) encouraged development with few restraints. In addition, weak state land-use laws limited the reach of proponents' more aggressive regulatory strategies. But due north of the city in Fulton County, where MARTA had been endorsed, with the result that bus service and eventually two rail lines served the area, a different scenario unfolded.

When the first buyout of an entire post-World War II neighborhood for new office development was proposed in the early '80s, Fulton County planners, seeking both to preserve the neighborhood and to protect adjacent neighborhoods, worked diligently with preservation-minded local residents. The planners and the community successfully resisted the entreaties of developers offering inflated prices for Ardmore Forest homes. Two years later, however, the prospect of windfall profits proved too strong, and Ardmore Forest was sold to developers of offices. Planning staff and several county commissioners concluded that developers with checkbooks were stronger than planning principles or community attachments.

But north Fulton County, the eventual site of more than a dozen neighborhood buyouts, retained an active resistance movement. Annual forays by citizens and their elected representatives to the State Legislature with the aim of incorporating much of north Fulton as a city, thereby severing itself from county control of land use and major segments of the budget, failed to convince a majority of the full Fulton County legislative delegation, a prerequisite to favorable action by the Legislature. Within the county government, opposition to city-status for part of north Fulton and effective control of the County Commission remained in the hands of city- and south-Fulton-based commissioners who, as black Democrats, received very few votes in the superficially nonpartisan elections from the almost exclusively white, overwhelmingly Republican north end of the county.

Not only did approving almost every proposal for new development in the north end of the county have insignificant electoral political consequences for City of Atlanta and south-Fulton-based commissioners, it paid political dividends as well. Increases in the county tax base deriving from new development allowed these commissioners to increase politically viable payments to the public hospital, to reward county employees, and to pay for constituent-pleasing projects in their electoral bases. Only when north Fulton developed enough residences to vote in a commission member from their area did the hegemony end. By this time, the early 1990s, it was too late. The volume of office and commercial development had set patterns that will take decades to run their course. Reversing direction was precluded.

Industrial Dispersal

The movement of retail space and prime office space to the northern suburbs has not been the only reason for the continuing decline of the central and the near-south-side area. Industry has also been migrating from the areas around the core, primarily to the suburbs in the north. Industry in Atlanta has always been somewhat decentralized. It started out this way because the city was a rail center, with strings of major delivery/distribution and manufacturing facilities located on railroad lines radiating from the city's center. Recent developments have brought about even more industrial dispersal. With the advent of manufacturing assembly lines in single-story buildings after World War II, and with the shift from railroads to trucks as the major means of transportation, industry began moving to outlying districts. The construction of the interstate highway system in the '50s and '60s accelerated this trend. And recent increases in bay widths and heights have put older, centrally located industrial districts at an even greater disadvantage. Predictably, this shift to suburban areas caused a serious decline in the market for industrial space in and around the downtown area.

Atlanta's largest concentrations of both industrial and warehouse space are on the north side, which has 40.9 percent and 41 percent of the respective markets. The central area has only 14.3 percent of the city's industrial space and 8.6 percent of its warehouse space. Industrial and warehouse areas around the airport and along the Chattahoochee River south of the city account for slightly more than one-third of each market. The highest rents and the fewest vacancies are on the north side. The same holds true for the higher-priced, more prestigious research-and-development space: Nearly two-thirds (65.9 percent) is located on the north side. The central area has only 13.4 percent and the south side only 9 percent.[12]

Commercial Development in the South Metro Region

In most measures of economic strength, the south side of town lags far behind the north. Whereas nine large shopping malls have appeared on the north side, only three have appeared on the south side, one on the Perimeter, serving upper-middle-class black southwest Atlanta, and two on the far south side, serving the relatively smaller suburban white population south of the Atlanta ghetto. The east and west sides have one regional mall each, twelve to fifteen miles beyond the Perimeter Highway. Seven new major office submarkets have appeared on the north side, but the only office concentration on the city's south side is around Hartsfield Airport and in the former railroad towns of Hapeville and College Park. In 1998 this area contained slightly less than 4 million square feet of primarily (57.2 percent) class B space. Greater economic activity in the north than in the south has of course meant greater job growth in the north. In 1970, the north metro area had only 29 percent of the area's jobs; by 1990 the northern suburbs had 52 percent of regional employment. The only area on the south side to gain in employment during this period was around the newly constructed airport.

The disparity in economic growth between the north and south metro areas would have been even greater had it not been for a major redevelopment project in the late '40s and early '50s. In an effort to provide jobs for World War II veterans, Fulton County developed an industrial park next to the Chattahoochee River southwest of the city. The county chose to develop this site for two reasons. First of all, it already owned much of the land. The area consisted of a public-works camp, a prison, and an adjacent farm. Second, choosing this site continued a pattern of industrial land use in the immediate area; there had previously been mills along this section of the Chattahoochee River. The county established a development authority, provided sewer, water, rail, and other infrastructure, and managed the project. The state assisted by constructing Fulton Industrial Boulevard as a primary artery through the area.

The other major source of jobs on the south side is the city's new airport. When Maynard Jackson, the city's first black mayor, was elected in 1973, he was committed to redirecting economic development to the stagnating south metro area. Business leaders were urging that a new airport be built, and they and some airlines wanted a new facility constructed northwest of the city. They argued that this was the best location, since fully 80 percent of the airlines' customer base lived in the north. But Jackson wanted the airport on the south side to help counter the growing economic dominance of the north. The facility would be a $400 million construction project, and once completed would generate 10,000 direct jobs and many more indirect jobs. Jackson was determined to use newly enacted affirmative-action programs to gain construction jobs for black firms and a large portion of airport jobs for other blacks. Since the city managed the airport, Jackson had considerable leverage, and he finally prevailed.

In 1998, the airport area accounted for 55 percent of all industrial square footage in the south metro area. The Fulton Industrial District accounted for nearly 45 percent. Were it not for these two south-side industrial areas, more than 60 percent of the industrial space in the Atlanta region would be in the north.

Distribution of Jobs By Race and Sex

In the Atlanta job market, the distribution of jobs is still largely determined by race and by sex. White men still dominate the best-paying, most prestigious jobs. In recent years, however, the share of the best jobs held by white men has been declining. More and more white women have been entering the job market, and their representation in the best jobs has been increasing. The numbers and proportions of black women in white-collar jobs have also increased, but largely on the bottom (clerical-support) rung. Black men, too, have entered the job market in large numbers, but the percentage of black men holding the best jobs relative to their overall numbers in the workforce has actually been declining, and their proportions in the least desirable service and blue-collar jobs have increased.

The occupational data we will look at in Table 3 are from 1980 and 1990. In 1980, 58.7 percent of all white men in the labor force in the Atlanta metro area held white-collar jobs (the first five types of jobs in the table). By 1990 the figure had increased to 64.5 percent. But while the percentage of white men holding these kinds of jobs was growing, their overall share of such jobs was actually shrinking. In 1980, white men held 42.4 percent of all jobs in the top four categories of white-collar employment. By 1990, they held 38.2 percent of these jobs.

With regard to executive, managerial, and administrative positions, the top category of white-collar jobs, white men dominated. But their share of these jobs declined between 1980 and 1990. In 1980, 64.3 percent of all executive, managerial, and administrative positions in the metro area were held by white men. By 1990, they held only 50.2 percent of these jobs. To look at it another way, in 1980 the percentage of these kinds of jobs held by white men was 1.42 times parity—that is, 1.42 times that of their percentage in the workforce. By 1990 the percentage of white men holding these top jobs had shrunk to 1.26 times parity. Though white men had lost some ground in this top job category, they were still overrepresented in these jobs by 126 percent of their percentage in the workforce.

During this period, the share of white-collar jobs held by white women stayed about the same, decreasing from 41.8 percent in 1980 to 41.2 percent in 1990. At the same time, white women made a slight gain in parity in these jobs, going from 93.8 percent of parity to 95.2 percent. In other words, while the percentage of white-collar jobs held by white women stayed about the same, there was a slight increase in the percentage of white women holding these jobs relative to the overall percentage of white women in the workforce.

In executive, managerial, and administrative jobs, white women did quite well during this period. They went from holding 25.4 percent of these jobs in 1980 to 34.4 percent in 1990. And the overall representation of white women in these jobs also improved. They went from 77.7 percent of parity in these top jobs to 103.3 percent of parity. It should be emphasized, however, that the parity that white women have achieved in this job category does not mean parity in pay. The percentage of all white women in the workforce who have these top jobs has been growing, but the pay they receive for these jobs has not caught up with the pay that white men receive.

White women also did quite well during this period in the professional specialty occupations. Between 1980 and 1990 their share of these types of jobs went from 36.8 percent to 43.6 percent. In 1980 white women were already overrepresented in professional occupations, with a parity of 112.5 percent. The proportion of white women in the workforce with these kinds of jobs kept growing, and by 1990 they were at 130.9 percent of parity. But even though white women are doing especially well in this job category, the data do not show just what this means in terms of income. For instance, the figures don't show how many white female professionals are teachers with modest incomes and how many are lawyers or doctors with six-figure incomes.

In 1990 nearly a third (30.5 percent) of the white female labor force worked in administrative-support or clerical jobs—the lowest-paid, least prestigious white-collar category. This was the largest single category of jobs held by white women. Over one and a half times more white women were employed in these kinds of jobs than in any other kind of white-collar occupation. The proportion of white women in these clerical or secretarial jobs, however, had actually declined since 1980. In 1980 they were at 186.2 percent of parity in these jobs; in 1990 they were at 161.3 percent of parity. What had happened was that white women were replaced by black women. In 1980, white women held 60.9 percent of these jobs and black women held 15.3 percent. By 1990, the share of these jobs held by white women had gone down to 53.7 percent, while the share held by black women had increased to 22.5 percent. Between 1980 and 1990, black women went from 143.2 percent of parity in these jobs to 177.2 percent. In 1990, while

Table 3. 1980 and 1990 Distribution of Occupations by Race and Sex, Atlanta Metropolitan Statistical Area

	1980 Atlanta MSA							
	Black				White			
	Male		Female		Male		Female	
Occupation	Number	Percent	Number	Percent	Number	Percent	Number	Percent
Executive, managerial, and administrative	6,347	6.9	5,871	6.0	76,445	19.6	30,254	10.7
Professional specialty occupations	5,471	5.9	12,275	12.5	49,914	12.8	39,465	14.0
Technicians and related support	1,827	2.0	2,948	3.0	15,493	4.0	8,203	2.9
Sales occupations	4,743	5.1	7,620	7.8	54,463	14.0	37,798	13.4
Administrative-support occupations, including clerical	10,709	11.6	27,732	28.3	32,198	8.3	110,155	39.1
Private household occupations	311	0.3	5,022	5.1	120	0.0	1,220	0.4
Protective service occupations	2,598	2.8	631	0.6	7,409	1.9	1,315	0.5
Service occupations, except protective and household	13,255	14.4	20,409	20.8	18,215	4.7	29,614	10.5
Farming, forestry, and fishing occupations	1,239	1.3	184	0.2	3,368	0.9	847	0.3
Precision production, craft, and repair occupations	13,328	14.5	2,203	2.3	72,972	18.7	5,826	2.1
Machine operators, assemblers, and inspectors	10,291	11.2	8,440	8.6	22,009	5.7	10,964	3.9
Transportation and material-moving occupations	11,035	12.0	857	0.9	19,041	4.9	2,218	0.8
Handlers, equipment cleaners, helpers, and laborers	11,024	12.0	3,717	3.8	17,770	4.6	3,727	1.3
Total	92,178	100.0	97,909	100.0	389,417	100.0	281,606	100.0

Table 3. *Continued*

	1990 Atlanta MSA							
	Black				White			
	Male		Female		Male		Female	
Occupation	Number	Percent	Number	Percent	Number	Percent	Number	Percent
Executive, managerial, and administrative	12,882	7.3	18,665	11.7	10,3201	20.6	70,644	16.9
Professional specialty occupations	9,627	5.4	21,106	13.3	69,844	14.0	77,739	18.6
Technicians and related support	5,055	2.8	6,375	4.0	23,857	4.8	14,752	3.5
Sales occupations	11,506	6.5	18,585	11.7	88,221	17.6	60,059	14.4
Administrative-support occupations, including clerical	18,949	10.7	53,227	33.4	37,459	7.5	127,270	30.5
Private household occupations	208	0.1	3,120	2.0	135	0.0	1,530	0.4
Protective service occupations	6,136	3.5	1,451	0.9	9,143	1.8	1,781	0.4
Service occupations, except protective and household	28,938	16.3	18,061	11.3	23,358	4.7	40,112	9.6
Farming, forestry, and fishing occupations	2,574	1.4	235	0.1	6,540	1.3	1,408	0.3
Precision production, craft, and repair occupations	20,252	11.4	3,844	2.4	79,325	15.9	7,256	1.7
Machine operators, assemblers, and inspectors	11,408	6.4	8,881	5.6	18,273	3.7	8,098	1.9
Transportation and material-moving occupations	16,575	9.3	2,061	1.3	21,748	4.3	3,175	0.8
Handlers, equipment cleaners, helpers, and laborers	33,552	18.9	3,548	2.2	19,159	3.8	3,699	0.9
Total	177,662	100.0	159,159	100.0	500,263	100.0	417,523	100.0

Source: 1980 and 1990 U.S. censuses.

a third of white women worked in these jobs, 45.2 percent of black women did.

Black women made moderate progress in the Atlanta job market during the '80s. Their share of white-collar jobs went from 10.4 percent to 13.9 percent, and they went from 91.2 percent of parity in these jobs to 109.4 percent. They also increased their share of executive, managerial, and administrative jobs, holding 4.9 percent of these jobs in 1980 and 9.1 percent in 1990. And even though black women remained underrepresented in this top category of white-collar employment, their proportion in this category did increase significantly, going from 43 percent of parity to 71.6 percent of parity.

Black men entered Atlanta's job market in large numbers during this period. They increased their presence in the metro-area labor force at nearly twice the rate of white men, white women, or black women. At the same time, however, the proportion of black men who held white-collar jobs declined somewhat, going from 50.5 percent of parity in these kinds of jobs to 47.9 percent. They lost ground in executive, managerial, and administrative positions, their parity in these top jobs shrinking from 49.5 percent in 1980 to 44.4 percent in 1990. The percentage of black men in professional jobs shrank even further, going from 47.7 percent of parity to 38 percent. In the next three categories of white-collar jobs, the proportional representation of black men actually increased. In jobs as technicians and in related support jobs they went from 59.8 percent of parity to 71.1 percent. In sales occupations, they went from 42.1 percent of parity to 45.7 percent. And their presence in administrative-support jobs increased slightly, from 55.1 percent of parity to 56.3 percent. But their increased representation in these three categories of white-collar jobs was outweighed by their declining representation in the top two categories. Between 1980 and 1990, the proportional representation of black men in the combined five categories of white-collar employment decreased by 5.1 percent.

There is no simple explanation for this decline in the representation of black men in white-collar jobs in Atlanta. The increasing number of white women entering the job market is certainly part of the reason. But so are patterns of black migration, changes in other sectors of the economy, and growing disparities between blacks and whites in education.

Another noteworthy feature of black male participation in white-collar jobs is that black women actually hold a larger share of these jobs than black men do. This is true even if we leave out administrative-support jobs, which have traditionally been dominated by women. In 1980, black men held 5.1 percent of the jobs in the top four categories of white-collar employment; black women held 8 percent. In 1990, black men held 6.4 percent of these jobs while black women held 10.6 percent. The problems faced by blacks in general in the white-collar job market are affecting black men more than black women.

One occupational category that underwent dramatic changes during this period in its sexual composition was the service sector, the fastest-growing segment of the metro area's economy. At the start of the decade, service occupations were dominated by women. In 1980 there were 50,023 women in these kinds of jobs, compared with 31,470 men. By 1990, women in service jobs outnumbered men only by 58,173 to 52,296. In 1980, 61.4 percent of these jobs were held by women; by 1990, the share of these jobs held by women had shrunk to 52.7 percent. Between 1980 and 1990, women went from 128.8 percent of parity in service jobs to 107.2 percent. Men went from 76.3 percent of parity to 93.9 percent.

The main reason for the shrinking difference in the representation of men and women in service occupations was that over the course of the decade the number of black men in service jobs increased significantly, eventually surpassing the number of black women working in these jobs. Between 1980 and 1990, the number of black women in service jobs shrank from 20,409 to 18,061, while the number of black men in these jobs more than doubled, from 13,255 to 28,938. In 1980, black women held 25 percent of all service jobs; black men held 16.3 percent. By 1990 the situation had been reversed: Black women held 16.3 percent of service jobs, and black men held 26.2 percent. Black women's parity proportion consequently declined from 219.3 percent to 128.3 percent, and black men's increased from 152.3 percent to 177.5 percent.

Analyzing blue-collar jobs also yields revealing data about Atlanta's black workforce. Because relatively few blue-collar jobs are held by women (black women hold 7 percent of blue-collar jobs and white women hold 8.5 percent), we will analyze the racial composition of just the male blue-collar workers.

During the 1980s, black men were heavily concentrated on this lowest rung of the employment ladder. In 1980, nearly half (49.7 percent) of all black men in the labor force held blue-collar jobs. By 1990, the proportion of black men in these kinds of jobs had shrunk only slightly, to 46 percent. In comparison, the proportion of white men in blue-collar jobs during this period declined from slightly more than one-third (33.9 percent) to 27.7 percent. Black men were heavily over-represented in this job category. In 1980, black men were at 198.1 percent of parity in blue-collar occupations; white men were at 73.9 percent of parity. By 1990, black men were at 221.1 percent of parity, white men at 133.1 percent. Looking at changes in the total job picture for black men between 1980 and 1990, we see that their over-representation in both blue-collar and service occupations was growing, while their relative participation in white-collar occupations was declining.

In both 1980 and 1990, the highest proportion of white men in blue-collar jobs was in the best-paid and highest-skilled category: precision production, craft, and repair occupations. In 1980, 18.7 percent of white men were employed in these kinds of jobs. In 1990 the proportion of white men in jobs of this kind had shrunk to 15.9 percent. In 1980, more than half (55.3 percent) of all white men in blue-collar occupations held the highest-skilled, best-paid jobs. By 1990 this proportion had increased to 57.4 percent. In 1980 the lowest proportion of white men employed in blue-collar jobs was in the lowest-paid, least-skilled occupations. In 1980 only 4.6 percent of white men were employed as handlers, equipment cleaners, helpers, or laborers. By 1990, only 3.8 percent were employed in jobs of this sort.

In 1980 the second-highest concentration of black men in blue-collar jobs was in the best-paid, highest-skilled occupations; 14.1 percent of black men were employed in precision production, craft, and repair jobs. By 1990 the proportion of black men in these kinds of jobs had increased to 18.3 percent, but during the same period a growing percentage of black men moved into the lowest-paid, least-skilled blue-collar jobs. In 1980, 12 percent of black men were employed as handlers, equipment cleaners, helpers, or laborers. By 1990 the proportion of black men in these occupations had grown to 18.9 percent, slightly more than the percentage of black men at the top of the blue-collar hierarchy. This growing concentration of black men on the lowest level of blue-collar occupations was caused by a combination of factors: racial discrimination, expanded participation of black men in the labor force, the low-level skills of many of the black men entering the job market, and the lock that white men still have on the best-paying, highest-skilled blue-collar occupations.

When it comes to low-paying, low-prestige jobs, one occupational category deserves special mention. Table 3 lists one job category as "private household occupations." Most of these jobs are as domestic help or maids—vanishing vestiges of slavery. In 1980, 75.2 percent of these jobs were held by black women. By 1990, the proportion of such jobs held by black women had dropped to 62.5 percent, and the proportion of black women in the labor force working as maids had dropped from 5.1 percent to 2 percent. But even though fewer and fewer black women work as domestic servants, MARTA still operates several weekday morning and late afternoon "maids' buses," whose routes go past white-owned mansions on the north side.

Unemployment

In the Atlanta-area economy during the 1980s, not only was race a factor in job distribution, it was also a factor in unemployment rates. While white unemployment decreased during the decade, black unemployment increased. We will analyze here the unemployment data for both the city itself and the metro region.

In the city proper, white male unemployment decreased from 4.2 percent in 1980 to 3.6 percent in 1990 (Table 4). White female unemployment declined slightly, from 3.9 percent to 3.8 percent. In 1980, 10.9 percent of the black male labor force was unemployed; by 1990 the figure had risen to 13.4 percent, a 22.9 percent increase. For black women during this period, unemployment increased from 10.2 percent to 12 percent, a 17.6 percent rise. In relative terms in 1980, more than two and a half times as many blacks as whites, male and female, were unemployed (Table 5). By 1990 the ratio had risen to more than 3-to-1. In 1990, the black male unemployment rate was 3.7 times the white

Table 4.   Atlanta and Regional Unemployment Rates (Percent), 1980 and 1990

	1980		1990		Percentage Change	
Race by Sex	City of Atlanta	Atlanta MSA	City of Atlanta	Atlanta MSA	City of Atlanta	Atlanta MSA
Black men	10.9	9.5	13.4	11.1	22.9	16.8
White men	4.2	3.2	3.6	3.4	−14.2	6.3
Black women	10.2	9.3	12.0	9.3	17.6	0.0
White women	3.9	3.9	3.8	3.9	−2.6	0.0

Source: 1980 and 1990 U.S. censuses.

male rate, a 42.3 percent increase from 1980, and black women's unemployment was 3.2 times as high as that of white women.

In the region as a whole, the change was only moderately different. White male employment increased slightly, from 3.2 percent in 1980 to 3.4 percent in 1990. Black male unemployment increased by one-sixth, from 9.5 percent to 11.1 percent. White female unemployment remained stable at 3.9 percent. Black female unemployment also remained stable, but at the much higher rate of 9.3 percent. For men, the ratio of black to white unemployment increased by 10 percent, from 3 percent to 3.3 percent. For women, the ratio remained the same, with 2.4 times as many blacks as whites unemployed.

The movement of jobs away from black Atlanta neighborhoods to the predominately white northern suburbs has almost certainly been part of the reason for the growth of the overall black unemployment rate. In 1968, John Kain did the first analysis of the geography of race and employment and the effect of these factors on black employment. Kain found that in Detroit and Chicago, both residential segregation and the suburbanization of jobs aggravated black unemployment.[13] There has been extensive research on this subject, now called spatial mismatch research, since Kain's study, and there have been conflicting analyses. But the most recent authoritative research done on the subject has concluded that the preponderance of the evidence showed that spatial mismatch has a significant effect on black employment and earnings.[14] Keith Ihlanfeldt and David Sjoquist followed their review of the research with the observation that a combination of factors work to keep blacks from obtaining suburban jobs. Beyond

Table 5.   Atlanta and Regional Ratio of Black to White Unemployment

Sex	1980 City of Atlanta	1980 Atlanta MSA	1990 City of Atlanta	1990 Atlanta MSA	Percentage Change City of Atlanta	Percentage Change Atlanta MSA
Men	2.6	3.0	3.7	3.3	42.3	10.0
Women	2.6	2.4	3.2	2.4	23.1	0.0

Source: 1980 and 1990 U.S. censuses.

residential segregation and the suburbanization of jobs, which the research documents, Ihlanfeldt and Sjoquist argue that the evidence suggests "an absence of information on suburban job opportunities, a reluctance to search in white areas for fear of not being socially accepted, greater hiring discrimination against blacks in suburban areas, and the inability to commute from the inner city to suburban employment centers via public transit."[15]

Prescriptions for policy range from increasing mobility and accessibility in the short term to redeveloping inner-city economies and desegregating suburbs. Over the long term, action on all three fronts is required, for it is clear that continuing involuntary racial segregation and the suburbanization of employment extract substantial economic costs from the people least able to afford them.

Participation Rates

Unemployment rates present only a partial picture of the percentages of people actually working. They do not include people who have become discouraged and stopped looking for work, people who devote their time to child-rearing or homemaking, people who are institutionalized, or people who earn their livelihoods from the underground economy. To supplement employment data and to take into account all the people who fall into these categories, labor-force participation rates are used. They count all people over sixteen years old. Like the unemployment rates we have analyzed, the labor-force participation rates in Table 6 are based on data from 1980 and 1990, and include both Atlanta itself and the larger metro area.

Table 6.   Atlanta and Regional Labor-Force Participation Rates (Percent), 1980 and 1990

Race and Sex by Participation Rate	1980		1990		Percentage Change	
	City of Atlanta	Atlanta MSA	City of Atlanta	Atlanta MSA	City of Atlanta	Atlanta MSA
Black civilian labor force participation rate						
Total	58.0	63.9	59.6	71.8	2.8	12.4
Female	53.0	59.1	56.0	68.9	5.7	16.6
Male	64.0	69.8	64.2	74.5	30.0	6.7
White civilian labor force participation rate						
Total	59.7	68.6	67.9	73.0	13.7	6.4
Female	48.7	56.2	57.8	64.4	18.7	14.6
Male	71.2	81.5	76.0	82.2	6.7	0.9

In both 1980 and 1990, participation rates were higher for white men than for black men. In 1980 in the city proper, the white male participation rate was 71.2 percent, while the black male participation rate was 64 percent. By 1990, the rate for white men had increased to 76 percent, but the rate for black men had increased only marginally, to 64.2 percent. In 1980 in the metro area as a whole, the participation rate for white men was 81.5 percent, and the rate for black men was 69.8 percent. By 1990 the rate for white men had increased to 82.2 percent, and the rate for black men to 74.5 percent—a higher increase than in the city but still 9.4 percent less than the increase for white men. The lower participation rates for black men throughout the decade, particularly in the city, can be accounted for by a greater proportion of discouraged workers, substantially higher rates of incarceration, and greater participation in the underground economy.

Participation rates for women, notably white women in the city, also increased. In 1980 the participation rate for white women was 48.7 percent. By 1990 it had grown to 57.8 percent, an 18.7 percent increase. During the same period, the participation rate for black women in the city started out at 53 percent, higher than for white women, but the rate grew more slowly, and by 1990 it was at 56 percent, lower than the rate for white women.[16] This rapid growth of labor-force participation by white women had several causes: the growth of two-income households in the white population, large numbers of younger white women moving to the city, and an increase in the number of white households dependent on a single female worker.

The same pattern did not hold for the larger region. The participation rate for black women was higher to start with (59.1 percent against 56.2 percent for white women), and it remained higher, increasing by 16.6 percent to a level of 68.9 percent. White women's participation rate also increased substantially—by 14.6 percent—but at 64.4 percent in 1990 it remained lower than that of black women.

Race, Sex, Marital Status, and Income

One of the most revealing ways of analyzing the Atlanta area's economy is to examine the distribution of income by race, sex, and household composition. Table 7 presents household income data for 1980 and 1990, categorized by race and household makeup. Data are from both the city and the five core counties in the Atlanta region.

The data show that in 1980, white, married-couple households earned 1.59 times the income of black, married-couple households in the city proper and 1.47 times that of black, married-couple households in the five-county metro region. By 1990 the ratio had increased substantially in the city, to 2.24, but had narrowed slightly in the region, to 1.44. The primary cause of the lessening racial gap in incomes in the metro area as a whole and the increasing racial gap in incomes in the city was that affluent blacks as well as whites were moving to the suburbs, leaving behind in the city a growing concentration of black poverty.

In 1980 there were wider racial gaps in income between households headed by women than between married-couple households. In the city, households headed by white women earned 2.31 times as much as households headed by black women. The regional figure was 1.87. Over the next ten years the gap narrowed somewhat. The ratio by 1990 was 2.17 in the city and 1.73 for the region. Major parts of the explanation are continued wage discrimination on the bases of race and sex; higher birth rates by younger single women, particularly in the city; and overall

Table 7.   Inequality in Household Income by Race and Family Type, Atlanta Region and City of Atlanta, 1980 and 1990

| | Median Household Income by Year | | | |
| | City of Atlanta | | Atlanta Region | |
Race and Family Type	1980	1990	1980	1990
White				
Married couple	$26,328	$73,577	$27,488	$55,498
Female head	$14,027	$30,594	$14,397	$30,391
Black				
Married couple	$16,521	$32,882	$18,713	$38,614
Female head	$6,064	$14,057	$7,709	$17,587
White-to-Black ratio				
Married couple	1.59	2.24	1.47	1.44
Female head	2.31	2.17	1.87	1.73

Source: Calculated from U.S. Bureau of Census Public Use Micro Sample Areas 2002, 2003, and 2004, which closely approximate but do not exactly correspond to city of Atlanta borders. Atlanta Region consists of Fulton, DeKalb, Cobb, Gwinnett, and Clayton counties.

American wage stagnation, which has led to a decreasing capacity of households supported by single wage earners (particularly female and especially black female wage earners) to earn sufficient incomes. Other factors include inferior primary and secondary schools, class discrimination in access to higher education, and public policies that emphasize subsidies to employers and deemphasize full employment.

Income Inequality

In 1987, David Smith, an English geographer, published a study of economic inequalities between blacks and whites in Atlanta, covering the period between 1960 and 1980.[17] Among the measures of economic status that Smith looked at was median family income by census tract. Table 8 presents the figures for median incomes derived by Smith and expands the scope of Smith's study by adding data from the 1950 and 1990 censuses. The table shows that blacks in Atlanta began this forty-year period with significantly less income than whites, and that the inequality has grown substantially since then. In 1950, the mean value

of median family income for predominantly white census tracts in
Atlanta was just over twice the figure for black census tracts. The gap
expanded to 2.66 by 1960, but then contracted to 2.13 in 1970. The
1970s and '80s saw significant increases in income inequality between
the races. The ratio increased by 56.8 percent to 3.34 in 1980, and by
an additional 58.1 percent to 5.28 in 1990. By 1990, the income inequality between whites and blacks was more than two and a half times
(261.4 percent) what it had been in 1950.

Smith also found growing income inequality within the black population. He used a statistical tool called a coefficient of variation to measure the degree of growth in income equality or inequality within the
white and black populations.[18] Table 8 presents the coefficients of variation for the period studied by Smith, and adds the coefficients of variation for 1990 and 1950. The larger the coefficient, the larger the degree
of inequality. The data show that the coefficient of variation for white
incomes went from 32.83 in 1950 to 48.21 in 1970, a 46.84 percent
increase. Between 1970 and 1990, however, the coefficient shrank to
33.69, only slightly higher than in 1950, meaning that by 1990 income
inequality among whites was about the same as it had been forty years
earlier. For the black population, on the other hand, there was a steady
trend of growing income inequality over this forty-year period. Income
inequality was initially much less for the black population, largely
because incomes were generally low and very few black families had

Table 8.   Inequality in Family Income Between Predominantly Black and
White Atlanta Census Tracts, 1950 to 1990

| Year | Median Family Income | | | Degree of Inequality (Coefficient of Variation) | |
	White	Black	Ratio	White	Black
1950	$3,007	$1,491	2.02	32.83	15.41
1960	$6,380	$2,396	2.66	47.93	23.83
1970	$12,146	$5,710	2.13	48.21	29.24
1980	$31,612	$9,473	3.34	38.49	49.08
1990	$88,029	$16,667	5.28	33.69	57.4

Sources: 1950, 1990, calculations by author; 1960–1980, David M. Smith, *Geography, Inequality, and Society* (Cambridge: Cambridge University Press, 1987).

high incomes. The coefficient of variation for median black-family income increased from 15.41 in 1950 to 49.08 in 1980 and 57.40 in 1990. By 1990 the coefficient of variation for black incomes was 3.72 times as high as it had been in 1950, and it was substantially higher than the figure for the white population.

Analyzing income data reveals two important facts. First, even though white and black Atlantans have made economic progress over the past forty years, whites as a group have made much more progress than blacks have. Second, even though more and more blacks have moved into well-paid jobs, many have been left behind. Over the past four decades, black Atlanta has become increasingly divided economically into two separate communities.

Part of the explanation is that the city has become home to the wealthiest concentration of white people in the state. Fewer poor whites remain in Atlanta, for several reasons: Some have left to escape the expanding black ghetto; others have been pushed out by land-use regulations limiting inexpensive housing, and others have chased jobs to the periphery of the region, where they can live more stably and cheaply. To be sure, some poor white people remain in Atlanta, but the predominant white groups in the city are the very wealthy and the middle classes, often but not always gentrifiers.

The increasing inequality among blacks is first a reflection of the fact that some segments of the black population have begun to earn middle- and upper-class incomes. Many factors help to explain the advance of segments of the black population: the civil-rights movement; a damping down and in some cases an elimination of the most overt and insidious forms of segregation; transitory attempts to correct long-standing racial inequities in public education; affirmative action; a partial correlation between political power and economic advancement; and the robust expansion of an economy that itself produces inequities as well as growth. But the data also clearly show that inequality within the black population exceeded white inequality by 1980 and by 1990 was 1.7 times as great. The combination of one of the most consistently expansionary local economies in the country and black political ascension has not been sufficient to even ameliorate the pervasive poverty that underlies these data.

Race, Class, and the
Atlanta Housing Market

tlanta enjoys a progressive image as a city with fairly benign race relations. After the white primary was declared illegal by the courts in 1946, Mayor William Hartsfield maintained close contact with established black leaders and accommodated some black requests for reform, most notably accepting black voter registration and hiring a small number of black police.[1] In the '60s, Mayor Ivan Allen Jr. continued to maintain close contact with the city's black leaders, and he eventually supported significant portions of the civil-rights movement and school desegregation. Indeed, Atlanta was an administrative center of the black struggle for equal rights during the 1960s. It was from Atlanta's Ebenezer Baptist Church that Martin Luther King Jr. led the Southern Christian Leadership Conference. Because of King and the movement's enduring influence, and because of the willingness of the city's white leadership to accommodate some black interests, there has been a somewhat more civilized tone to race relations in Atlanta than in many other cities.

But beneath this surface civility harsh facts prevail. The evidence presented in Chapter Two makes it clear that race still determines to a great extent what kinds of jobs blacks get, and it further shows that the economic gap between whites and blacks is actually widening. In this chapter we'll

41

look at the way in which race has affected the Atlanta housing market. If we look at the city's history and at current data, we find that racial discrimination has been a major factor in determining where African Americans live, the opportunities they have to own their own homes, and the quality of their housing. When it comes to residential living patterns, Atlanta is one of the most segregated cities in the country. Furthermore, racial inequalities in housing have widened over the past fifty years. This is due in part, of course, to inequality in incomes. But lending institutions, the real-estate industry, and local government have all been active in various ways in promoting this inequality.

Residential Segregation

The degree of racial segregation and integration in a geographic area can be measured with a dissimilarity index. This is a tool used by demographers and sociologists to describe the distribution of different groups within a geographic area. This distribution is expressed as a ratio. The ratio is 1.0 if groups in an area are completely separated geographically; if groups are distributed throughout an area in exactly the same proportions as the overall proportions of the groups living in the area, the ratio is 0.[2]

Table 9 (p. 44) shows a series of dissimilarity indexes measuring racial segregation in Atlanta between 1940 and 1990. Between 1940 and 1960, levels of segregation increased in both the city and the metro area. Between 1960 and 1980, however, levels of segregation decreased. Between 1980 and 1990, depending on the frame of reference one uses,[3] levels increased slightly in the city but continued to decrease in the metro area as a whole. The overall trend over the fifty years is that segregation has decreased slightly in the city but has increased in the metro area.

In 1970, the dissimilarity index for the city was .801; for the metro area it was .834. Each of these figures was higher than the 1970 national average of .792. In 1980, the index was .753 for the city and .765 for the metro area—again higher than the national average, which was .694.[4] In 1980, eleven metropolitan areas in the country were more segregated than Atlanta,[5] but Atlanta was more segregated than any of the six other

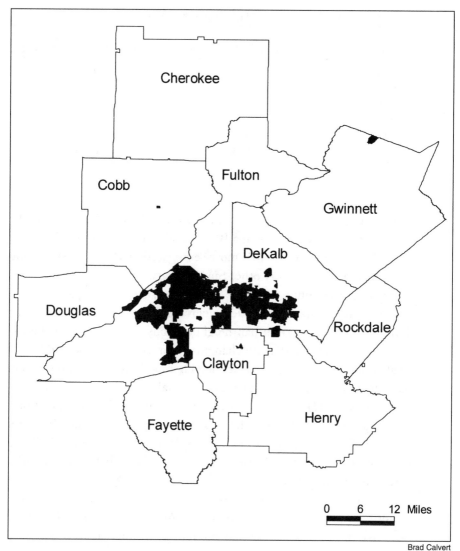

Cherokee

Cobb

Fulton

Gwinnett

DeKalb

Douglas

Rockdale

Clayton

Fayette

Henry

0   6   12 Miles

Brad Calvert

Map 4.   Census Block Groups More Than 80 Percent Black, Atlanta Metropolitan
Region, 1990

Table 9.   Residential Dissimilarity of Blacks and Whites, 1940 to 1990

Year	City of Atlanta (Consistent 1940 Boundaries)	Atlanta Metropolitan Area (Consistent 1940 Boundaries)
1940	0.809	0.695
1950	0.819	0.734
1960	0.828	0.838
1970	0.801	0.834
1980	0.753	0.765
1990	0.756	0.746

Calculations by author.

large metropolitan areas in the South: Birmingham, Miami, Nashville, New Orleans, Norfolk–Virginia Beach, and Tampa–St. Petersburg.[6] In 1990 the city was the fourth-most-segregated city in the nation and more segregated than any other Sun Belt city.[7]

There are currently only one or two truly stable integrated neighborhoods in Atlanta. The modest degree of integration that does exist derives mainly from suburban neighborhoods at the edges of the expanding black ghetto that are changing from white to black, and from a smaller number of gentrifying city neighborhoods that are changing from black to white. For the most part, residential integration is only temporary. Map 4 (p. 43) depicts the areas of concentrated black population.

It could be that this high level of racial separation came about not because of overt discrimination but simply because blacks prefer living with blacks. But national research does not show that this is a widespread urge. Research has shown fairly consistently that a majority of blacks prefer racially integrated neighborhoods, so long as a substantial minority of the integrated community is African American.[8] So it must be active discrimination that has brought about this highly segregated pattern of living in Atlanta.

Eliminating Black Residential Clusters

One important way in which a high degree of segregation was achieved in Atlanta was the elimination of black residential clusters in white areas of the city. There used to be a number of these clusters in the northern part of the city, but all but a few have now vanished. Very lit-tle is known about most of these isolated pockets of African American population, since historical research has been done on only a small num-ber of them. But if one compares census surveys of 1940 and 1960, one discovers that at least fifteen such clusters were either partly or com-pletely eliminated during this period.

City government played a central role in eliminating several of these clusters. One example is how it undermined the Blandtown commu-nity. Blandtown is a small, predominantly African American neighbor-hood located on the primarily white northwest side of the city. It sits just below the crest of one of the highest hills in the city, which com-mands exceptional views of downtown, the Peachtree Street ridge to the east, the Georgia Institute of Technology to the south, and the heavily wooded residential areas below it.

Before the Civil War and the end of slavery, the land upon which Blandtown is located was owned by a white woman, Mrs. Viney Bland. When slavery was officially ended, Mrs. Bland willed the land to one of her former slaves, Felix Bland, who had taken his former owner's sur-name and had attended Tuskegee Institute in Alabama at her expense. In the 1870s, Mr. Bland had the property taken from him by the local government for nonpayment of taxes, and land agents acquired the property. In the 1880s a man named Bob Booth obtained title to the land and partially developed it as a residential area. In the following decade, Seaboard Railroad constructed several rail spurs from its main line to an area just west of the neighborhood, where the hills begin their descent to the Chattahoochee River, three and a half miles farther to the northwest. Soon after that, a mill, a fertilizer factory, and a stock-yard opened in the area.

Blandtown was in one of Atlanta's first industrial areas. Because jobs were available there, and because transportation for poor blacks from other areas was not available, Blandtown continued to develop as a res-idential area for black workers. It became an established community, with a school, four churches, a public health clinic, and several small businesses: a bar, a barbershop, and a dime store.[9]

Now we move forward half a century. In its 1952 "Plan of Improve-ment," fast-growing Atlanta expanded its boundaries by annexing several north-side residential, commercial, and industrial areas from Fulton County. One of the primary objectives of this expansion was to dilute the voting power of the city's growing African American population so that whites could continue to control city government.[10] Blandtown was included in this annexation. Four years later, the city council ignored the residential character of the area and rezoned the neighborhood from its R-4 category, Small Single Family Residential, to the I-2 category, Heavy Industry. Apparently this was done without any discussions with the residents. All of Fulton County's previous zoning designations for the annexed areas had been subjected to review, but none of the older, long-term residents of Blandtown can recall any consultations with the neighborhood before the 1956 rezoning. Soon afterward, the Georgia Department of Transportation classified Blandtown's four main streets as Truck Routes, allowing semitrailer trucks to pass through the neighborhood in any direction.[11]

Industrial zoning constituted a death sentence for Blandtown. The Atlanta zoning ordinance stipulates that residences in industrially zoned areas may not be repaired if damage exceeds half of the property's value. New residential construction is prohibited, city and federal housing programs that could be used to rehabilitate deteriorating structures are banned, and financial institutions refuse to even consider making mortgage loans in these areas.

The zoning change for Blandtown had predictable consequences. In 1960 the community had 370 residents, most of them black. There were eighty-four housing units. Between 1960 and 1990, the neighborhood's population declined by 71.9 percent. The number of households shrank from eighty-four to forty-four, a 47.6 percent decrease. Twenty-five homes were demolished in this period, and fourteen of the fifty-nine housing units remaining were vacant. The decline in population, housing, and households occurred almost wholly within the rental sector. The number of owned homes dropped from thirty in 1960 to twenty-five in 1990, while occupied rental units declined from fifty-two to nineteen.[12]

People in the neighborhood eventually began to understand the changes in government policy that were gradually destroying their community. In the late 1980s, Blandtown's remaining residents began to push for relief from these destructive policies. They sought residential zoning, eligibility for government programs, and access to mortgage finance. They were assisted in this fight by their city councilwoman, Clair Mueller, a white woman and a veteran of north-side highway fights.

Industrialists in the area, led by the Nottingham Chemical Company, which was adjacent to the neighborhood, fought the residents at every step. They tried to mislead the community about the previous existence of residential zoning, claiming that the area had always been zoned Heavy Industry. They formed a separate neighborhood organization with themselves as officers, then presented themselves publicly as "the neighborhood." They tried, sometimes successfully, to intimidate the residents by telling them that their property would decline in value if residential zoning were obtained.[13] They hired lawyers and planning consultants to attack and try to discredit the residents' positions. And finally, in their most cynical move, they created a nonfunctioning charitable foundation, supposedly designed to aid residents in need. This foundation existed only on paper and never dispensed any money to anyone.

In 1991, the city revised its Comprehensive Development Plan. As part of this overall plan, the residents and Clair Mueller managed to get Blandtown designated a low-density residential area. But the other side intervened at this point and blocked the next step, which would have been the actual rezoning. The issue was legislatively stalemated for nearly a year while it was studied by both the Community Design Center of Atlanta and the city's Bureau of Planning. Both groups eventually recommended changing the zoning to reflect residential land use, a change that would have opened up the area to city programs, given it access to finance, and ended the prohibition against repair and possible redevelopment. But the Zoning Review Board was not convinced. Facing Nottingham Chemical's legal and technical experts and the same set of arguments for a second time, the board again refused to reinstitute residential zoning. Blandtown retained its designation as a low-density residential area on the land-use map of the Comprehensive Development Plan, but it was never actually rezoned for residential use.

Another example of city government eliminating black residences was the "back-alley dwelling law" of 1955. This law was aimed at eliminating an unknown but large number of homes along alleyways in affluent white areas of the city. These were largely inhabited by blacks. They had originally been constructed as quarters for domestic workers, and since domestic work continued for a long time to be a primary source of employment for African Americans, the houses and their occupants had endured. What prompted passage of this law were a series of school-desegregation lawsuits preceding *Brown v. Board of Education* that made it clear that school desegregation was very likely to occur.

Empirical observations imprecisely document the pattern. For example, in 1940, in an area bounded by Peachtree Street on the west, Briarcliff Road on the east, North Avenue on the south, and Fourteenth Street on the north, there were 267 city blocks. In this predominantly white residential district, more than half of the blocks (54.7 percent) had some black residents. Forty-two blocks had a black population of between 10 percent and 49 percent, while 104 blocks had some blacks but fewer than 10 percent. Most of the residences occupied by blacks in these integrated areas of the city were homes accessible from mid-block alleys.

The back-alley dwelling law used the same types of restrictions and prohibitions on repair and improvements as the zoning law had imposed on Blandtown. The law, coupled with the closing of most of the alleys, eventually eliminated most of these dwellings, and the area is now almost entirely white. Improving housing quality was the ostensible reason for eliminating these dwellings, but it was obvious that a major consequence would be the segregation of a previously integrated area.

Local government has also used outright public condemnation of property to eliminate black clusters. We see this in the case of Macedonia Park in Buckhead, an area just north of the city limits before the 1952 annexation. Macedonia Park was a black subdivision that had been developed as a sixty-acre residential area in 1921. Modest homes were constructed on small, narrow lots bordering a creek. These housed working-class African Americans who tilled the nearby farms, worked in the village of Irbyville (later Buckhead), and performed domestic service in the white-owned houses scattered around the village.

In the 1930s and '40s the white Garden Hills subdivision developed to the south and west of the Macedonia Park neighborhood. Once they were established in the area, white residents sought to force African Americans out and convert their community into a whites-only park and ancillary uses. Between 1945 and 1953, Fulton County purchased all of the homes in Macedonia Park, sometimes using its power of eminent domain and sometimes using the threat of forced purchase. More than 400 families, 71.6 percent of whom were renters, were removed from the area. This was done without the compensatory relocation payments that federal and state redevelopment legislation would later require in such situations.

After the black neighborhood had been eliminated, Fulton County constructed a County Health Center, a building that housed the Northside Women's Club, a baseball field, and a park on the site. Bagely Street, the only street in the subdivision, provided the name for the park until 1980, when it was renamed Frankie Allen Park. All that now remains of the African American presence in the area are a few tombstones in a cemetery that once adjoined the black church.[14]

Something similar happened to the community of Johnstown, a black subdivision less than a mile northeast of Macedonia Park. It was settled by blacks in 1912, before many white families had moved that far north. Until 1982, thirty black families lived in the neighborhood on twenty-three–by–143-foot lots. In 1956 the Lenox Square shopping center was built adjacent to the neighborhood. Then, in the late '60s, the city began making plans for its rapid-transit system. In a referendum plan offered to the voters in 1968, part of Johnstown was named as the site for parking for the Lenox Square rail station. The referendum failed, and an upper-income apartment complex was built where the station would have been. A new referendum, presented to voters in 1971, called for a rail station to be built where the neighborhood itself was located. This referendum passed, and in 1979 the rapid-transit authority began taking steps to eliminate the Johnstown community.

Federal relocation law had improved somewhat by this time, and the city started a process whose basic intent was to treat the displaced residents in an equitable manner. Theoretically, the process would have captured for the residents some of the increase in land values

surrounding the rail station. But what actually happened was that profits from an air-rights real-estate deal went to only nine landowners and
the man who packaged the deal, an associate of the mayor. Most Johnstown residents, apparently, received no more than federally mandated
relocation payments.[15]

The elimination of a black neighborhood for a public purpose also
seems to have happened in the Candler Park area on the east side of
Atlanta. This is now a white gentrified neighborhood. The 1940 census maps show that a three- or four-block area next to a park was 100
percent black. The area is now part of the park. We do not know for
sure why this pocket of black residents disappeared, but given the pattern of past events, it seems highly likely that this African American
community was done away with to allow expansion of the park.

Black clusters have also been eliminated to make way for private use
of land. In the late 1970s and early '80s, the Oak Ridge Condominiums
were built along LaVista Road in suburban DeKalb County. The con-
dos took part of their name from the Oak Grove community, an African
American neighborhood that had been partly destroyed to make room
for them. The church that served this community, the Mount Zion
African Methodist Episcopal Church, still exists, and both former and
present residents still attend it. According to some of the remaining residents, Oak Grove was initially a rural black farming community. It
evolved into a neighborhood in which most of the employed men
worked in a north-side automobile plant and many families owned their
own homes. As the areas around the community developed into residential suburbs in the '60s and '70s, upwardly mobile families sold their
Oak Grove homes to move to higher-priced housing. These and subsequent sales were eventually aggregated into a contiguous plot on
which the Oak Ridge Condominiums were built. Approximately twenty
residences remain in the diminished community.[16]

An indeterminate sequence of real-estate transactions transformed
the African American neighborhood that once surrounded Mt. Moriah
Baptist Church in north Atlanta. This church sits on a hill just beyond
Interstate 85, just off North Druid Hills Road. It overlooks a shopping
center constructed in the 1960s. This church, too, is still attended by
former residents of the neighborhood, which sat in the valley where the

shopping center now stands. As with the black cluster in Candler Park, we do not know how this community disappeared, because research has not been done. What we do know is that commercial development now exists where once there was a black neighborhood.

Restrictions on Housing

Another reason for the high degree of residential segregation in the Atlanta metro area is that various local governments have prevented developers from building the kind of housing that a sizable portion of the black population could afford. Several local jurisdictions have erected legal barriers against building smaller, lower-cost housing units. One such barrier, established by many jurisdictions, is a requirement for minimum floor areas. The city of Buford in Gwinnett County requires that all apartments, whether efficiencies, one-bedroom, two-bedroom, or three-bedroom units, be at least 1,100 square feet. In the same county, the cities of Lawrenceville (the county seat), Dacula, Loganville, and Norcross require that efficiencies and one- through three-bedroom units be a minimum of 1,000 square feet. The city of Roswell in Fulton County has the same requirement; so does Clarkston in DeKalb County. McDonough, the county seat of Henry County, requires 960 feet for an efficiency or a one-bedroom unit, 1,000 square feet for a two-bedroom, and 1,100 square feet for a three-bedroom unit.[17] As a result of these requirements, the only apartments that developers can afford to build are high-priced two- or three-bedroom units. The clear message is that these jurisdictions do not want smaller apartments, and that whatever apartments are built must be large and expensive. One exception to this pattern is Atlanta city government. It has eliminated size restrictions and lets the housing market determine minimum acceptable sizes.

Another way local governments have prevented developers from building low- and moderately priced housing is through the application of zoning. Local governments have zoned increasingly more land for single-family residences, and there has been a trend toward larger minimum residential lot sizes. In the mid-'80s, Fulton County established a minimum size of two acres for single-family lots on some of the land in the northern part of the county. In the '90s, Cobb and Cherokee counties joined Fulton County with two-acre minimum lot sizes as their most exclusionary category. By 1998 six counties—Bartow, Coweta, Fulton, Fayette, Cherokee, and Rockdale—had some single-family residential land zoned for more than two acres. Bartow added a three-acre-minimum category, and Fayette added a five-acre-minimum category.

Local governments have used other zoning strategies to prohibit low-priced rental developments. Fulton County, for instance, has used restrictions on rezoning. In Fulton, as in almost all jurisdictions, no vacant, developable land is zoned for multifamily housing. If a developer wants to build apartments, land zoned for some other use must be rezoned. Fulton County analyzed multifamily rezonings between 1987 and 1994, and found that most had previously been zoned as either office or commercial. So the county passed an ordinance for its higher-income northern sector that prohibited changing office and commercial zoning to multifamily zoning.[18] Neighboring Cobb County has chosen to limit the density of multifamily development as a way to keep out low-priced apartments. Even though garden-apartment densities of fourteen to twenty dwelling units per acre are typical nationwide, and even though most recent metro Atlanta development has occurred at the higher end of this range, the highest-density residential development permitted by Cobb is currently six to twelve units per acre. This means that only larger, higher-priced apartments are economically feasible for developers to build. On the other hand, Cobb allows densities of thirty-six to sixty-six units per acre for luxury high-rise developments near major shopping centers. This insures that all residential high-rise developments in the county will be high-priced.[19]

Local governments have also tried to keep out new rental developments by enacting moratoriums on rezoning. Fulton County's 1994 revision of its zoning ordinance followed a one-year moratorium. Cobb County had a moratorium in place from June 1994 to March 1995. Gwinnett County refused to issue any multifamily permits in 1996. Clayton County enacted a rezoning moratorium in the fall of 1997. In 1997, suburban Atlanta political jurisdictions enacted thirty-eight such moratoriums.[20] In the most extreme manifestation of class discrimination against renters, Fulton County paid $2.7 million—$600,000 more than the appraised value—to purchase a tract previously zoned for multifamily apartments in order to block the development of 360 apartment units.[21]

Each of these ordinances had other stated purposes besides prohibiting low-priced residential development, but the primary undeclared purpose was to increase the cost of housing. Builders and developers know that there exists a market for smaller-size, lower-income units, so they chafe under these restrictions. In 1990 a local homebuilders' organization started planning a federal lawsuit that would challenge these regulations. Lawyers consulted by the organization considered two ways to do this. The first was to argue that the minimum sizes of lots and units required by the ordinances were not related in any material way to protecting public health, safety, and welfare. According to most public-health data, minimum housing sizes should range from 450 square feet for efficiencies to 750 square feet for two-bedroom units. The other approach was to argue that the ordinances had racially discriminatory effects. Because race is a protected category under United States housing law, the lawyers decided that the second approach had a much better chance of succeeding in the courts. They calculated that $130,000 in legal costs would be needed to bring the case through the U.S. Supreme Court to completion. But some members of the builders' organization were apprehensive about filing a racial-discrimination lawsuit against government officials upon whom they depended for approval of development plans. Only $50,000 was raised, and the lawsuit was abandoned. In 1997, the same organization began planning a similar lawsuit in the Georgia courts, again assembled lawyers and experts, and commissioned analyses. This time, substantially weaker Georgia fair-housing laws and lawyers' skepticism that Georgia judges would enforce these laws aborted the litigation centered on fair housing.

Misuse of a Government Housing Program

In the early 1980s, the Reagan administration put in place a program for financing the construction of mixed-income rental projects. The ostensible purpose of the program was to foster racially and economically integrated housing, mostly in the suburbs. Local government agencies, usually housing authorities, financed the housing with bonds exempt from federal taxes. In the Atlanta area, between 1981 and the restructuring of the program in 1986, more than $200 million in bond revenues was raised and 3,000 units were constructed.

This program should have begun to counterbalance the exclusionary practices of local governments in metropolitan Atlanta. But the Reagan administration, developers, and local governments implemented the program in such a way that they subverted its intent. The federal bond regulations stipulated that 20 percent of the units built be reserved for households making less than 80 percent of the area's median income. In the Atlanta area, this meant an income limit of $29,040. The regulations also stipulated that people with incomes of more than 225 percent of the area's median income would not be eligible. In the Atlanta area this meant an upper limit of $81,675. But the federal government did not provide money for enforcement and put no pressure on local governments to provide enforcement from their own resources, so most local governments in the Atlanta area chose not to enforce any of the eligibility limits.

Another flaw in the program was that there were no limits on the size of eligible households. To satisfy the requirement that 20 percent of the units go to renters making less than 80 percent of the median income, developers built efficiencies and one-bedroom units that were too small for moderate-income families. As a result, younger, single people became the primary market for these apartments. Another problem was that the program was not effective in achieving racial integration. It did not require that efforts be made to recruit black residents, and no such marketing efforts were undertaken.

Most of these projects were in the suburbs, but a few were built in the city. One of them, the Concorde, a thirty-one-story, 295-unit luxury apartment building (now converted to condominiums) in Buckhead, was one of the most egregious offenders against the program's stated intent. The project was financed by the Urban Residential Finance Authority, the city's housing-bond agency. Rents for the efficiencies ranged from $500 a month on the ground floor to $635 a month on the twenty-ninth floor. If the required 20 percent of the units had been rented to residents making less than $29,040 annually, fifty-nine units would have been rented to residents in this income category. But a detailed examination of the rent rolls reveals that only fifty-seven units were rented to residents below this income level, and these fifty-seven units were rented not to low-income families but to single men and women with a median age of 25.5 and a median income of $24,430. Incomes for the households in the non-efficiency units, excluding one tenant who made $150,000 in one year, averaged just under $115,000. This is $30,000 per year over the mandated cap of 225 percent of median area income. Ten percent of the units were rented by corporations, and incomes for these businesses were not calculated.[22] Clearly, the program was not assisting households and families who needed assistance.

Discrimination in the Mortgage-Lending and Realty Industries

Not only has racial discrimination been a major factor in creating a high degree of racial separation in Atlanta, it has also caused serious disadvantages for African Americans in the housing market. Currently, in the city proper, 52.4 percent of whites own their own homes, versus 37.5 percent of blacks. In the metro area as a whole, the numbers are 70 percent and 40.4 percent.[23]

Among the reasons for this inequality in home ownership are the present inequality in incomes and the long-term income inequality that has retarded savings and the ability to accumulate enough money to make down payments. Job discrimination and inequality in educational resources and other forms of historical discrimination have also contributed. But active discrimination has also played a major role. Discriminatory practices on the part of local mortgage lenders and the ineffectiveness of government in ending these practices have made it much more difficult for African Americans to buy and own decent homes than it is for whites.

Racial discrimination in mortgage lending was the subject of a series of articles titled "The Color of Money," which appeared in *The Atlanta Journal-Constitution* in May 1988 and won a 1989 Pulitzer Prize for reporting. They were written by Bill Dedman, based on research done by Dedman, Stan Fitterman, Calvin Bradford, and Charles Finn. What the research found was that between 1982 and 1986, regulated financial institutions in the Atlanta metropolitan area made 90,000 home-mortgage loans to whites and only 19,000 to blacks. When the data were adjusted to account for the different levels of income between whites and blacks, it showed that lending institutions had made five times more loans to whites than to blacks.[24]

The series stimulated responses from the national government, Atlanta financial institutions, and local politicians. Nationally, the Department of Justice, which had previously been reluctant to pursue lending-discrimination cases, began inquiries that eventually led to successful fair-housing litigation against two Atlanta financial institutions. Local lenders, who had been negotiating for more than a year with the Atlanta Community Reinvestment Alliance (for whom Fitterman was the lead researcher), responded to the public pressure with remedial measures. Nine banks and savings-and-loan institutions organized a pool of slightly discounted mortgage money that initially amounted to $20 million. They called their joint effort the Atlanta Mortgage Consortium. They planned to make between 1,000 and 1,500 loans with these pooled funds. Three other institutions, acting individually, pledged an additional $45 million, some of which was also to have carried discounted interest rates. A member of the Empire Real Estate Board, an organization of African American real-estate professionals, was appointed to the Atlanta Mortgage Consortium advisory group. Other African American leaders were consulted by local lenders as part of community-outreach efforts.[25]

Over the next three years, the Atlanta Mortgage Consortium made a total of 730 loans for $34,712,479. Between 60 percent and 66 percent of the loans were to black householders; between 27 percent and 34 percent were to whites.[26] There has been no publicly reported analysis of the lending programs promised by the three banks acting on their own, because these banks will not say whether or to whom the loans were made.

Black political leaders in Atlanta searched for positions that would be acceptable to both the influential financial industry and their constituents. Marvin Arrington, president of the city council, led a drive in the council to form an "action committee" of politicians, bankers, and citizens to investigate lending practices. Arrington wanted "hard recommendations" within twenty days.[27] This committee held an initial series of hearings and divided itself into six subcommittees. Then it ceased actively functioning for nearly a year. Prodding from the *Journal-Constitution* and threats of resignations by committee members finally led to the publication in the spring of 1989 of a quickly assembled twenty-seven-page summary of subcommittee recommendations, none of which was endorsed by the full committee, as Arrington was seeking politically neutral ground. The unendorsed recommendations covered a broad array of possible actions to help minority businesses and communities. The home-ownership subcommittee suggested that city government shift its bank deposits to those financial institutions that followed the recommendations.

But there was no subsequent demand from anyone that these recommendations be put into effect. African American political leaders had for years maintained close and reciprocal relations with the white business community, and they were therefore unwilling to be too aggressive in forcing the issue. When the series of articles appeared in the newspaper, Mayor Andrew Young was conciliatory in his remarks. "I would hate to think we've slipped," he said. "It's the kind of thing you want to hope we've moved beyond. If there is serious redlining, it's not good for the city." Young went on to say that he hoped that regulation by the city government would not be necessary, and that the banks had responded earlier to his personal pleas for loans to Underground Atlanta, a downtown shopping complex, and Atlanta's hosting of the 1988 Democratic National Convention.[28]

Michael Lomax, chairman of the Fulton County Commission, who had been mentioned in the newspaper series after his request for a loan was refused by two Atlanta banks, initially complained publicly. But Lomax was planning a 1989 run for mayor, and he began to moderate his tone. When asked about proposals that city government bank deposits be linked to their lending practices, Lomax said, "I've never encouraged that in Fulton County. My preference would be to raise the issue with the banks in a positive way."[29] Maynard Jackson, who would oppose Lomax in the 1989 election, declined an offer of "equal time" in the *Journal-Constitution* series, and later commented moderately in an interview. "I like to try to negotiate things first," Jackson said. "You're talking about conservative institutions. That's not going to change. There are probably banks that are going to be more responsive than others; we have to find those institutions and work with them, organize their efforts. To whatever extent we can legally and economically leverage city money, I'm willing to consider that."[30] But suggestions that the city actively use municipal financial deposits to support nondiscriminatory lending institutions were quashed in his campaign policy papers and not considered in his mayoral administration.

At the time the series was published, *The Atlanta Journal-Constitution* was edited by Bill Kovach. Kovach, who had hired Dedman, sought to reestablish the newspaper as a significant, independent regional voice. But the unusually dissonant posture that "The Color of Money" series brought to Atlanta's normally cohesive politics was not sustained. Within a year both Kovach and Dedman were gone, and although the paper collaborated on an update of the research two years later, it declined to publish the results, explaining unconvincingly that "the banks had not had time to respond."[31]

When the series of articles had appeared in the newspaper, one local financial institution had defended itself by arguing that mortgage-brokerage firms were taking care of a substantial portion of African American business. It is true that the mortgage-banking system has historically initiated and serviced more than half of all black mortgage loans. But the primary reason for this is that blacks have had to turn to mortgage banks as a last resort because of persistent discrimination on the part of conventional banks and savings-and-loan institutions. Blacks were channeled into mortgages insured by the Federal Housing Administration because widespread discrimination made it difficult to get conventional mortgages. Another reason that many African Americans have FHA-insured mortgages is that such mortgages require lower down payments, Many mortgage brokers, particularly during the '70s and '80s, specialized in initiating and selling FHA paper, and so ended up originating a large number of mortgage loans to blacks.

The Atlanta Mortgage Consortium lasted for nine years; then its constituent banks disbanded it. In its last six years it made 1,100 loans worth $60.2 million, an average of 183 loans per year. Over its lifetime it originated 1,815 loans worth approximately $95 million.[32] In comparison, annual single-family mortgage-loan volume between 1992 and 1996 averaged 43,790 loans worth more than $4.2 billion in the seven-county Atlanta metropolitan area.[33]

Ten years after "The Color of Money" series, Elvin Wyly and Steven Holloway repeated for 1992 through 1996 the research that Fitterman and others had done for 1982 through 1986. They found that for middle-income households, the white-to-black conventional-loan ratio had dropped from 5.16 to between 4.24 and 4.66, depending on the particular method used to construct comparable measures. In other words, the ratio for middle-income-level conventional loans, although declining by somewhere between 9.6 percent and 17.8 percent, remained remarkably stable, with well over four times as many loans per owner-occupied structure for whites than for blacks. Ten years of substantial changes in mortgage finance had produced only modest declines in extremely stable racial and geographic disparities.[34]

Local response to discrimination's persistence in 1999 was much more muted than at its discovery in 1988. After the Fannie Mae Foundation, which funded the replication of the research, called a press conference to announce the results, *The Journal-Constitution* ran only a 700-word article in its Saturday business section. No local political or financial figures were interviewed,[35] and none subsequently issued public comments. The initial documentation of the extent of discrimination engaged the press, financial institutions, and local politicians for several months and produced some modest reforms. Rediscovery a decade later led to virtual silence.

The Atlanta real-estate industry has been just as guilty of discriminatory practices as have Atlanta's lending institutions. According to a national study of local real-estate practices released by the U.S. Department of Housing and Urban Development in 1991, 49 percent of blacks looking for homes in the Atlanta area in 1989 reported that they had been discriminated against by real-estate agents. In about 10 percent of these cases, discrimination was blatant: The agent simply refused to do business with a black person. In other cases the discrimination was more subtle: Blacks looking for homes were misinformed about available housing, were offered unfavorable terms and conditions, did not receive assistance in looking for financing, or were shown only certain homes by agents, a practice referred to as "steering."[36]

More than fifty years ago, in response to widespread discrimination in the Atlanta housing market, African American real-estate agents formed their own separate professional organization called the Empire Real Estate Board. Like its predominantly white counterpart, the Atlanta Board of Realtors, the Empire Board provides its membership with professional development, market, and property research, and opportunities for networking and socialization. The members of the Empire Real Estate Board, seeking to distinguish themselves legally and professionally from "Realtors," referred to themselves as "realists," a term that conveyed succinctly the reason for the organization's existence. Real-estate brokers play a central role in transmitting information about the location of housing and the availability of financing. When segregation was enforced by law, the existence of an exclusively black brokers organization was essential. But today, the existence of two racially separate organizations of real-estate brokers, whose members operate in racially separate geographic areas, serves to perpetuate segregated housing markets.

State and local governments have not done much to end discrimination in the Atlanta housing market. If a state government wishes to, it can obtain federal funding to implement measures promoting fair housing. To be eligible for these funds, it must pass a fair-housing law that complies with federal law. But the states are under no legal compulsion to do this. Until the late 1980s, Georgia had a fair-housing law that was weaker than the federal law, and it funded its own efforts at promoting fair housing. The agency it established to do this was a subdivision of the Equal Employment Opportunities Commission. The state funded this operation only very modestly, and it had little noticeable effect. More recently, however, the state Legislature did pass two laws—the first in 1989, the second in 1991—that brought Georgia into compliance with federal statutes. These were hopeful signs. But though these state laws make federal funding available, the amounts the state is eligible for are also very modest, and have not led to a vigorous or widespread effort to encourage fair housing practices.

Efforts on the local level have been just as limited. The Fulton County Commission did pass a fair-housing law in 1988, in the aftermath of "The Color of Money" series. But no funding was provided to enforce the law. Enforcement of national fair-housing laws on the local level in metropolitan Atlanta has primarily been the responsibility of Metro Fair Housing Services. This nonprofit agency gets its core funding from the city of Atlanta ($21,000 to $25,000 annually), Fulton County (approximately $40,000), and DeKalb County ($40,000 to $45,000). This money, which remained relatively steady from 1987 to 1996, supports a core staff of three to five professionals. Periodically the agency is successful in supplementing local funding with federal grants, but the availability of these funds fluctuates widely, depending on the commitments of different national administrations to fair housing.[37]

The national fair-housing bill enacted in 1990 shows some promise of strengthening enforcement, and some of the far too few legal staff members at HUD's regional office in Atlanta are earnest in their pursuit of fair housing. But the city remains more timid than its civil-rights reputation would suggest. According to Joseph Shifalo, executive director of Metro Fair Housing Services, the city's financial commitment to promoting fair housing is "woefully inadequate." During Maynard Jackson's third term as mayor (1990 to 1994), he killed a proposal that federal funds be passed on to the agency for an analysis of mortgage-redlining. The mayor nixed the proposal even though City of Atlanta staff members ranked it higher than competing proposals—and much higher than projects that subsequently did receive funds. Jackson explained to his staff that, though he felt that someone should analyze mortgage discrimination, the analysis should not be funded by city government.[38]

Inequalities in Housing

Active racial discrimination in the Atlanta housing market has done more than produce a high degree of residential segregation and create serious disadvantages for African Americans trying to buy homes. It has also led to a growing inequality in housing conditions between the races. Inequality in housing conditions is due in part to inequality in incomes, but the kind of actions and attitudes discussed above have also been major factors. Three ways to measure housing conditions will be looked at here: values of owner-occupied housing, levels of rent paid by renters relative to their incomes, and degrees of overcrowding. The data for the

Table 10.   Inequality in Housing Values Among Predominantly Black and White Atlanta Census Tracts, 1950 to 1990

Year	Median Value of Owner-Occupied Housing		
	White	Black	Ratio
1950	$9,772	$5,156	1.90
1960	$14,763	$8,942	1.65
1970	$22,705	$12,124	1.87
1980	$85,272	$19,939	4.28
1990	$283,867	$43,739	6.49

Source: 1950, 1990, calculations by author; 1960–1980, David M. Smith, *Geography, Inequality, and Society* (Cambridge: Cambridge University Press, 1987).

period between 1960 and 1980 are from the study done in 1987 by David M. Smith on the economic inequalities between blacks and whites in Atlanta,[39] with figures derived from the censuses of 1950 and 1990 added.

Table 10 shows the differences in the median values of white-owned and black-owned housing. The figures show that in 1950 the ratio was just under two-to-one. By 1960 the ratio had shrunk to 1.65, a 13.2 percent decrease. Between 1960 and 1990, however, the gap widened considerably. The 1990 ratio was almost three and half times as great (341.6 percent) as the 1950 ratio. By 1990, the median value of a white-owned home was almost six and a half times as high as the median value of a black-owned home.

It should be mentioned here that there is an important element of national housing policy that has actually compounded the effects of racial inequalities in home ownership. Since the start of the federal income tax in 1913, those who own homes have been able to deduct interest and property-tax payments. This amounts to a federal subsidy to those who own homes.[40] Since a higher percentage of whites than blacks own homes in the Atlanta area, whites are subsidized to a far greater extent than blacks are. And because the median value of white-owned homes has always been greater than the median value of black-owned homes, white homeowners have received a disproportionate share of this subsidy. What's more, since the overall difference between the value of white-owned and black-owned housing has grown over the years, the disproportionate share of this subsidy received by white homeowners has been increasing.

There are also inequalities between black and white renters, though they are not as extreme as the inequalities between black and white homeowners. A higher percentage of black renters pay excessive amounts of rent relative to their income. A national standard for what percentage of income should go for rent has never been established, but traditionally more than 25 percent has been considered excessive. This was the percentage of income charged government agencies for public housing and required of privately owned but publicly subsidized housing. Between 1981 and 1985, the Reagan administration raised public and Section 8 housing rents from 25 percent to 30 percent of income. The Census Bureau followed suit, and used the 30 percent figure as a critical dividing line in presenting its 1990 data for housing expenditure.[41]

Table 11 shows the disparities between black and white renters who pay excessive rents. The percentages for both black and white renters have increased; by 1990, more than half of all renters paid excessive rents. But African American renters have fared somewhat worse than white renters. Between 1980 and 1990, while the percentage of white renters paying excessive rents declined, the percentage of black renters paying excessive rents increased. Between 1980 and 1990 the ratio of black to white renters in this category increased by 35.5 percent. In 1990, the percentage of black renters in this category was one-third greater than the number of white renters (60.9 percent as opposed to 40.9 percent). Since a much higher percentage of blacks than whites are renters, the growing inequality between white and black renters who

Table 11.   Inequality in Incidence of Housing for Which More Than 25 Percent of Income Is Paid for Rent, Atlanta, 1970 to 1990

| Year | Percentage of Housing for Which More Than 25 Percent of Income Is Paid for Rent | | |
	White	Black	Ratio
1970	37.4	44.7	1.20
1980	48.4	53.0	1.10
1990	40.9	60.9	1.49

Calculations by author.

Table 12.   Inequality in Overcrowded Housing Among Predominantly Black and White Atlanta Census Tracts, 1950 to 1990

	Percentage of Housing with More Than 1.0 Person per Room		
Year	White	Black	Ratio
1950	11.96	33.98	2.84
1960	6.48	33.06	5.1
1970	4.55	19.74	4.34
1980	0.83	8.80	10.6
1990	0.00	9.10	∞

Sources: 1950, 1990, calculations by author; 1960–1980, David M. Smith, Geography, Inequality, and Society (Cambridge: Cambridge University Press, 1987).

pay excessive amounts of rent has had a disproportionate effect on the African American population as a whole.

Overcrowding is another important measure of housing conditions. Overcrowding is defined as more than one person per habitable room in a housing unit. This problem has greatly diminished in the country as a whole. The reason for this is not that the American housing industry has been increasingly successful at housing large households, but that over the years the average household has grown smaller in all social classes and social groups. Overcrowding has diminished in Atlanta, as it has elsewhere, and it has done so for both blacks and whites. Table 12 compares percentages of overcrowded housing in predominantly white and predominantly black Atlanta census tracts between 1950 and 1990. In 1950, 11.96 percent of white households had more than one person per room. By 1980 the number had declined to 0.83 percent. Overcrowding also diminished in black areas: In 1950, 33.98 percent of black households had more than one person per room, but by 1980 the number had shrunk to 8.8 percent. Then, however, the trend reversed itself. Between 1980 and 1990 the percentage of overcrowded housing in black areas increased from 8.8 percent to 9.1 percent. In 1990 there were only five census tracts in white areas of the city that had any overcrowding, and the median percentage of overcrowded housing within white census tracts had declined to zero. By contrast, in 1990 all but one of the predominantly black census tracts had overcrowding, and the median percentage of overcrowded housing had increased by 3.4 percent since 1980. A consequence of these changes is that the ratio of black-to-white overcrowding has steadily increased, from 2.84 in 1950 to 10.60 in 1980 and to infinity by 1990. In the previous chapter we looked at coefficients of variation for white and black median incomes, a coefficient of variation being a statistical measure that describes changing equality or inequality in incomes within a group. Smith used this statistical measure to describe the change in equality or inequality in housing within the white and black populations between 1960 and 1980. Table 13 shows the coefficients of variation for white and black median housing values between 1950 and 1990. The data for white homeowners show slightly declining inequality in the distribution of housing values between 1950 and 1960; then a dramatic increase in inequality between 1960 and 1970, the coefficient rising by 37.12 percent, from 39.68 to 54.41; and then, between 1970 and 1980, a sharp decrease, back down to 41.58. Inequality rose again slightly to 43.64 in 1990, but that was still only slightly greater than it had been in 1950. African American homeowners, on the other hand, saw steadily growing inequality in housing values over this

Table 13.   Degree of Inequality (Coefficient of Variation) Among Predominantly White and Black Atlanta Census Tracts, 1950 to 1990

Indicator	Year	White	Black
Median value of owner-occupied housing units	1950	41.81	19.32
	1960	39.68	16.95
	1970	54.41	24.31
	1980	41.58	38.24
	1990	43.64	40.86
Housing with more than 1.0 person per room	1950	75.45	27.69
	1960	86.51	22.45
	1970	91.54	33.31
	1980	148.01	41.75
	1990	181.7	55.52
Housing for which more than 25 percent of income is paid for gross rent	1970	23.75	20.58
	1980	30.94	93.76
	1990	47.47	14.87

Sources: 1950, 1990, calculations by author; 1960–1980, David M. Smith, *Geography, Inequality, and Society* (Cambridge: Cambridge University Press, 1987).

forty-year period. The coefficient of variation went from 19.32 in 1950 to 40.86 in 1990, an increase of 211.5 percent. By 1990, blacks and whites were much closer to each other in this measure of inequality than they had been in 1950.

As for overcrowding, the coefficient of variation for whites has increased dramatically, going from 75.45 in 1950 to 181.70 in 1990, a 140.82 percent increase. Because the incidence of overcrowding has declined in the white population, this increase represents an increasingly wider distribution of increasingly smaller proportions. Overcrowding for whites has become a relatively insignificant problem. In 1990, there were only 101 overcrowded white households in Atlanta. For blacks, however, overcrowding remains a significant problem, and inequality in overcrowding has increased. In 1990, 9.10 percent of black housing was overcrowded, and between 1950 and 1990 the coefficient of variation doubled, going from 27.69 to 55.52. As with housing values, inequality in black overcrowded housing increased substantially.

Between 1970 and 1990, inequality in gross rent relative to income among white renters increased by 53.4 percent, the coefficient of variation going from 23.75 to 47.47. The problem of disproportionate rent decreased, however. During this period, the incidence of disproportionate rent among white renters went from 48.4 percent to 40.9 percent. For black renters, the coefficient of variation for gross rent increased sharply between 1970 and 1980, going from 20.58 to 93.76. But over the next decade the inequality in gross rent decreased just as sharply, the coefficient of variation shrinking to 14.87 in 1990. However, this decline in the inequality of gross rent for black renters has been accompanied by a steadily increasing incidence of disproportionate rent over the same period, with 44.7 percent of African American renters paying disproportionate rent in 1970, 53 percent in 1980, and 60.9 percent in 1990. (See Table 11.) Disparities in rent for blacks are not as great as they were twenty years ago, but proportionately more African Americans now pay excessive rents relative to their incomes.

The growing inequalities in housing values and overcrowding in the black population reinforce the data on the growing inequalities in income among blacks discussed in the previous chapter. All the data clearly show that over the past four decades of economic expansion in Atlanta, the black community has been divided into increasingly unequal economic classes. Two of the indexes describe usually distinct economic classes: renters and owners. The data say that within the ownership class, black inequality has increased nearly to the level of white inequality, and that white inequality, after some movement, has returned to roughly the same level as forty years ago. Within the economically weaker rental class, white inequality has doubled and black inequality has declined only because a sizeable majority is afflicted with disproportionate expenditures. Taken together, these data describe substantial regression in equality and a deterioration of economic equity that forty years of Atlanta's vibrant growth and expansion have not only not moderated but have actually exacerbated.

Race Versus Class

For a number of years there has been a debate over whether race or economic class is the primary cause of residential segregation. Recent research shows that race is a significantly more important factor in the high levels of segregation in Atlanta and other cities. The evidence shows that African American households are geographically segregated, irrespective of income.[42] Another debate concerns the relative significance of race and class in producing disparities in employment, education, and family stability. Resolving this debate is not easy, as there are higher levels of poverty among blacks, and racial segregation concentrates this poverty in black neighborhoods. We can, however, determine to some degree the relative influence of race versus economic class on the adverse conditions faced by blacks.

Let us assume for a moment complete racial segregation for the Atlanta metro area. In 1980, the poverty rate for whites was 5.1 percent and for blacks 25.7 percent. If class segregation had not been a factor, these would have been the poverty rates in white and black neighborhoods, respectively. But these are not the actual figures. Douglas C. Massey and Mitchell L. Eggers have calculated the actual concentrations of poverty among blacks and whites in what they term hypersegregated cities, of which Atlanta is one. The results of their research are presented in Table 14. In the Atlanta area in 1980, the average black family lived in a neighborhood that was 37.1 percent poor, whereas the average white family lived in a neighborhood that was 12.5 percent

Table 14.   Geographic Concentration of Poverty Among Blacks and Whites in
Atlanta

	1970	1980	Percentage Change
Percentage of poor in the neighborhood of an average black family	31.7	37.1	5.4
Percentage of poor in the neighborhood of an average white family	12.4	12.5	0.1

Source: Douglas S. Massey and Mitchell L. Eggers, "The Ecology of Inequality: Minorities and the Concentration of Poverty, 1970–1980," American Journal of Sociology 95 (1990), as
cited in Douglas S. Massey and Nancy A. Denton, American Apartheid: Segregation and the Making of the Underclass (Cambridge, MA: Harvard University Press), p. 129.

poor. Since the poverty level among blacks in 1980 was 25.7 percent,
and since racial segregation was high but not complete, most of the first
25.7 percent of the actual 37.1 percent concentration of black poverty
is attributable to racial segregation. The remaining difference of 11.4
percent, or about a fifth of the concentration of black poverty, must be
due to discrimination based on class.[43] What this research shows is that
the migration of black, middle-class families out of the inner city has
had some effect on the concentration of black poverty, but the much
larger determining factor has been the continuing pattern of racial discrimination.[44]

The research done by Massey and Eggers has important implications for public policy. If it were true that the out-migration of middle-
class blacks was the primary cause of the perpetuation of black underclass neighborhoods, then efforts to reduce racial segregation and thus
encourage this migration would have the perverse effect of further con-
centrating African American poverty. But since the research done by
Massey and Eggers convincingly demonstrates that residential racial
segregation is the primary cause of concentrated black poverty and the
ill effects that come from it, public policy ought to focus its efforts on
reducing racial segregation. The evidence tells us that if government
is to make any headway in improving the economic and social conditions of the black population, it should vigorously enforce fair-housing
laws, actively promote racially integrated housing, and make sure that
housing-assistance programs have the same goals.

Atlanta Politics and the Governing Elite

hroughout most of the past fifty years, Atlanta politics was
dominated by the city's downtown business leaders. The
power of the downtown business elite has waned recently,
but up until the early 1980s it was the central force in Atlanta
politics. With one exception, members of this downtown
elite wielded power not by holding political office but by
influencing major decisions made by elected officials. The
one exception to this was Ivan Allen Jr., a prominent member of the downtown elite who served two terms as mayor
in the '60s.

The major goal of downtown business leaders was to redevelop the downtown area. But downtown redevelopment
had very little appeal to the city's white middle class. So
beginning in the late '40s, white business leaders, in order to
hold on to political power and achieve their redevelopment
objectives, formed an alliance with political leaders from the
newly enfranchised black middle class. Through their control of city government, business leaders contributed to bringing an end to legally sanctioned segregation, and they also
supported efforts to acquire land for African American middle-class housing. In return, black political leaders enlisted
black electoral support for two successive mayors who represented downtown business interests; muted their objections

to highway and urban-renewal projects that displaced low-income blacks in the downtown area; and garnered black support for a rapid-rail plan that was heavily promoted by the white business elite.

When Maynard Jackson was elected Atlanta's first black mayor in the early '70s, he broke away from this biracial coalition. He tried to govern with the new coalition that had brought him to power: an alliance of African Americans of all classes, liberal white gentrifiers, and the city's small Jewish community. The city's business leaders were unhappy about having lost their preferential position and felt that Jackson was hostile to their interests. Private complaining soon became public criticism, and friction developed between the business community and the Jackson administration. The conflict prompted Jackson to change his political tactics. He concluded that in order to govern effectively he could not simply act on behalf of his political base but would have to act on multiple fronts.[1] Before the end of his first term he had decided to repair relations with the business community. He set about reestablishing the biracial coalition, and during his second term he developed much closer contacts with business leaders. Andrew Young, Atlanta's second black mayor, succeeded Jackson, and Young further strengthened the biracial coalition. During Young's two terms in office during the '80s, he fully supported downtown business leaders in their efforts to revitalize the downtown economy.

Because the primary governing power in Atlanta from the early '50s through the mid-'80s was an alliance between wealthy whites and middle-class blacks, social class played just as important a role in Atlanta politics as race during this period. Middle-class whites and the white and black lower classes had little influence, and the biracial coalition largely ignored their interests. Some of the major conflicts in Atlanta politics during this period were essentially class conflicts. On redevelopment, transportation, and other issues, middle-class whites and low-income blacks frequently found themselves at odds with the wealthy whites and middle-class blacks who dominated governance.

The Woodruff/Hartsfield Era

The single most powerful figure in Atlanta politics in the late '40s and through most of the '50s was Robert Woodruff, the Coca-Cola magnate and multimillionaire.[2] Woodruff and a small group of prominent businessmen exercised considerable influence on city government. The mayor during this period was William Hartsfield. Hartsfield was not a member of the inner circle of business leaders, but he was a friend of Woodruff and his political ally. Woodruff and this small group of businessmen also wielded their influence through various civic organizations, such as the Chamber of Commerce and the Central Area Improvement Association. In the early '50s Woodruff gradually withdrew from active participation in these organizations, but he continued to exert his authority through friends and associates who remained active in politics and the civic life of the city.

In *Community Power Structure: A Study of Decision Makers* (1953), Floyd Hunter examined the internal dynamics of this governing elite and the methods it used to achieve its political objectives. These power leaders, as he called them, were an especially cohesive group. They had strong social ties to one another, they all belonged to a highly exclusive athletic club, and most were natives of the state or the city. They formulated important policy decisions in private, informal meetings at their homes, at luncheons, at their athletic club, and at other exclusive clubs to which they belonged.[3] This inner circle of decision makers had a hierarchical command structure. Some had more power and influence than others, those at the top could rely on the cooperation of those beneath them, and those in the lower echelons always cleared their ideas with the upper echelon. There was also a larger group of men outside this inner circle who acted as "executives" and carried out its wishes.[4]

A clear example of the political power of this elite group and the political methods it used was the Plan of Improvement mentioned in Chapter Three. In the late '40s, city leaders devised a plan to expand the city's boundaries by annexing the upscale northern suburb of Buckhead; white, middle-class suburbs to the northeast and west of the city; and undeveloped land to the north, south, and west. The publicly stated purpose of this annexation was to relieve Fulton County of the burden of delivering government services to fast-growing areas outside the city. There is strong evidence, however, that the real purpose was to permanently dilute growing black voter strength in the city by adding more whites to the city's voting rolls.[5] In a referendum held in 1948, the annexation plan was approved by city voters but rejected by county voters in outlying districts. The city's governing elite then asserted its power and influence. It orchestrated a campaign to give the plan the appearance of a broad civic movement in the public interest. It worked in conjunction with the state Legislature to create a committee to formulate and implement strategy. Five members of the governing elite were members of this committee, and one of them became president of a prominent civic organization, with the purpose of generating support for the plan among the members of this organization. Through the strategy committee, supporters of annexation persuaded the Legislature to pass a "home rule" bill that stipulated that if a majority of voters in all areas approved the plan, districts that voted against it could also be annexed. A majority of voters approved the plan in a 1949 referendum, and it was implemented in 1952.

The Georgia Supreme Court later decided that the home-rule act was unconstitutional, and future annexations under the act were banned, but the 1952 annexation was allowed to stand. Had it not been for the Supreme Court's ruling, city leaders would have had a legal mechanism for maintaining a permanent white electoral majority. As it was, annexation of Buckhead and the other areas delayed a black electoral majority and the election of a black mayor by twelve or sixteen years.

The Biracial Coalition

Immediately after the end of World War II, Atlanta's African American middle class reorganized itself politically and began to play an increasingly important role in the city's politics. In 1946, Georgia's all-white primary-election law was declared unconstitutional. With the path cleared for more meaningful participation, blacks began holding voter-registration drives. In 1948, Atlanta's black Democrats and

Republicans combined efforts to form the Negro Voters League for the purpose of screening white candidates for local elected offices. Through the efforts of this organization and the Urban League, the city's black population managed to fashion a strong minority voting block. In a close 1949 mayoral primary, 27 percent of the electorate was African American. And even though the 1952 annexation diluted black voting strength, the city's black population and black electorate continued to grow.

In the late '50s, Atlanta's white business leaders wanted to redevelop the downtown area and make it an accessible and thriving business center, but they did not have support for downtown redevelopment from the city's white middle class. So the governing elite decided to strengthen its evolving alliance with the increasingly powerful black middle class. It maintained close contact with middle-class African American political leaders and guardedly supported initial moves toward desegregation. Mayor Hartsfield cautiously and slowly began the integration of the city's police department and negotiated an end to segregation in transportation and in many downtown hotels, restaurants, and department stores (but not theaters). Token desegregation of public schools also began during Hartsfield's administration.

Hartsfield's successor, Ivan Allen Jr., desegregated city hall, supported desegregation of the remaining public accommodations, warily supported an end to segregation in the public schools, and testified before a congressional committee for the national civil-rights bill. He also helped the black middle class acquire land on the southwest side of the city for housing. In return for this support, the white governing elite gained the backing it needed from middle-class black voters; the white elite was able to hold on to city hall and pursue the redevelopment of the downtown area.

In the '50s, the Hartsfield administration began construction of a highway system radiating from downtown. In the '60s, the Allen administration built a baseball stadium and a civic center/auditorium close to the downtown area. It also vigorously promoted a metro-region rapid-rail system. A schism in the coalition defeated a rapid-rail plan in a 1968 referendum, but Allen's successor, Sam Massell, gained support for a rapid-rail system from African American political leaders, and in a 1971 referendum, largely because of black voters' support, a rapid-rail plan was approved.

This biracial coalition broke down briefly during Maynard Jackson's first term as mayor—1974 to 1978—but Jackson began to reestablish the partnership before the end of his first term, and even though the coalition's power began to wane in the late '80s, it remained the dominant player in the city's politics.

Clarence Stone, in his 1989 work *Regime Politics: Governing Atlanta 1946–1988*, analyzed the political dynamics of Atlanta's governing coalition. Stone argued that the reason urban coalitions are formed and endure is their capacity for getting things done. Stone contended that in a capitalist society, coordinated action that achieves large objectives must occur on a multiple of fronts. Business enterprise is autonomous, and different groups and interests compete freely with one another politically. Furthermore, in the American brand of capitalism, government has limited powers. There is resistance to government interfering with and trying to regulate private endeavor, so government's capacity for bringing together different segments of society in a concerted effort is limited. Stone argued that coalitions are formed and endure because these extra-governmental groupings make coordinated action in a fragmented society possible. Informal alliances overcome institutions' and groups' limited capacities to accomplish political goals. They enable people to transcend the limitations of an incohesive society, making concerted action on a large scale feasible.

Another reason that coalitions are effective, Stone wrote, is their capacity to mobilize the resources needed for large-scale undertakings. Successful political alliances have ready access to capital and expertise, including organizational experience. Since business elites command exactly these kinds of resources, they are likely to be partners in long-lasting, effective coalitions.[6]

Over the past five decades, the two major organizations representing the interests of the white downtown business elite have been Central Atlanta Progress (CAP)[7] and the Atlanta Chamber of Commerce. These organizations have been well funded, well organized, and well staffed, and they have played a major role in the city's efforts at economic development. (There used to be a third such organization:

Research Atlanta, a private policy-research organization supported by corporate funds, which promoted policies acceptable to the business community. Diminishing revenues, a reflection of reduced corporate interest, led in 1992 to its present affiliation with the Andrew Young School of Policy Studies at Georgia State University. Research Atlanta's board is still extensively corporate, but its connection with an academic institution has brought more balance to its policy prescriptions.)

There are no similar organizations in the African American community, which is one of the reasons for white business dominance within the coalition. Both the Atlanta Urban League and the Atlanta Business League have very small staffs that concern themselves primarily with the immediate issues of affirmative action and the particular problems of smaller black-owned firms. Neither organization has the capacity to dissect issues and organize and propose action programs. The larger, white-controlled organizations do.

Another reason for the success of Atlanta's biracial coalition has been the social cohesiveness of both the city's white business elite and the city's black, middle-class leadership. Atlanta's black middle class organized itself politically during the '40s and '50s to gain electoral power, and it reorganized itself during the civil-rights struggles of the '50s and '60s. It was therefore politically conscious and politically organized, and these characteristics made it an effective political partner.

There are other reasons that the biracial coalition continued after African Americans gained control of city government in the early '70s. One reason is historical and institutional. A political partnership with the white business elite is part of the political heritage of black Atlantans from 1946 on. Because the biracial coalition was, in their own view, successful, it became the established procedure. Through vehicles such as the Action Forum, a monthly conclave of members of the white business elite and senior black business and political leaders, formed in the aftermath of a coalition schism, disputes are aired, compromises sought, and actions decided upon. Black opposition to a 1968 referendum on the rail system led to its defeat, and both groups sought to avert further public discord. The Chamber of Commerce's Leadership Atlanta program and the Atlanta Regional Commission's leadership-development program formally reinforce and help perpetuate coalition governance by inculcating its structure, values, and practices in networks of new generations of black and white politically active or ambitious citizens.

Electoral finance is a strongly reinforcing dimension of the enduring coalition. All candidates, black or white, have to seek corporate and business elite funding for election campaigns. The historic weakness of labor unions in the south renders them peripheral in financing local elections. The odd council member may mount a grassroots campaign for a particular district, but anyone seeking a higher office (citywide council seats, president of the council, or mayor) has to appeal to the business elite for contributions.

Another strong incentive for black elected officials to continue their close relationship with the white business elite is economic advantage. The African American community's history of underdevelopment underlines the fact that all black politicians have businesses or professional practices to maintain, and having political and social connections among the white elite provides business and professional opportunities.

A final reason that the coalition has endured is the social and class affinity of its members. Reared in parallel but similar societies, coalition members share fundamental values. Most are in business or in the professions that service business. Mores regarding the essence of the economic system, the centrality of work, the bases for trust, the virtues of democracy, and the correspondence of wealth and class are shared. For example, both Ivan Allen Jr.'s and Maynard Jackson's antecedents were socially prominent, politically active, respected members of their separate communities. The two men maintained personal contact during turbulent moments in Jackson's first term, in part because their socialization had prepared them to understand each other.[8]

Even though Atlanta has always had a large population of low-income African Americans, the city's governing coalition did very little to improve their living conditions in the four decades during which the coalition dominated the city's politics. Even after African Americans gained control of city government, black elected officials largely ignored the problem of black poverty. The coalition did very little to provide poor blacks with adequate housing, viewing this primarily as a federal responsibility. Instead of trying to revitalize low-income black neighborhoods, the city government, with coalition backing, tore down all or part of poor black neighborhoods in and around the downtown area. Nor did the coalition do much to improve public schools in the inner city or to establish job-training programs, beyond whatever small federal programs might be temporarily available. And the coalition did very little to improve or expand social-welfare services, seeing them as the responsibility of the county or state, not the city.

Not that Atlanta's black poverty has been easy to ignore. It has contributed to a high crime rate, high unemployment, an undereducated and undertrained workforce, widespread drug use, and a high rate of teenage pregnancy. The coalition managed to ignore it anyway. The coalition decided which issues should and should not be acted on, thus controlling the political agenda, and it generally excluded black poverty from that agenda. This is a good illustration of the dual dimension of political power: Power can be wielded not only by accomplishing things but by deciding which issues are acceptable for discussion and which are not. Those in power can assert themselves through action or through deliberate inaction.[9]

Transition

Sam Massell was elected mayor in 1969. His election was a clear sign that power was shifting toward a growing black electorate. Massell had good relations with the black community and won a substantial majority of the black vote in the general election. Another sign of change was that Massell, though a successful businessman, was not a member of the traditional white power structure, like Allen, or allied with it, like Hartsfield. He was Jewish and liberal, and he had strong ties to labor groups. During his campaign, Massell made it clear that he opposed the excessive influence that business interests had on city government.

As it turned out, Massell was not as antibusiness as he had seemed. He was just as supportive of the rapid-rail plan as business interests were, and he supported locating a state-financed business convention center, the Georgia World Congress Center, on the west side of downtown, the site favored by business. Despite his reputation as a political maverick, Massell ended up being an ideal coalition mayor. While supporting downtown redevelopment, he reached out to the black community. In his first year as mayor, he appointed African Americans to important city-government positions and pushed hard for affirmative action in hiring for city jobs.

Maynard Jackson's Turnaround

By the 1973 mayoral election, close to a majority of the city's electorate was African American. With the help of a relatively small group of white gentrifiers and Jewish voters, the city elected its first black mayor, Maynard Jackson. During his first term in office, Jackson was quite active in supporting the political and economic interests of his primary constituents. He appointed blacks to important positions in city government, and he lobbied aggressively for affirmative action, insisting that a percentage of city contracts go to minority businesses and urging businesses to promote blacks to important executive positions and appoint blacks to governing boards. Atlanta was about to build its new airport at the time, and Jackson insisted that a certain percentage of construction contracts go to minority firms. He also asserted control over the police and fire departments. When he encountered resistance from the white chief of police, he created the new position of Public Safety Commissioner and appointed a friend and political ally to the position, with the goal of instituting measures that would guarantee that more blacks got promotions.

But Jackson did more than just champion black interests. Just before he was elected mayor, Jackson had helped fashion the agreement to extend MARTA to the remote Perry Homes public-housing community, an agreement that was central to winning multiple-class black support for MARTA in the 1971 referendum. Against the background of the civil-rights movement, and with his election clearly marking black political ascendancy, Jackson came into office with a progressive style and agenda. He was a strong advocate of neighborhood interests and had campaigned on a platform of increased community participation in city government, which had gained him the support of liberal white gentrifiers. When he took office in 1974, he set about reforming city government to make it more inclusive and more responsive to neighborhood concerns.

A new city charter gave city government a much more democratic structure. Previously, all members of the city council had been elected to at-large seats. Under the new charter, twelve of the eighteen members of the council were elected to district seats, giving individual communities much more direct representation. Furthermore, under the new charter a neighborhood planning system was established. Twenty-four newly created neighborhood planning units allowed individual communities to participate in redevelopment decisions. Though these units did not have veto power over the city's redevelopment plans, they were given a central role in formulating the plans. Jackson vigorously supported this new neighborhood system and created a planning division to help neighborhoods formulate their own redevelopment plans.

Jackson's inclusive, pluralistic approach to government during his first term was a radical departure from government by an elite few, which had characterized Atlanta's politics for nearly three decades. Jackson tried to govern without the traditional coalition, relying instead upon the new alliance between a multiple-class black electorate and receptive elements of the white middle class. With Jackson at the helm, the white downtown business elite found its influence on city government diminished. Accustomed to a close relationship with city hall, downtown business leaders felt left out. Many were also put off by Jackson's personal style. Not only was he aggressive and outspoken in his demands for greater economic opportunities for blacks, but his manner struck them as arrogant, even pompous. Members of the business community began complaining openly, and the press began criticizing Jackson for being antibusiness. Many people felt that his progressive agenda and abrasive manner would hurt future economic development.

Jackson's estrangement from the business elite was neither complete nor permanent. He met periodically with Coca-Cola's Robert Woodruff, the don of the business elite, in Woodruff's offices.[10] He traveled to Paris with Ivan Allen III, son of the former mayor, to promote international air service to Atlanta.[11] In 1975 he announced the airport affirmative-action program, but he chose a meeting of the Action Forum, a coalition vehicle, to make the announcement.[12] Under pressure from the business elite, he retained Charles Davis, an appointee of Ivan Allen Jr., as the city's chief financial officer.[13] And eventually he engineered a rapprochement to bridge the gaps between coalition partners that did emerge.

The transition to African American electoral dominion almost inevitably caused a brief schism. Jackson may have had the tacit assent of some business leaders during his campaign,[14] but he was elected by an independent constituency that had substantive issues. Affirmative action and support for neighborhoods that opposed expressways backed by the business elite, combined with a procession of public lamentations by the elite, cast coalition members' differences in sharp relief for a time.

The rejuvenation of the coalition took the form of a series of informal meetings at city hall called the Pound Cake Summits (which did not work due to personal idiosyncrasies); the restoration of a painting of the Civil War's Battle of Atlanta, which resonated much more with white constituents than with black; the mayor's more energetic and visible promotion of the city and the downtown; and Jackson's receptivity to a plan favored by business for a mixed public-private corporation that would channel government subsidies and incentives to economic development. On the other side, talk of annexation or metropolitan government stopped, and both the newspaper and Ivan Allen Jr. endorsed Jackson for a second term.[15,16]

Jackson was reelected, and over the next four years he continued to change course politically. He moderated his reform agenda and became more accommodating in his relations with the business community. He reorganized the city's planning department along functional lines (parks, transportation, and so on), which effectively broke the ties that individual neighborhood planners had developed with "their" neighborhoods. He traveled more with the business elite on trips to promote the city, and to attract continuing investment he followed through with the public-private development corporation to oversee large development projects and channel subsidies to private developers.

Jackson had come to believe that the electoral alliance that had twice put him in office could not provide him with what he needed to govern effectively. To undertake economic-development projects, he felt, he needed the cooperation of business leaders, not only because conflict with them made such projects more difficult and cost too much politically, but also because the organized effort required for such projects would be much easier and more likely to succeed if he could rely upon the cohesiveness, the expertise, and the resources of the business elite—the characteristics that had made it such an effective political force in the past. By his second term in office, Jackson had concluded that even though African American politicians now had control of city hall, certain political and economic realities remained the same: Cooperation between white business leaders and black political leaders was still necessary.

Andrew Young and Full Regime Restoration

Maynard Jackson was succeeded by Andrew Young, Atlanta's second African American mayor, in 1981. Young had retained the white gentrifiers as members of his initial electoral coalition, but they were not an essential political ingredient, as the city's electorate was now more than 60 percent black. The new mayor was eager to further invigorate the governing coalition. In the context of the civil-rights movement, Young had often functioned as the lead negotiator with business coalitions over the terms of access to businesses and public accommodations, and he had gained an appreciation for the power businesses often had in local political affairs. By nature a conciliator, and well aware of the multiple advantages of concerted action, Young moved immediately to strengthen the traditional coalition.

Though he had not been supported by the downtown business elite during his 1981 campaign, he developed an especially close relationship with downtown business leaders during his two terms in office. Shortly after his inauguration, in an alliance with former President Jimmy Carter and the business sector, he reversed his opposition to the east-side expressway—the touchstone issue for the gentrifiers through whose neighborhoods the road would travel. Simultaneously, downtown business interests were intensifying their efforts to revitalize the downtown area, and Young joined them. His administration worked closely with Central Atlanta Progress to revive a failed shopping complex on the south side of the downtown area called Underground Atlanta. This was a complicated, costly, and risky undertaking, but the Young administration persisted in supporting the project until the complex was built. CAP was also focusing increasingly on downtown residential development. A CAP task force and others conducted a series of studies between 1984 and 1987 that examined ways of using multiple subsidies to encourage middle- and upper-income housing in the downtown area. Young supported these efforts and served on the task forces for two of the studies (though the effort was temporarily halted when the Atlanta residential real-estate market went into its steepest recession in twenty-five years[17]). Young was also an enthusiastic supporter of the efforts made by downtown business leaders to bring the 1996 Summer Olympic Games to Atlanta—so enthusiastic that he backed the city's bid for the Games over the objections of his advisers, who feared that playing host to the Olympics would end up costing the city money and would distract Young from his other responsibilities.[18]

Though Young allied himself with downtown business interests, he faced a different political situation than his coalition predecessors had. While he was fully reestablishing the coalition of business and black officials, the coalition was gradually losing its dominant position in Atlanta politics. There were multiple reasons for this.

First, the continuing decline of the downtown area as a business center meant a decline in the importance of the downtown business elite: The rapid growth of the northern suburbs and rapid commercial expansion in the north metro area were diminishing the power and influence of downtown business leaders. Not only were there new points of development activity outside the city, there were new corporate headquarters, new executive housing developments, and new political issues. Even in mildly regulated suburban Atlanta, new development required approvals and new or reorganized infrastructure, and each of these required political engagement. At the municipal level, accommodating new development meant only that there were now non-Atlanta focuses for political tussles. At the regional and state levels, however, new development meant direct competition for governmental approvals and resources. Completing the Lakewood Freeway or the Stone Mountain Tollway in the city now had to compete for Georgia Department of Transportation dollars with the widening of the Perimeter Expressway or extending Georgia 400 from the perimeter to the mountains—both well outside the city.

But development is not the only source of business-led influence on state and local politics. Governance involves multiple other areas in which businesses have interests: unemployment compensation, insurance regulation, health and welfare regulation and expenditures, and others. Growth in the number of corporate headquarters and firms outside the city, with many different political agendas, dispersed the influence that Atlanta-centered corporations and firms had once had. To be sure, interests often aligned and were not always competitive, but often enough, different corporations and businesses pursued different ends.

A second factor contributing to the diffusion of business influence was residential diffusion. With senior and middle-level executives living in widely separated parts of a growing metro area, local interests and causes become more diverse. How much development should be permitted on the Chattahoochee River is a far more important issue to a resident of the northern suburbs, where the river runs through several neighborhoods, than whether Atlanta should have a new downtown arena and a new hockey team to go with it.

Business influence also grew more diffuse as corporate culture changed in response to the internationalization of the economy. Executives were relocated and changed jobs more often, so they knew each other less well; this made it difficult to establish the type of stable, informal hierarchy that had previously supported cohesive decision making. This mobility also weakened interest in local issues, and it made long-term involvement in local civic affairs by businesspeople less likely. Although civic engagement remains a required dimension of successful corporate behavior, people now move too often and change jobs too frequently to develop the influence and effectiveness that come from long, continuous activity. One recent example: The man who had worked his way up to heading the United Way's annual campaign, in the past a gateway to greatly increased business responsibility, was promoted out of the city in the middle of the fund-raising campaign.

Internationalization of the economy also meant that more and more commercial real-estate investment was coming from outside the city, that a number of foreign banks established offices in Atlanta, and that more and more national, multinational, and foreign companies were establishing regional headquarters in the city. An increasing number of new Atlantans were focused on competing in national and international markets, not on local issues. Atlanta was becoming part of the global economy, and it was losing some of its local identity to what Charles Rutheiser, author of *Imagineering Atlanta,* has called an "ageographic and generic urbanism."[19] As a consequence, local government no longer had the same connection with the community. Economically, culturally, and politically, metropolitan Atlanta had become too complex and too externally focused to allow any one group to govern as effectively as the coalition once had.

Young adapted to the changes in the economy by trying to bring more foreign business to the city, traveling abroad frequently and drawing on the international contacts he had developed as U.S. ambassador to the United Nations during the Carter administration. He responded to the increasing dispersal of economic activity within Atlanta by supporting economic growth in areas of the city besides the downtown area. Atlanta experienced a boom in commercial real estate during the '80s, with most of the development occurring in three areas: the Midtown area, a few miles north of the central business district; Buckhead, several miles north of Midtown; and the north metro region, along the Perimeter Expressway. The Midtown district and Buckhead had politically assertive pro-growth factions representing their respective economic interests, and during Young's eight-year tenure, conflicts arose between these factions and neighborhood activists. In each case, Young sided with the pro-development faction.

A number of office towers and high-rise apartment buildings were constructed in the Midtown area during this period, and much of the investment was nonlocal; some was international. Intense commercial development in the area created conflict between pro-development interests and those who wanted to preserve the character of the district. A number of old apartment buildings with attractive architectural features were demolished, and others were threatened. Midtown was also the city's theater district, and the theaters were being threatened in another way. Because there was so much competition for land and because the city had weak land-use regulations that imposed very few restrictions on development, property values were rising rapidly. This meant that rents in the area were also rising, and theaters could not afford the higher rents.

The old apartment buildings and the theaters contributed to the area's vibrant personality. Residents of adjacent neighborhoods and those who found the area appealing wanted to preserve Midtown's distinctive nightlife. They wanted restrictions imposed on development to save the old buildings and to prevent the theaters from moving. They feared that Midtown would come to resemble the downtown area— a district of office towers with empty streets at night. But CAP and the Midtown Business Association opposed restraints on commercial real-estate developers. Mayor Young negotiated with preservation and neighborhood interests, but he made it known that he was much more interested in new development than in preserving old buildings. Eventually, with business interests and city hall favoring office and commercial development, all the old apartment buildings were torn down and all but one theater had to move.

Young not only supported development in several parts of the city, he supported links to the expanding suburbs. The Buckhead area had experienced rapid commercial growth over the previous two decades, and the pace quickened in the '80s. Buckhead business interests had for years wanted an expressway that would link Buckhead with the Georgia 400 highway, which ended several miles north of Buckhead at the Perimeter Expressway. Georgia 400 passed through the suburbs in north Fulton County, and the proposed extension would greatly improve access to Buckhead from these suburbs. During Young's second term, the Buckhead business community intensified its lobbying for this expressway. But the proposed link would cut a swath through several middle-class neighborhoods, and these neighborhoods organized resistance. Neighborhood leaders presented multiple arguments, one of which was that rapid transit, instead of yet another highway, should be used.

Young had spoken out against the expressway during his 1980 campaign, but as the issue came to a head in the mid-'80s he shifted his position and supported it. The project required approval by both the City Council and the Fulton County Commission. The commission chairman, Michael Lomax, also supported the road. Lomax was an African American politician who wanted to become mayor, and he both believed in the merits of the road and wanted to solidify his political support in the Buckhead business community. After a protracted political struggle, the Georgia 400 extension was approved, and the road was built as a tollway.

Young had faced a similar controversy earlier in his tenure. In 1982, former President Jimmy Carter began making plans to build a presidential library and policy center on the east side of the city, near the downtown area. The governor of Georgia and the state's transportation department wanted to build a parkway in conjunction with the Carter Center and Library that would link several east Atlanta suburbs with the central business district. A number of gentrified and gentrifying city neighborhoods along the route of the proposed parkway believed that the road would seriously damage their communities, and they organized active resistance. Carter favored the parkway because he wanted improved access to his center and library.

Though he had campaigned as an opponent of the parkway, Mayor Young reversed himself shortly after the election and actively supported the proposal. He argued that the parkway would actually be an asset to the neighborhoods, since the proposed plan included parks, jogging trails, bike paths, and land for housing. To anyone familiar with Atlanta's recent past, there was obvious irony in Carter's aloof endorsement and Young's advocacy. The parkway would follow the same route as an expressway that had been proposed in the early 1960s. This highway had been opposed by both Carter, who was then governor of Georgia, and by Young, who was then serving in the U.S. House of Representatives, and their opposition had been a major factor in defeating the plan.

Young's position contained certain elements of the old partnership between the downtown business elite and black political leaders. Downtown business interests favored the transportation department's proposal, because the parkway would improve access to the downtown area. And Young garnered black support for the project by insisting that African American businesses would participate in construction of the road. But the old coalition was just one of several major factions involved in the struggle, and the outcome provided evidence of the coalition's diminished importance. The alliance between the coalition and state government eventually won only a partial victory. Under pressure to resolve the issue in time for the 1996 Olympics, and after a prolonged legal battle between the Department of Transportation and the neighborhoods, a truncated, scaled-down version of the road was built in the early '90s, long after Young had left office.

In both highway battles, Young sided with business and against white, middle-class neighborhoods; he resembled his coalition predecessors not only in his commitment to downtown redevelopment but also in his opposition to the conflicting interests of the city's white middle class. Another similarity was that Young, like previous coalition mayors, did very little to address the needs of the city's black underclass. Class insularity and class bias may have been part of the reason for this, but Young also believed that the economic development he sought was a partial antidote to black poverty and that the issues of poverty, low-income housing, and social programs were largely national and not local responsibilities.[20] It is also important to remember that Young was mayor during the Reagan era. His pro-business stance and his reluctance to address poverty more directly reflected the conservative mood of the country during his time in office.

Redevelopment,
Atlanta Style

n 1960, while Ivan Allen Jr. was president of the Atlanta
Chamber of Commerce, just before he started his campaign
for mayor, he delivered a speech to the chamber that he
called the "Six-Point Program." It was a kind of civic mani-
festo, in which Allen outlined what he thought the city's
redevelopment goals should be. Allen had formulated this
program with Jim Robinson and Ed Smith, respectively
chairman of the board and president of the First National
Bank, and it reflected what the city's downtown business
leaders wanted. It proposed six major redevelopment objectives: continued construction of expressways, urban renewal,
a rapid-transit system, a major-league baseball stadium, a
civic center/auditorium, and advertising for the city. This
ambitious program would serve as Allen's campaign platform
in the upcoming mayoral election.[1]

Allen's two terms as mayor were the start of a new era of
downtown redevelopment. Construction was completed on
an extensive system of highways that joined up to the east
of the downtown area, and Allen's administration built the
baseball stadium and the civic center. His administration
also vigorously promoted rapid transit, and in the '70s construction of a rapid-rail system began. The '60s and '70s saw
robust private commercial development in the downtown

area, initially office towers and subsequently offices, hotels, and some mixed-use development. By the late '60s, business leaders were eager to make Atlanta a convention city, and in the '70s a state authority built a business convention center on the west side of the downtown area next to the Omni, a multiuse complex constructed earlier by major local developer Tom Cousins.

Despite all this private development and despite all the redevelopment undertaken by the city, downtown Atlanta began to decline as a business center in the '80s. And at night, despite the city's convention business, downtown streets remained empty. After dark, conventioneers rarely ventured outside hotel enclaves and mixed-use complexes— or what Ruledises aptly characterizes as an "archipelago of fortified fantasy islands."[2] In the late '80s, in an effort to give the downtown area some semblance of nightlife and to attract the city's own residents to the area, Mayor Andrew Young and Central Atlanta Progress managed to get Underground Atlanta built, using mostly public financing. But this shopping and entertainment complex failed to draw enough visitors to sustain itself. Many businesses left or closed, the city had to subsidize the operation, and eventually the city sold the complex to a private buyer at a substantial loss.

White, middle-class voters were generally unwilling to pay for all this downtown redevelopment with higher taxes. The downtown business elite could depend on political leaders in the coalition to try to persuade the black electorate to pay higher taxes for redevelopment, but it was a hard case to make, and there was no guarantee that the black leaders would be successful. So the coalition relied heavily on federal and state money to finance its redevelopment plans. It also devised ways to use local taxpayer money without having to go to the voters for approval.

Despite these ambitious redevelopment projects and all the federal, state, and local money spent on them, the governing elite's vision of downtown Atlanta as the vital center of the metro region's economy had not yet been realized by the late 1990s. One reason for this was that the rapid expansion of the northern suburbs continued to decentralize the area's economy. But another reason was that with the exception of the convention center, all the redevelopment projects were ill-conceived from an economic standpoint. Though the Georgia World Congress

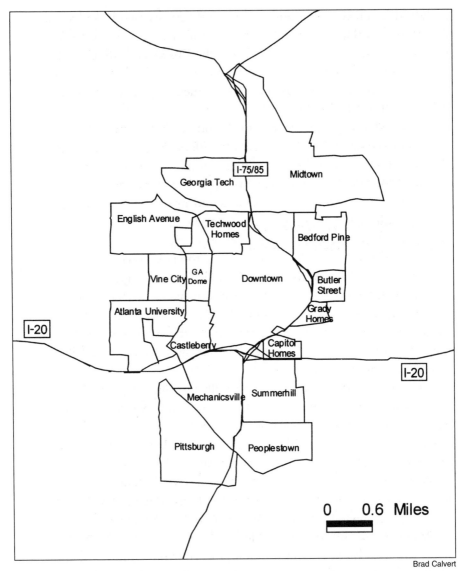

I-75/85
Midtown
Georgia Tech

English Avenue
Techwood
Homes
Bedford Pine

GA
Vine City Dome
Downtown
Butler
Street

Atlanta University
Grady
Homes

I-20

Castleberry
Capitol
Homes

I-20

Mechanicsville Summerhill

Pittsburgh Peoplestown

0   0.6 Miles

Map 5.   Atlanta's Central Neighborhoods

Center (convention center) brought more tourists to the downtown area, the baseball stadium, civic center, and rapid-rail system contributed very little to the downtown economy, and Underground Atlanta was a notable failure. As for the highway system, though it improved access to the downtown area, it also helped accelerate dispersal of economic activity to the suburbs. Though these redevelopment efforts added to Atlanta's prestige as a modern, progressive city, and though they gave city leaders a sense of pride, they did not have enough of an effect on the downtown economy to make downtown Atlanta the thriving, growing, exciting place that the governing coalition wanted it to be.

Removal of Low-Income Blacks From the Downtown Area

Immediately after World War II, Atlanta's business leaders organized the hiring of consultants to devise a transportation plan that would improve access to the city's central business district. The result was the 1946 Lochner Report. This report advocated a network of expressways radiating outward from the CBD to all four quadrants of the city. The highway configuration recommended by the consultants bypassed the area to the west through the old and increasingly vacant industrial districts that had developed along the west-side rail lines fifty to seventy years earlier. This approach would have minimized the destruction of neighborhoods. The destruction of neighborhoods, however, was exactly what Atlanta's business leaders wanted.

In the end, the consultants recommended that a north-south expressway partly encircle the CBD to the east. The final version of the Lochner Report reflected one of the major but unstated goals of the city's downtown business leaders. They wanted to remove as many poor blacks from the downtown area as possible, and a highway built just to the east of the CBD would cut through several low-income neighborhoods and eliminate portions of them.[3] They also hoped that the highway and future development alongside it would create a buffer between the CBD and the remaining portions of these neighborhoods. In addition, they wanted to create a reserve of land on the CBD side of the highway for eventual expansion of the business district.

Once the north-south expressway had been built, the city used the federal urban-renewal program to clear land for redevelopment on both sides of it. The combination of highway construction and urban renewal eliminated half of the low-income white neighborhood of Home Park and portions of several poor black neighborhoods: Buttermilk Bottoms (subsequently renamed Bedford Pike), Old Fourth Ward, Summerhill, Peoplestown, Mechanicsville, and Vine City. Map 5 (p. 90) illustrates the dissection of the central neighborhoods by the two expressways. The north-south expressway also cut through the middle of Auburn Avenue, historically the main black commercial district. The Allen administration chose to build the stadium on a site where parts of the neighborhoods of Summerhill and Peoplestown had been eliminated. The publicly declared purpose of this segment of the Atlanta urban-renewal program was to rehabilitate low-income neighborhoods by replacing deteriorating housing with improved housing and by bringing industrial jobs to the renewed area.[4] In building the stadium on this cleared land, the Allen administration blatantly disregarded the stated intention of urban renewal and the legal justification for tearing down housing. His administration did the same thing in building the civic center/auditorium. The city used the urban-renewal program to raze a portion of the poor neighborhood of Buttermilk Bottoms, northeast of the downtown area. After the civic center had been built, it used the urban-renewal program to tear down the rest of the neighborhood.

The Allen administration damaged the interests of poor black people with urban renewal in another way. The program stated that adequate replacement housing should be provided for residents of housing that was torn down.[5] But the Allen administration was able to partially respond to this provision because the federal government did not fully enforce it and in any case did not provide enough additional funding to build or acquire enough replacement housing. Not until 1968 was enough funding made available by the federal government to build all of the public housing that had been authorized by the 1949 Housing Act to provide much of the replacement housing. Not until 1971, when Congress passed the Uniform Relocation Act, was full legal and financial protection given to displaced residents.

Consequently, the immediate effects of urban renewal in Atlanta were the uncompensated displacement of much of a white neighborhood and large numbers of poor blacks, and overcrowding in black areas of the city. Since the urban-renewal and expressway programs did not require accurate accounting, no one really knows how many Atlantans were displaced. Estimates by knowledgeable local planners are that 68,000 people were forced to move, that nineteen out of every twenty people displaced were black, and that these 68,000 people represented between 19,000 and 22,000 households.[6] In the twenty-two years between the beginning of urban renewal in 1949 and the passage of the Uniform Relocation Act, the Atlanta Housing Authority built 3,667 public-housing units for families and 1,095 units for elderly people—a total of 4,762 potential replacement units. This means that at least 14,000 and perhaps as many as 17,000 households that were forced to move did not receive replacement housing. It is true that an unknown number of federally subsidized rental units were built during this period by local nonprofit organizations, usually churches. But their efforts could not possibly have provided enough replacement units to make up the difference. It is also true that some households received replacement housing in the existing stock, but in historically tight low-income housing submarkets there are usually very few vacancies meeting housing codes.

Another serious problem with the urban-renewal program was that once an area was targeted for renewal, low-income communities would live for years under the threat of being eliminated. Under these circumstances, poor neighborhoods slated for "renewal" deteriorated even further. Property values declined, rental property was no longer maintained, and social and other municipal services were withdrawn. Many people left before the process of property acquisition had even begun.

Even though the African American community in Atlanta was highly organized and active politically, the massive displacement of poor blacks met with little organized resistance from the black community as a whole. There were two reasons for this. First, during the '50s and '60s black political leaders were not able to focus their attention on this issue. African Americans were struggling to acquire basic civil rights; trying to protect themselves from white extremists; protesting police brutality; trying to change the racial composition of the police force; trying to contest city elections; attempting to gain seats on planning and development boards; and making efforts to improve, expand, and integrate public schools.

The second reason was that black leaders were trying to get the city to set aside land for construction of middle-class black housing. The focus of this effort was undeveloped land on the southwest side that the city had annexed in 1952. Long-established patterns of residential segregation had circumscribed the areas in which middle-class blacks could expand: neighborhoods surrounding the Atlanta University Center, a consortium of predominantly black colleges, a graduate school, and a theological school southwest of the central business district. The growing black middle class needed more land than was available in these interior neighborhoods, but they were separated from undeveloped peripheral land by middle-class and lower-middle-class white subdivisions. Because leaders in the city's governing coalition were middle-class, and because they had a limited amount of political capital, they in effect chose a political trade-off: In return for the land they needed for middle-class expansion and progress on some of the larger desegregation and access issues, they offered only tepid resistance on issues related to urban renewal. By 1956, access to the southwest side of the city for middle-income blacks had led to construction of 3,450 new owner-occupied houses and 3,100 private rental units. By that same year, only 2,444 new public-housing units had been built for low-income blacks.[7]

City leaders further displayed their bias against low-income African Americans in the way they went about building public housing. First of all, even though the federal legislation that initiated urban renewal stipulated that replacement public housing could be built on land cleared for redevelopment, city government, business leaders, and the Atlanta Real Estate Board all agreed—informally and illegally—not to do so. The obvious motive behind this agreement was that city leaders did not want any low-income housing adjacent to the downtown area. Furthermore, the locations chosen by the city for public housing segregated poor blacks not only from residential areas on the northeast and northwest sides of town, where whites lived, but also from areas on the southwest side, where middle- and upper-income blacks lived. The Carver Homes public housing development, with 990 units, opened in 1953. It was located in southeast Atlanta, east of the north-south expressway, a little more than two miles south of the CBD. Perry Homes, with 944 units, opened in 1955. It was on the undeveloped far northwest side, just south of and adjacent to the Inman Rail Yards, which defined the northern limits of black residential expansion. Harris Homes, with 510 units, opened in 1956 on the near west side, between the black colleges and the east-west expressway. It was separated by the expressway from the area designated for residential expansion for middle-class blacks.

The same pattern prevailed in the 1960s. Bowen Homes opened in 1964, and Bankhead Courts and Hollywood Courts opened in 1969. The three developments contained a total of 1,352 units, all built beyond Perry Homes on the remote, undeveloped far northwest side, an all-black area. One hundred twenty-eight units were added to Perry Homes in 1969. In 1965, John O. Chiles Homes, a 250-unit public-housing project for elderly people, was appended to Harris Homes. The only apparent exception to this pattern—not building public housing in the southwest quadrant reserved for middle-class black expansion— was the building of the McDaniel-Glenn Homes, which opened in 1968. But in fact, this 496-unit development was separated from black, middle-class areas by the industrial belt that followed the rail lines south beyond the CBD and west of the development.

The four public-housing developments built in the sparsely populated northwest area had very few services available. The 3,000 residents of the Perry Homes development had only one small grocery store. There was no pharmacy, one very modest clinic, and extremely limited recreational facilities. Those who had defended building public housing in this remote area had argued that the area would soon be overtaken by suburban development, and that the public housing there would become an integral part of surrounding communities. But the forty-five years since the development was built have seen no additional residential development in the area. Railroad switching yards, landfills, dumps, and industries producing toxic waste existed in the area when Perry Homes were built, and more would come. These noxious land uses have kept developers away.

Atlanta/Fulton County Stadium

The first step Mayor Allen took toward getting the stadium built is recounted in the book that he and Paul Hemphill wrote about Allen's administration. In 1963, the mayor invited Charles O. Finley, owner of the Kansas City Athletics, to come to Atlanta, hoping to persuade Finley to move his team there. During a secret visit, local sportswriters gave Finley a tour of the city, including a number of possible sites for a new stadium. According to Allen, Finley was not impressed with any of the sites. Then, just before Finley was to leave, Allen, in a sudden moment of inspiration, showed him the land cleared for urban renewal in the Summerhill/Peoplestown area, a site in the southeast quadrant of the intersection of the north-south, east-west expressways. Finley's reaction: "This is the greatest site for a stadium that I've ever seen."[8]

A different account of why Allen chose this site for the stadium appears in a recent book by Ronald Bayor. The story that Bayor tells is more prosaic and more complicated than Allen's. According to Bayor, the Allen administration originally wanted middle-class housing built in the Summerhill/Peoplestown area. But they abandoned this idea and decided instead to demolish the existing housing there and replace it with white public housing. There were several reasons for this change of plan. First, they found a lack of private-sector interest in building middle-class housing in the area. Second, the federal government was putting pressure on the city to build public housing to replace the housing being destroyed in its urban-renewal efforts. Third, white public housing would satisfy white business leaders who wanted a buffer between the CBD and the remnants of nearby black neighborhoods.

This plan, however, met with opposition from African Americans. They argued that the city should build black public housing in the area to compensate for all the low-income black housing being eliminated. According to Bayor, Allen finally chose to build a stadium on the site to satisfy the business community and avoid a direct confrontation with his black constituents. The choice preserved his informal agreement with the business elite and the real-estate industry: that public housing would not be built on urban-renewal land. It also accommodated business leaders who wanted a buffer between the CBD and the remnants of nearby black neighborhoods, and to some degree it mollified African Americans who opposed building white public housing on the site.[9] Map 6 shows the stadium's location within the Summerhill, Peoplestown, and Mechanicsville communities.

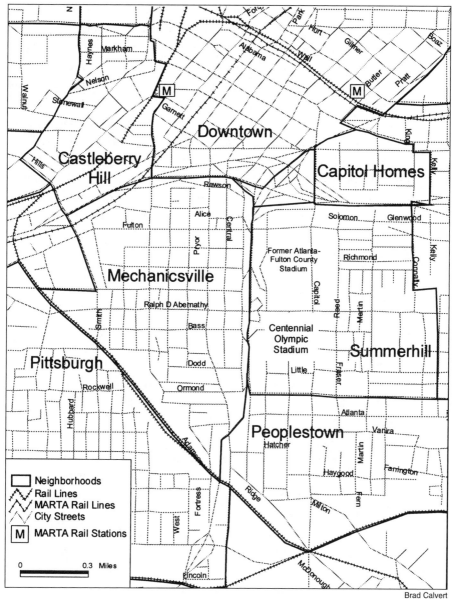

Brad Calvert

Map 6. Summerhill/Peoplestown/Mechanicsville and Surrounding Neighborhoods

Six weeks after Finley's visit, Allen asked Mills B. Lane, president of the Citizens and Southern National Bank, to put together financing for the project. Lane agreed enthusiastically. He moved quickly and put up nearly half a million dollars in front-end money for architectural and site planning. He had Allen make him treasurer of the Atlanta/Fulton County Recreation Authority board, and had him appoint Arthur Montgomery, an executive of the Coca-Cola Bottling Company, board chairman. Acting in concert, Allen, Lane, and Montgomery transformed the recreation authority. Part of the original mandate of the organization, and the rationale behind its dedicated tax revenue, was to expand, improve, and maintain the city's park system. But now half of the tax money the authority received was diverted to financing the stadium project. The money was spent first on planning and building the stadium, and in the future would be used to maintain the stadium and to pay off the bonds used to finance it.

Lane committed the front-end money for the project before either the City of Atlanta Board of Aldermen or the Fulton County Commission had met to discuss it. It remains unclear whether the initial money Lane contributed was his own or the bank's. What *is* clear is how much power Lane appropriated to himself in acting on a project that would be financed with public money. According to Allen, when Allen learned what Lane had done, he warned the banker that he was taking a risk by committing so much money without any security. Lane's reply, according to Allen, was: "You go back over to City Hall and run the City's business, and let me run this show."[10] Lane's attitude was evidently that even though the stadium would be financed with taxpayer money, the project now belonged to him and his bank, and public officials need not be concerned.

Construction of the stadium was completed in 1965. A generous contract was eventually negotiated with the Milwaukee Braves, and the team moved to Atlanta in 1966. The contract guaranteed a minimum annual revenue, and annual shortfalls in promised revenue since then have been made up by taxpayer money—an average of 2.25 percent per thousand dollars of assessed value of the city's tax base. Taxpayer money that was originally dedicated to improving the city's park system has been used instead to subsidize the baseball corporation. And because public money has been diverted from the park system to subsidize a baseball team, Atlanta's park system remains to this day inferior to those of comparable cities.

The timing of the revenue transfer particularly damaged the interests of black citizens. With civil-rights legislation dismantling the operation of previously segregated parks and recreation systems, courts began to recognize claims for equitable access to those facilities. In 1960, the closest date for which data are available, the racial subdivision of park and recreational facilities was as follows:

football fields: whites 20, blacks 0
recreation centers: whites 16, blacks 3
swimming pools: whites 12, blacks 8
baseball fields: whites 22, blacks 3
tennis courts: whites 119, blacks 8
parks: whites 42, blacks 8.[11]

The diversion of dedicated revenue to the stadium meant less money in the Recreation Authority's budget that could be used to rectify the segregation era's unequal distribution of facilities.

In Allen's view, the actions he took to build the stadium and to obtain a major-league baseball team for Atlanta were examples of bold leadership. Years later, looking back on what he and Mills Lane had accomplished, Allen commented, "We built a stadium on ground we didn't own with money we didn't have for a team we hadn't signed."[12] Allen certainly displayed a great deal of initiative in accomplishing what he did, and he obviously derived a great deal of satisfaction from his accomplishments, but his actions displayed a disregard for the interests of the public, especially the interests of poor black Atlantans. To some, his actions may seem bold, vigorous, and even creative, but to those who believe that government should be inclusive and representative, his misuse of federal money, his disregard of federal guidelines intended to protect poor people, his willingness to commit government to act independently of the Board of Aldermen and the Fulton County Commission, and his diversion of taxpayer money to subsidize a private corporation—all these constitute abuse of power.

To the residents of the Summerhill and Peoplestown neighborhoods, Allen's actions seemed like betrayal, for they had been promised that their neighborhoods would be redeveloped.

The Allen administration ignored the damage that the stadium would inflict on what was left of the surrounding neighborhoods. It imposed the stadium on adjacent neighborhoods without realistic planning, and the result was a further deterioration of these communities. The city did have a feasibility study for the stadium done in 1964, but the study was aimed primarily at justifying the stadium and persuading a baseball team to move to the city. Consequently, it focused on ways to organize financing and did not closely examine how the facility would affect surrounding neighborhoods.

First, the study proposed a plan for parking that was far from adequate. The study assumed that there would be four persons per car coming to the stadium, and it proposed 4,100 parking spaces.[13] This would allow 16,400 persons to arrive by car. The study projected that 3,250 people would come on fifty buses, for which parking would also be provided. So parking space would be provided for a total of 19,650 fans. The stadium, however, had a seating capacity of 55,000, so there were far too few parking spaces for heavily attended games. When the Braves agreed to move to Atlanta, they insisted that the city provide an additional 2,500 parking spaces within ten years. The city complied, eventually increasing the total number of spaces to 6,600, but this was still far from adequate. The number of people per car was actually a little over three. Realistically, therefore, when a game was sold out, 12,642 cars had to find parking.[14] The 6,600 official parking spaces available accommodated only about half (52.2 percent) of the fans. The other 6,042 cars had to find parking in the surrounding neighborhoods.

Owners of property in the neighborhoods surrounding the stadium realized that they could make more money by selling parking space than by renting their property. A zoning change—from residential to commercial use—was supposedly required in such cases, but the city did not enforce its regulations, and many owners never bothered to obtain approval. Some demolished houses to make room for parking, and others burned houses down. The result of all this demolition was a vacant no-man's-land, two to three blocks deep, around the stadium's official parking lots. When more than 6,600 cars came to a game, the additional drivers parked in these "gypsy" lots, usually paying two to six dollars.

Despite the damage that was done to the neighborhoods, the city refused either to provide sufficient parking or to enforce land-use regulations that barred informal parking on residentially zoned land.

Not only did stadium planners come up with a parking plan that considerably damaged surrounding neighborhoods, they also came up with a traffic plan that caused considerable inconvenience to neighborhood residents. The plan stated that an hour and a half before a game, almost all streets in the adjacent neighborhoods be converted to one-way streets carrying traffic toward the stadium. For more than an hour after the game, the streets would be one-way in the other direction.[15] Residents of these streets wishing to leave their homes by car before a game had to go against the traffic flow using emergency vehicle lanes and avoiding the policemen directing traffic. It was impossible for them to return home right after a game.

There were other inconveniences. The stadium put on noisy fireworks displays to celebrate victories, and the city refused to impose a curfew on the length of games or on how late the fireworks could be set off. After one extra-inning victory in 1993, residents were awakened by fireworks at 4:15 a.m. The fireworks could be dangerous as well as irritating: There were cases of the fireworks setting houses on fire.

Before the stadium was built, the Summerhill/Peoplestown area had a vibrant community life. In 1960, Peoplestown, the neighborhood immediately south of the stadium parking lots, was an integrated neighborhood of 6,831 people. The population was 49.8 percent black and 50.2 percent white. The white population was predominantly Jewish, who lived in Victorian homes on the west side of the neighborhood and included merchants who owned and operated stores in a neighborhood shopping area along Georgia Avenue. After construction of the stadium, the vitality of the area largely disappeared. By 1970, the population of Peoplestown had been reduced to 5,169, of whom 89 percent were black.[16] Henry Phipps, a black man who lived in Peoplestown and who worked to improve the neighborhood, has described what the area was like before urban renewal and the stadium:

> In this neighborhood we took a census about how many kids would be coming in and going out of school for the next three years—how many would be in school. Mr. John Calhoun helped us and we went before the board. The

next year they started building the school up here . . . around 1953 or 1954. I drew up the petition. I had five boys and two girls. Everyone of them went to school up there. My wife was PTA President.

After we got the gas and the street paved and the school and the park, everything looked good. We used to do our shopping on Georgia Avenue. They had a big supermarket there. They had a chicken house there and they sold chicken and fish. And then they had a theater on the corner of Crew Street and Georgia Avenue. Then below that they had a shoe shop, a bakery and on the other side of the street they had Fritz's Ice Cream. [17]

This shopping district along Georgia Avenue, which also included a small hospital, a hardware store, and a butcher, was demolished to make way for the stadium and its parking lots. This further contributed to a decline in the quality of life in the area. The stadium severely damaged the soul of the community surrounding it.

When Allen first proposed building the stadium in his speech to the Chamber of Commerce in 1960, and then made it part of his platform in his campaign for mayor, he presented it as a way to stimulate the downtown economy by bringing people to the area after working hours. But the site he ended up choosing actually had limited economic potential. Not only was there a three-expressway interchange between the stadium and the downtown area, but the state Capitol and government office buildings lay between the stadium and the commercial part of the central business district. So the downtown area was not really convenient to the stadium; people came to the games and left without lingering in the area. Downtown Atlanta remained largely unpopulated at night, and the partial destruction of two downtown neighborhoods further depopulated the area. The stadium actually diminished downtown commercial activity: It added to Atlanta's prestige as a major-league city, the Braves provided Atlantans with a new form of entertainment, and getting the stadium built gave Allen a feeling of pride and a reputation for being an energetic, skilled politician, but it contributed very little to the downtown economy.

The Civic Center/Auditorium

At the same time as it was building the stadium, the Allen administration was building a combination civic center and auditorium. The site that the city chose for this facility was in the neighborhood of Butter-milk Bottoms, just east and north of the CBD. The city had a two-phase plan for the area: It would first acquire and clear just enough land for the civic center/auditorium, and then acquire and clear a larger area for further redevelopment, which would include some upper-income housing.

Buttermilk Bottoms was a low-income, mostly rental neighborhood of shotgun and modest wood-frame houses. It lay in a valley between two parallel ridges. Stretching along the ridge to the east was Peachtree Street, and on the ridge to the west was Boulevard Avenue. In the early part of the century, wealthy whites lived in homes along these streets. Most of the original residents of the valley were black domestic work-ers who had jobs in these homes. A major fire in 1917 burned down the homes along Boulevard Avenue, and the homes along Peachtree were replaced by offices and other commercial development, but the more than 3,000 homes in Buttermilk Bottoms remained.

In 1963, in order to build the civic center/auditorium and redevelop the surrounding area, the city renewed its application for urban-renewal funding. In recent years there had been increasing competition among cities for urban-renewal money, which meant that by the time Atlanta renewed its application, the federal Urban Renewal Administration had greater leverage in enforcing its guidelines. One of the requirements that the URA threatened to enforce more strictly was that housing be built to replace housing that was torn down. Mayor Allen had ignored this requirement in the past: His informal agreement with the Board of Aldermen and business groups was that no new public housing would be built in these areas. Allen now persuaded the aldermen and busi-ness groups to make an exception to this agreement for the Buttermilk Bottoms area. Business groups agreed largely because they viewed the URA requirement as a convenient way to dispose of "the least salable areas" in the urban-renewal land inventory.[18] The Board of Aldermen also went along, but did so in ways that undermined the real purpose of the federal requirements. The aldermen agreed to apply for 1,000 units of public housing, but only if the city was not obligated to build these units with its own money. Also, the aldermen did not want any of this public housing to be built near the civic center/auditorium, so the land they designated for it was not in the Buttermilk Bottoms area but across the north-south expressway from the stadium and adjacent to an industrial area south of the CBD. Furthermore, the federal government did not adequately or fully enforce its stricter requirements for replacement public housing. The government allowed the city to count 300 units of the Bowen Homes public-housing development, even though this development was already being used to satisfy earlier replacement requirements.[19]

The Urban League began negotiating with the city to try to protect the residents of the Buttermilk Bottoms area. They reached an agreement with the city's planning department that the renewed area would be large enough to include substantial upgrading of the substandard housing in the area, and that relocation of displaced residents be an integral part of renewal plans. But Mayor Allen chose to keep his broader plan for redeveloping the entire area a secret. In order to expedite acquiring the land for just the civic center/auditorium, the city submitted a request to the Urban Renewal Administration for "early land acquisition," but the administration did not mention its long-range intention to develop the larger area. It wanted to avoid revealing to residents of Buttermilk Bottoms that their neighborhood was slated for destruction, and it also didn't want it known that displaced black families would be seeking housing in nearby white neighborhoods.[20] Once again, the federal government did not do enough to insure that the renewal process would be fair to residents of the affected area. Instead of requiring that the city submit public plans for developing this larger area when it submitted its request for smaller-than-allowable early land acquisition, all that it required was that the city apply for an eventual planning study for this larger area.

Construction of the civic center/auditorium was completed on schedule in 1965. It was then that the city announced its plans for redeveloping the larger, adjacent area. Residents of the neighborhood now learned that 1,000 households were going to be displaced. In an effort to prevent further destruction of their neighborhood, they created an organization they called U. Rescue, an acronym for Urban Renewal Emergency: Stop, Consider, Understand, Evaluate. This organization included not only residents but local merchants, most of whom were white. Two years earlier, residents of the area had organized to protest the closing of an elementary school in the neighborhood.[21] They had sought the help of the larger black community in this effort. The result had been that the controversy over closing this school had been broadened to include the city's overall approach to desegregation, and thus the efforts to protect the neighborhood had been diluted.[22] This time, having learned important lessons, the neighborhood did not seek help from the black community at large. U. Rescue operated solely as a neighborhood organization. It held mass meetings and made specific demands. It urged that an advisory committee be formed with official power to participate in decisions regarding the neighborhood. It sought assurances that the area would remain not only residential but also affordable to current residents. It tried to guarantee that an adequate amount of housing would be built to replace the housing that was destroyed. And it tried to prevent the destruction of a church in the area that had already been moved by an earlier renewal project.

The Atlanta Housing Authority, acting as the city's redevelopment agency, tried to mollify U. Rescue by proposing that a new advisory committee be formed that would replace U. Rescue's leadership. But U. Rescue opposed this and gained official recognition as the neighborhood liaison.[23] The neighborhood then won some minor victories. Part of the redevelopment plan was to widen one of the primary north-south streets, which would have meant further demolition of houses. U. Rescue managed to get this postponed. The group also successfully resisted a plan to enlarge a park in the area from twelve to twenty-five acres, which would have meant displacement of residents, and U. Rescue enjoyed partial success in getting new public housing in the area. The group sought construction of 650 units. The city filed an application for 350 units, and eventually, over objections from the business community, built 144 units along North Avenue, the seventy-one–unit U. Rescue Villa, a high-rise for elderly people, and an additional seventy-three units of family public housing.[24]

But U. Rescue's small victories hardly mattered. As it turned out, the city kept putting off its commitment to redevelop the neighborhood. Most of the cleared land in the area, which was renamed Bedford Pine, lay vacant for the next two decades while a succession of community groups tried to get the city to follow through on its commitment. Then, in 1973, Central Atlanta Progress formed a subsidiary called Park Central Properties, and even though it was not the low bidder, Park Central was assigned responsibility for continued redevelopment of Bedford Pine. In 1974, the Project Area Committee, a federally mandated watchdog agency, extracted a commitment from the city that 25 percent of any new housing in Bedford Pine be subsidized for low- and moderate-income residents. Nothing was done, however, and the land continued to lie fallow.

While Buttermilk Bottoms was being razed, the Atlanta Housing Authority had provided 110 mobile and modular units as temporary housing, to allow a very small proportion of the residents to stay in the area and retain some of the social community that was being destroyed. But since the city kept failing to redevelop the entire area, and since the replacement units it did build were far too few, and since even these replacement units ended up taking three or four years to build, this so-called temporary housing lingered on, an embarrassing reminder that the city had failed to live up to its promises. Eventually the housing authority decided that retaining the temporary housing was not cost-effective, and it was destroyed.[25]

In the mid-'80s, after years of inertia, Park Central finally fostered the development of multifamily complexes in the Bedford Pine area: more than 1,400 units, most of them reserved for upper-income residents. What finally provided the impetus for residential development in Bedford Pine were the vigorous reestablishment by the Andrew Young administration of the coalition of business and black elected officials, and a renewal of the effort to attract upper-income people to live in the downtown area. In effect, Park Central transmitted the urban-renewal subsidies to developers. Also, to attract prospective residents, the city forgave property taxes on the housing for five years and offered a gradually declining abatement of property taxes for five years beyond that. The Project Area Committee had long since folded, so there was no longer any pressure on CAP or elected officials to honor the 1974 agreement that 25 percent of the units built in the area be subsidized for low-income people. Including the earlier public housing built in the area, only 218 units of Bedford Pine housing were subsidized for low-income residents—less than 16 percent of the total and far fewer than the number of low-income housing units that had been destroyed. The city claims that in exchange for the tax abatements some units were reserved for moderate-income people, but this provision was not enforced, so there is no way to verify this claim.

Transforming Atlanta into a Convention City

In the late '60s, downtown business leaders decided they wanted to make Atlanta a convention city, and they started making plans to build a business-convention center in the downtown area. In pursuing this project, they were confronted with a new political situation. When Sam Massell was elected mayor in 1969, the downtown business elite lost control of city hall, and could no longer rely upon city government to help it reach its redevelopment goals. So downtown business interests turned to state government to help them build the convention center.

In 1970, the Georgia Legislature appropriated $175,000 for preliminary planning for the proposed center. Senate and House advisory committees formulated legislation that would finance both construction of the center and a statewide tourism-promotion program. The bill was supported by the Georgia Hotel-Motel Association, whose members would be taxed to fund the promotion program. Supporters created a committee called the Georgia International Congress Center to shepherd the bill through the Legislature. Jimmy Carter, the recently elected governor, was named honorary chairman of the committee, and Mayor Massell was named honorary vice chairman.

Midway through the legislative session, as the bill moved toward passage, opposition began to develop. Mayor J. R. Allen of Columbus objected to using a statewide hotel and restaurant tax for the benefit of Atlanta. "Some special-interest groups up in Atlanta are attempting to quietly secure passage of a bill in the State Senate Thursday which would rob the citizens of Columbus of up to a half-million dollars a year to build a civic center in Atlanta," Allen said.[26] The Georgia Municipal Association, a political-action group of statewide elected municipal officials, also came out against the bill. The GMA wanted the revenues for tourist promotion to go to local governments instead of being routed through state government.

A compromise was worked out, but passage of the legislation was delayed until the next session. In the meantime, a fight developed over the site for the proposed center. John Portman, a prominent Atlanta developer, had persuaded the Legislature in its early planning to consider a site in the still-vacant Bedford Pine area, just east of his Peachtree Center hotel/office/shopping complex. Tom Cousins, another large-scale developer, had purchased the air rights over the railroad gulch on the west side of the CBD, and he campaigned to have the convention center built on his property. Eventually the Legislature chose the site on Cousins' property. Mayor Massell refused to take sides, either because he felt he ought to remain impartial or because he feared the consequences of backing the losing proposal, so the city had no role in deciding the location of a substantial land-use project that would have a major impact on future development of the downtown area.

The desire of city leaders to make central Atlanta a middle-class shopping and entertainment area was one of the reasons that the Ivan Allen Jr. administration had used the urban-renewal program to eliminate poor black neighborhoods adjacent to the downtown area. In the '60s and '70s, residents of these neighborhoods made up much of the pedestrian traffic in downtown Atlanta. City leaders did not want prospective new consumers to have to mingle with large numbers of poor blacks, and eliminating these nearby neighborhoods reduced the number of poor blacks frequenting the downtown area. For the same reason, the city used urban renewal to eliminate the poor neighborhoods surrounding the site of the convention center.

The city also reduced the amount of low-income black pedestrian traffic around the Five Points MARTA station. This station is the major transfer point for commuters traversing the city. Before the rapid-rail system was built, the Five Points area, the original center of the CBD, contained small grocery stores, drugstores, sporting-goods stores, and clothing and jewelry stores. These shops had clustered around the areas where lower-income black workers transferred between the buses that took them to their jobs and the buses that took them home. When the Five Points MARTA station was built, bus-to-rail transfers were dispersed to peripheral stations, and most bus routes in the central area were eliminated. This was done partly for efficiency but also to eliminate the cluster of shops patronized by low-income blacks. Furthermore, the layout of the rail station did not provide convenient access to the stores around it. As a result, the businesses died or moved away. A faint echo of this once-vibrant business district remains, in the form of street vendors who set up their tables in front of the station each day. But these vendors are harassed by the police, and Central Atlanta Progress keeps trying to get rid of them through legal means.

Making downtown Atlanta safe and attractive for out-of-town visitors also heavily influenced private downtown development. After the convention center was built, Tom Cousins, the developer who had won the fight to have the center built on his property, built next to it a combination sports arena, hotel, and shopping and entertainment complex called the Omni. Conventioneers never had to venture outside the complex. John Portman's Peachtree Center is a similar self-contained multiuse complex. And Underground Atlanta, a downtown shopping and entertainment complex built in the '80s but since shut down, embodied much the same concept, providing a self-contained, secure environment for out-of-town visitors, but contributing very little to street life.

As a result of all these efforts to make Atlanta a viable convention city, many downtown streets are almost empty at night. Because developers and business leaders were afraid of letting conventioneers mingle with the city's black population, they created a downtown that lacks a natural, vibrant, nighttime street life. After business hours, conventioneers do not walk the streets. They stay in their hotels, take cabs to other hotels, or leave the central area. The location of the convention center and the Omni contributes to this problem. Because they are situated on the very western edge of the downtown area, conventioneers find it inconvenient to walk from them to the heart of the central business district. Nor do many Atlantans visit a largely vacant downtown after business hours. The city built Underground Atlanta to revitalize the downtown area at night, but the nighttime shopping and entertainment offered by the complex failed to attract many Atlantans. In addition, Underground Atlanta's isolation and inward focus minimized the contribution to street life made by those who did patronize it. In other words, after the city and private development had reduced night-time pedestrian traffic in the downtown area, both by eliminating adjacent low-income black neighborhoods and by driving out downtown businesses patronized by low-income blacks, it spent millions of dollars in an unsuccessful attempt to fix a problem that its own actions had helped to create.

Underground Atlanta

During the Jackson administration, Central Atlanta Progress became enamored with the idea of building an underground shopping complex on the south side of the CBD to help revitalize the area. An earlier Underground Atlanta had failed after several years of operation, but CAP revived the idea because festival marketplaces were enjoying national popularity as ways of reinvigorating moribund downtown areas. The Rouse Company was the major East Coast developer of such facilities, and during the Jackson administration CAP began talking to the Rouse Company about resuscitating Underground Atlanta. After Andrew Young became mayor in 1982, his administration hired Rouse to a do a serious assessment. At the urging of CAP, Young also formed a private corporation, the Underground Festival Corporation, to plan and organize the project.

The project was a risky one. To be successful, it had to attract not only out-of-town visitors but also both black and white Atlantans, and potential private investors had serious doubts about whether whites and blacks would be willing to go downtown and mingle in significant numbers. But CAP persisted despite the private sector's reluctance, and Young continued to go along with what CAP wanted. The project was finally undertaken, but most of the initial capital investment was public money. The Rouse Company itself did not invest any equity capital. Instead, it negotiated an annual management fee.

Putting together financing proved especially complicated. Backers of the project wanted most of the financing to come from bonds issued by the Downtown Development Authority. But even though the bonds were to be issued by the DDA, they would be backed by the city.

Because state law requires a referendum for this type of large issue of city-backed bonds, and because neither CAP nor the mayor wanted to submit the project to a vote, bond lawyers had to find language that would commit the city to repaying the bonds but would evade the referendum requirement. Finally, after two unsuccessful and highly expensive court tests, a financing package was put together. It included $85 million in bonds issued by the Downtown Development Authority but backed by the city. The city also decided to contribute several million dollars in revenue from a new sales tax. Georgia law requires that the amount of a new sales tax be offset by a corresponding reduction in property taxes. But even though a new sales tax is supposed to be revenue-neutral, an additional sales tax is attractive to local governments because there is a one-year time lag during which property-tax collections continue at the old rate while the new sales tax increases revenues. As a result of increasing its sales tax, the city enjoyed a $39 million revenue windfall, of which $12.1 million was dedicated to the Underground Atlanta project.

The project received $18.5 million in pass-through federal funding: a Community Development Block Grant for $8.5 million and an Urban Development Action Grant for $10 million. Urban Development Action Grants were intended to leverage private money for redevelopment projects. Community Development Block Grants are aimed at the housing, community, and economic-development needs of poor people. The Reagan administration made the restrictions on the latter grants more lenient, loosening requirements that recipients demonstrate that the money is being used on projects that actually improve the conditions of poor people. One of the arguments made in support of Underground Atlanta was that it would provide jobs for poor people, but because of these loosened requirements, the grant was made with no confirmation that this would happen.

CAP and the Young administration felt no compunction about having taxpayers shoulder almost all of the initial expense for an enterprise that they hoped would yield substantial profits for private investors and the businesses involved in the project. The total public money invested in the project amounted to $121.6 million; total private investment was only $15 million. Furthermore, local investors made this private equity investment as a tax write-off. So an accurate assessment of how much investment in the project was actually public money should also include the cost to the federal government of tax revenues forgone through write-offs. Because private records are not available for examination, such an assessment is not possible. But if the $15 million in private investment is taken at face value, the public investment in the project amounted to 89 percent of the total capital required.[27]

This second version of Underground Atlanta was a seriously flawed undertaking. It did not bring large numbers of people to downtown Atlanta, and a number of businesses in the complex either closed or moved out. As a consequence, the complex continued to be a burden on taxpayers. The city reserved rights to some of the profits from the complex, but Underground Atlanta performed so poorly that instead of receiving profits from the enterprise the city had to subsidize the debt service. From its opening in 1989 through 1997, a total of $36.1 million in city revenues subsidized the complex—an average of $4.2 million a year.[28] When the initial investment and these subsidies are added together, the amount of public money spent on the complex through 1997 comes to $162.7 million. Similar excesses in public underwriting of private development schemes characterized the late 1980s throughout the country. No one has ranked these public-private partnerships in terms of their reliance on public money, but Underground Atlanta would almost certainly be near the top of such a list.

Underground Atlanta did so poorly that in 1996 the Rouse Company declined to renew its management contract. Finally the city decided to cut its losses. In March 1999 it sold Underground Atlanta to a private firm. To sell the complex, the city had to write off an additional $38 million in unpaid public debt.[29] So almost all the public investment in this risky, ill-conceived project ended up being a total loss.

6

MARTA

A major part of Atlanta's downtown redevelopment efforts was its construction of a rapid-rail system. Plans for a rail system were formulated beginning in the early '60s, and construction began in the early '70s. The most striking feature of this undertaking was that it was essentially an effort to enhance the city's image, not a realistic solution to the region's transportation needs. A study issued in 1967 maintained that an expanded and improved bus system would serve the city just as well and far less expensively than a rapid-rail system. Two years later, another study argued with what seemed like irrefutable logic that rapid rail did not make sense economically because of Atlanta's low population density. In 1997 a retrospective analysis of MARTA's actual performance concluded that the earlier studies had been correct.[1] City leaders appear to have promoted an extensive rail system mainly because they wanted Atlanta to have a modern, "big city" transportation system. They ignored facts and practical considerations because they wanted to be part of a highly visible project that would bring prestige to their city.

The plans for the configuration of the rail system and for the means of funding it had to be approved in multiple referendums, so its supporters had to devise a rationale for the system to counter the argument that it did not make economic sense. They argued that if the city and the other participating jurisdictions enacted land-use regulations that

113

concentrated high-density development around rail stations, ridership would increase, justifying the cost of building and operating the system. But after voters approved the rail plans, the implicit promise that local governments would enact regulations focusing development near rail stations was not kept. In the city itself, developers objected that such regulations would be too restrictive, and they lobbied city government for a laissez-faire zoning ordinance. Elected officials yielded. This meant that the city had no way of insuring that high-density development would be coordinated with rail lines and stations. In the suburbs, the subject of zoning never came up at all after the final referendum had passed.

Race has always played an important role in Atlanta's politics, and it was an important element in the effort to get the rail plan approved by metro-area voters. The original rail plan formulated during the Ivan Allen Jr. administration did not have strong popular support, and largely because it proposed more rail service to white areas of the city than to black areas, it was not supported by black political leaders in the city's governing coalition. As a result, when the plan was presented to voters in 1968, in what was to have been the final referendum, it was rejected. White leaders then sought black support by promising more rail service to black areas, a minority contracting program, and low fares for a fixed period. A compromise agreement was presented to metro-area voters in another referendum in 1971. Largely because of the support of African American leaders, this revised rail plan passed in the city and in Fulton and DeKalb counties. Had it not been for cooperation between white and black partners in the governing coalition, a rail system would never have been built. The white business elite, as it had done several times in the past, allied itself with black political leaders in pursuing its redevelopment goals, and once again this biracial political alliance demonstrated its effectiveness.

In the mid-'80s, the transit authority began formulating plans for a second phase of rail construction. The change that had taken place in the political dynamics of the governing coalition since blacks had taken control of city hall was evident in the planning process. One of the central provisions of the 1971 agreement between black and white leaders had been that a rail line would connect the downtown area to the Perry

Homes public-housing development on the far west side of town. This line had not yet been built, but white business leaders now wanted the north rail line extended to the northern suburbs. The northern route would be more expensive than a line to Perry Homes, yet the transit authority decided to build the northern line and to postpone the Perry Homes line indefinitely. Some African American leaders objected, but in general the city's black leadership put up very little resistance. This was just one example of the real balance of power that has prevailed in the governing coalition since blacks gained control of city government. Even though white business leaders no longer directly control city hall, they still get what they want because black elected officials usually let them have it. The city's biracial governing coalition still exists, but instead of being made up of pro-business whites inside government and African American leaders outside, it is now an alliance between white business leaders outside government and pro-business blacks inside.

Early Planning and Early Successes

In the 1940s and '50s, transportation policy for the Atlanta area had focused entirely on building highways. But as early as 1954, the Atlanta Region Metropolitan Planning Commission (ARMPC) issued an overview of future development priorities, in which it suggested that the city would need a rapid-transit system "within a few years."[2] At the time, the Atlanta region had a population of less than a million, and the report remained vague as to exactly when such a transportation system should be built.

In 1960, Ivan Allen Jr., who was then president of the Atlanta Chamber of Commerce, announced his "Six Point Program." One of the six goals Allen proposed was a rapid-transit system.[3] In February of that year, the ARMPC began an eighteen-month study of rapid transit; it issued its study just before Labor Day in 1961. This was the first of what would become a succession of rail plans. The study recommended a sixty-mile, fixed-rail system that would connect the city proper with five metro-area counties: Fulton, DeKalb, Cobb, Gwinnett, and Clayton. It proposed that there be six radial lines, three in the north and one each on the east, west, and south sides of town, and that these six lines intersect in the CBD. The estimated cost of the entire system was $3 billion.[4] It was evident even in this initial study that serious consideration was not going to be given to an expanded bus system. In recommending a rail system, the ARMPC report dismissed the value of buses, characterizing them as a "second rate" means of transportation.[5]

Excepting only the line under Peachtree Street in the central area, the ARMPC plan proposed that the rapid-rail system be built along existing rail lines. Atlanta was originally a railroad junction, and there were at least nine existing lines to choose from, most of which radiated outward from the city's central area. The rights of way along these rail lines were continuous, which would make the construction easier. And, of course, building rapid-rail lines along these routes would cost less than building them through developed areas. This approach would, however, mean that the system would not serve areas that were not accessed by these existing lines.

The approach of following existing lines would be used by all future rapid-rail plans. The other precedent set by the ARMPC study was that the plan it proposed would provide less service to the African American areas of the city than to the white areas. The predominantly black south side was to be served by one line. This was to be the airport line, which would run from the white, working-class, suburban town of Forest Park through black neighborhoods to the central business district. The west line, the shortest of the primary lines, would provide service to the black, middle-class communities around and beyond the Atlanta University Center on the near west side. The east line would provide service to the white suburb of Avondale Estates. Along its route to the CBD it would skirt the edges of black neighborhoods to the south and white neighborhoods to the north, and would reinforce the boundary between them. On the white north side of the city there were to be three lines: a line from Marietta (Cobb County) to the CBD, one from Norcross (Gwinnett County) to the CBD, and a branch line that would connect Emory University/North Druid Hills (DeKalb County) with the east line. Overall, there were to be three lines serving white areas; one line, the west line, serving an African American area; and two lines, the south and east lines, serving both black and white areas. A total of five lines with twenty-nine stations would serve white areas; a total of three lines with ten stations would serve black areas. This disparity in proposed service between black and white areas did not reflect the balance of population in the metro area. It did, however, reflect a geographic reality: Because of racial discrimination, blacks were confined to a smaller area of the city than they would have lived in otherwise, given their percentage of the population.

Initially there was a legal obstacle to any rapid-transit system: The state Constitution did not recognize the legal authority of local governments to provide transportation services. In the winter of 1962, rapid-transit proponents in the state Legislature introduced a proposed amendment to the Constitution to change this. They also created the Metropolitan Atlanta Transportation Study Commission to formulate a new regional transportation plan.[6] But the constitutional amendment did not have statewide support among voters. It was defeated in the November 1962 general election, although it did pass in Fulton and DeKalb counties. Despite this setback, promoters of the rapid-rail plan continued their efforts. The next Legislature received the study commission's plan, and created a Committee of 100 to come up with a way to overcome constitutional obstacles. At the end of the legislative session, members were appointed to this committee, including representatives from the six metro-area jurisdictions included in the rail plan. Ernest Vandiver, former governor of Georgia, was named to head this body.[7]

The constitutional amendment the committee drafted required that only the six metro-area jurisdictions included in the transportation plan had to vote in favor of the amendment for the measure to pass. It also authorized the state to create a governmental entity to "frame, build, and operate a commuter service for the Atlanta area." The way the amendment was framed went a long way toward insuring its passage. It restricted the vote to those areas most likely to pass the amendment, it did not specify the actual source of revenue for the system, it did not specify the exact route alignment, and it did not state that a vote in favor of the amendment was a binding commitment to build the system. The proposed amendment got the unqualified support of the newspapers and the business community, and in a 1964 referendum it passed in all six metro-area jurisdictions.[8]

The 1965 Legislature created the shell of the Metropolitan Atlanta Rapid Transit Authority (MARTA), the government entity authorized by the amendment, but legislators were hesitant to go ahead and fully establish this entity. They were aware that problems with racial issues and local autonomy lay ahead, so they required that another referendum be held to let voters decide whether MARTA should be fully constituted. This time, however, the referendum did not require that all six jurisdictions vote in favor of it; those areas that passed the measure would form MARTA, and those that defeated it would not be included.

Supporters chose an early election date, one that was awkward and inconvenient, in an attempt to minimize voting, which they hoped would maximize the favorable vote. They scheduled the referendum for the week after Memorial Day, the first week of June, when many middle- and upper-class voters, the likely opponents, would be occupied with the end of the school year, making vacation plans, and starting new summer routines. The strategy was successful: It reduced the vote to 48.1 percent of the vote in the previous referendum, and the referendum passed in every jurisdiction except Cobb County. In Gwinnett County only 2,705 voters turned out, and the measure won by 137 votes. In Cobb County, even though the total vote was down by 57.3 percent, MARTA was defeated soundly, 56.5 percent to 43.5 percent. Consequently, Cobb's seat on the MARTA board and its participation in the system were dropped.[9]

After six years of preliminary studies and political maneuvering, a government entity for planning and building a rapid-rail system had been legally established. Proponents of a system had won substantial victories. MARTA now hired two consulting firms that had worked on San Francisco's Bay Area Rapid Transit system: Parsons, Brinckerhoff, Tudor, Bechtel; and Hamer, Greene, Siler Associates.

The 1968 Referendum

Despite their early successes, proponents of rapid rail faced serious obstacles. One of these was growing dissatisfaction in the African American community with the disparity in proposed service between white and black areas. Black political power was growing, and one sign of this was the formation in 1963 of the Summit Leadership Conference, a coalition of nine black organizations whose initial focus was a master plan for the "total desegregation of Atlanta" in housing, jobs, public accommodations, and the criminal-justice system.[10] The Leadership Conference became more prominent than the more narrowly based Negro Voters League, and included in its membership some of the more aggressive members of the Atlanta civil-rights movement. In late 1966, the conference voted to oppose the construction of the rapid-rail system unless the west line was extended farther than planned, to provide better service for blacks on the west side.[11]

MARTA supporters were soon presented with another challenge. Atlanta's bus system was owned and operated by a privately owned company called the Atlanta Transit System. In June of 1967, the ATS issued a report that advocated a 32.3-mile radial bus system that would either precede completion of the proposed rail system as a transitional, intermediate system or constitute an alternative to it. According to this report, the bus system could be put in place in a matter of months, would provide service levels approaching those of a rail system, would be linked directly to the existing bus system, and would cost only $52 million, a fraction of the estimated multibillion-dollar cost of the rail system.[12]

MARTA planners moved quickly to insure that the ATS proposal would not be taken seriously. Less than five weeks after its appearance, they issued a report entitled "Metropolitan Atlanta Rapid Transit Authority's Review of Atlanta Transit Systems 'Rapid Busway' Proposal." The authors of this report stated that the decision to build a rapid-rail system had already been made, and that discussion of an alternative was therefore pointless. Actually, a decision had not yet been made: The final line configuration and the means of financing a rail system still had to go before the voters. The MARTA planners also denied that a rapid busway system would be a useful intermediate system while the rapid-rail system was being built. They estimated that the cost of the rapid busway plan would be more than $150 million, far more than the estimate of $52 million in the ATS proposal, and they questioned whether it made sense to spend this amount of money on a means of temporarily relieving traffic congestion while a rail system was under construction.

The ATS study raised important issues, but neither its proposals nor MARTA's response prompted any public debate. Because a rail system had the prestige of being a modern means of transportation, and because the rail plan at this point had so much political momentum, no elected officials and no one in the business community paid any attention to the ATS study or questioned MARTA's arguments.

MARTA planners now turned their attention to the means of financing the rail system. They started working out the details of the bond issue they would have to present to metro-area voters. The financing arrangement used to build rapid-rail systems in other cities across the country was to have them paid for partly by local taxpayers and partly by matching funds from the federal government. But the amount of federal funding fluctuated annually in response to appropriations and nationwide demand. It was legally capped at two-thirds of the total cost of a system. These fluctuations made it difficult for local governments to develop reliable projections of their share of the cost. This was the most difficult challenge faced so far by MARTA planners. A local bond referendum raises a specific amount of money. If the amount turns out to be insufficient, a local government has a choice of finding more financing, shrinking the project, or going back to the voters for more money.[13]

Mayor Allen and the MARTA board had decided by the fall of 1967 that the bond issue should go before the voters in 1968. Because new rail systems were also being built in San Francisco, Seattle, Los Angeles, and Washington, D.C., MARTA planners made a conservative estimate of how much of the cost would be paid for by the federal government: 40 percent. This meant that the local share would be just over $375 million. But deciding how much each local government would contribute proved vexing. At the conclusion of these negotiations, problems with the financial plans of the San Francisco rail system prompted MARTA planners to revise their own calculations. This led to a lengthy second round of negotiations among the participating local governments over who was to pay how much. These extended negotiations caused MARTA to delay presenting the bond issue until three weeks before the election.[14]

Also working against passage of the bond issue was a feature of the contracts negotiated by the participating local governments. Minus the federal share for the first phase, these contracts stipulated that all long-term obligations had to be cited on the ballot—not only the $377.6 million of capital costs, in other words, but the estimated $615.4 million in underwriting fees and interest charges as well. This large difference between the previously advertised cost of the project and the figure that would actually appear on the ballot would almost certainly cause an unfavorable reaction among voters.[15]

Another major problem that hurt MARTA's efforts was its lack of political foresight. All the local governments involved in the MARTA referendum had appointed businessmen with no political background to the MARTA board of directors. They did this because it was a business-led initiative, because they viewed the rail system as something that would primarily benefit downtown businesses, and also because they felt that businessmen would be less susceptible to political pressure and corrupting political influences than local politicians would be. But this tactic allowed local politicians to remain somewhat removed from the campaign,[16] which meant that the board had insufficient knowledge of how to attract the political support MARTA needed. Partly as a consequence of this, as the shortened campaign to persuade voters to approve the bond issue entered its final stages, most local politicians avoided taking a position on the referendum.[17]

This lack of political expertise and political responsiveness created especially serious problems for MARTA when it came to gaining the support of the African American community. The limited rail service planned for black areas of the city had become a major issue among black leaders, opposition to MARTA in the black community was gathering momentum, and without the support of a substantial number of African Americans, the bond referendum would have trouble passing. The 1970 census showed that African Americans accounted for 51.5 percent of the city's total population. When the bond issue was voted on in November 1968, the racial composition of the city was just about even, and whites held only a 57-percent–to–43-percent advantage in registered voters. A black electoral majority was imminent.

African American politicians were especially sensitive to the inadequate level of rail service planned for the city's public-housing developments. In 1968 there were nearly 15,000 public-housing units in

Atlanta, and with the exception of units reserved for the elderly, almost all of them were occupied by blacks. More than 15 percent of the city's black population lived in public housing. The most isolated developments, which needed access to public transportation the most, were on the northwest side. The largest of these was the Perry Homes development, with more than 3,000 occupants. At one point just before the election, some of these occupants organized a march across empty fields and through industrial areas to city hall. There they held a demonstration demanding improved access to public transportation.

The day before the election, the Summit Leadership Conference came out in opposition to the bond issue, accusing MARTA of ignoring "modest requests" for improved service. Jessie Hill, an insurance executive who was cochairman of the Summit Leadership Conference (the other cochairman was the Reverend Sam A. Williams, who also headed the city's Community Relations Commission), said that the conference had met numerous times with MARTA, and that he had hoped up to the last minute to be able to endorse the plan, but that MARTA would not give sufficient assurances regarding services to black areas.[18] Opposition among black leaders was not unanimous. Alderman Q. V. Williamson, State Senator Leroy Johnson, and State Representative Grace Hamilton all supported MARTA. But the fact that there was any opposition at all was a sign that black leaders were aware of the growing political power of the black community. A new generation of more aggressive African American leadership was more insistent on getting better terms in political deals with white business leaders.

On November 5, 1968, voters in the city of Atlanta and Fulton and DeKalb counties defeated the bond issue. DeKalb came closest to approving it, with a 48.9 percent favorable vote. In the city, only 41.9 percent of more than 90,000 voters approved the measure.[19] Black areas voted against it more than 2-to-1. With a few exceptions, the only areas where the measure succeeded were white wards in northern residential areas.[20] These were wards dominated by the city's white business elite.

A Compromise Plan and the 1971 Referendum

Mayor Allen did not let this setback stop his efforts to build a rail system. He moved quickly to address the issues he considered responsible for the defeat of the bond referendum. He asked the MARTA board "to restudy the route structure to make it more acceptable to all Atlantans, particularly Negro Atlantans."[21] He also pledged a reassessment of the financing package to see whether more of the costs of the project could somehow be shifted to the federal government. Finally, he tried to co-opt the opposition by appointing Jessie Hill, cochairman of the Summit Leadership Conference, to the MARTA board.[22]

But MARTA now faced another problem as well: a new study that was critical of the basic rationale for a rapid-rail system. A year before the 1968 referendum, the five jurisdictions involved in the MARTA transportation plan had jointly hired a consulting firm, A. M. Voorhees and Associates, to conduct a broad overview of regional transportation needs. Voorhees issued a study called the Draft Technical Report in April 1969. This report tried to strike an objective balance among overall regional needs, not only for a rail system but also for buses and highways. The defeat of the 1968 referendum increased the importance of this study, and its conclusions revealed that the MARTA plan had put a disproportionate emphasis on rail.

Unlike the MARTA plan, the Voorhees plan followed conventional transportation-planning logic in interpreting Atlanta's needs. According to this logic, only when there are significant concentrations of both residences and jobs does a rail system attract enough riders to justify the substantial investment. Voorhees argued that the constraints of a fixed-rail system did not make it the best transportation solution for a city like Atlanta, because Atlanta, having experienced most of its growth during the automobile era, is a low-density city with widely dispersed residences and jobs.

Like the earlier study done by the Atlanta Transit System, the Draft Technical Report recommended an expanded bus system. It concluded that only the Peachtree Street northern corridor had enough density to justify a rail system, and proposed busways in place of the east-west and south rail lines.[23] This plan, besides offering an empirically rational solution to the city's transportation needs, would cost a quarter of what the much more ambitious MARTA plan would cost. MARTA planners and its backers were aware that a rail system did not really suit Atlanta's low population density, but they argued that proper land-use regulations would draw high-density development to the stations and rail lines. What MARTA was arguing, therefore, was that building a rail system would create the conditions that would justify building a rail system.

MARTA further justified its plan by using inflated figures in projecting future employment in the CBD. Whereas transportation models of the time estimated an increase in employment in the CBD from the 1960 figure of 187,469 to between 206,000 and 218,000 by 1995, MARTA used a figure of 404,000.[24] The Voorhees study used this fig ure, but it noted that if the CBD grew this rapidly it would experience "an extraordinarily high rate of growth, with few cities in the world anticipating such development."[25] Even accepting this exaggerated employment projection, Voorhees did not give rapid rail the prominence it had in the MARTA plan.

Through press releases and public statements, MARTA attacked the Voorhees plan as unrealistic. It maintained that the plan underestimated the right-of-way acquisition costs and construction costs involved in building busways, that it neglected to include in construction costs the cost of emergency lanes and road dividers, and that it underestimated the eventual increase in the number of riders. MARTA also seized upon Vorhees's recommendation of articulated buses, arguing that no one knew how well these would work.[26]

MARTA also challenged the Voorhees plan as not being politically viable. In April 1970, the chairman of the MARTA board wrote to the supervisors of the study and told them: "Inasmuch as no system can be built without the political approval of the subdivisions which it serves, political acceptance is the key criteria. MARTA has been advised that east-west busways and a north-south rail line are an unacceptable combination."[27] MARTA knew that providing only bus service to African American neighborhoods on the east, west, and south sides of town while providing rail service to the white north side would be unacceptable to blacks. MARTA had learned from the defeat of the referendum that political as well as technical factors had to be taken into account.

The political landscape changed dramatically when Sam Massell was elected mayor in the fall of 1969. Massell was Atlanta's first Jewish mayor and the first to come from outside the city's white power structure. He had strong ties to the black community and owed his election largely to black voters, having garnered 92 percent of the black vote and only 27 percent of the white vote. Massell supported the MARTA plan for a rapid-rail system, but he directly addressed black concerns by supporting a busway connecting Perry Homes with the west rail line. His political masterstroke was a proposal that there be no charge for riding the transit system, which of course had great appeal to low-income voters. Furthermore, to gain support for the system from the city's property owners and raise the money for free service, he proposed that the local share of funding for the system come from an income tax rather than a property tax. This would mean that the burden of funding the system would fall partly on suburban commuters who earned their incomes in the city. He also tried to broaden the political base of the MARTA board by appointing as its chairman the president of the Atlanta Labor Council, one of the few times in Atlanta political history that a labor representative has occupied an important policy position.

The city's governing coalition now began to exercise its influence. Having split earlier on the issue along racial lines, the coalition began to coalesce through a new civic organization called the Action Forum. This biracial group of business leaders had been founded by Mills Lane, a bank president, and W. L. Calloway, a prominent black real-estate agent, after the defeat of the bond referendum. With black political power increasing, and with blacks on the verge of taking over control of city government, Lane and Calloway wanted black and white business leaders to work together to maintain a strong business influence on city hall.[28]

The first major issue addressed by the Action Forum was financing for the rapid-rail system. White suburbanites were naturally opposed to Massell's proposal that an income tax be used to pay for the system, so the Action Forum worked out a compromise between Massell's proposal and the sales tax favored by suburbanites. The group proposed that a penny earmarked for the transit system be added to the sales tax and, to partly offset the sales tax's regressive effects, proposed a fifteen-cent fare and a commitment that the fare would not be raised for seven years. This compromise would require state legislation, since Georgia law at the time prohibited local governments from imposing new sales taxes. The previous governor, Lester Maddox, had been a foe of rapid transit, but he had been replaced by Jimmy Carter. With Carter supporting rapid transit, and with leaders of the business community supporting the compromise worked out by the Action Forum, the state Legislature voted by substantial majorities to allow the local governments involved to offer their voters a sales-tax referendum.[29]

MARTA had presented its plan for the 1968 bond referendum to the voters only three weeks before the vote, and one thing it had learned from its defeat was that it needed more time to campaign. It presented its plan for the upcoming sales-tax referendum on April 7, 1971, more than seven months before the November vote and more than four months before the board had to put the plan into its final form. The new plan proposed a four-county, 52.1-mile rapid-rail system with forty stations, an immediate takeover of the private bus system, 17.6 miles of busways connecting with eight stations, and, including the busways, an 86 percent expansion of the bus system. The plan promised a fifteen-cent fare, although it did not promise how long this fare would last.

The busways and the expanded bus service were meant to appeal to both black and white voters. The plan proposed that a Proctor Creek busway connect Perry Homes with the Ashby Street rail station, running through all-black sections of northwest Atlanta with stops at Bankhead Highway, Grove Park, and Jackson Parkway. A busway on the east side was to run south of the east-west rail line, parallel to Moreland Avenue; it would serve the black communities of Reynoldstown, Kirkwood, East Atlanta, and Thomasville. White areas of the city would be served by busways between Lenox Square and Sandy Springs and between East Lake and the North DeKalb Shopping Center.[30]

As soon as the plan was made public, black leaders began pressing their demands. A busway to Perry Homes rather than a rail line quickly became a controversial issue. At a public hearing held at the high school in the Perry Homes neighborhood, Jessie Hill, the man whom Ivan

Allen Jr. had appointed to the MARTA board to represent black interests, announced that MARTA was studying the possibility of replacing
the busway with a rail line. Two other major issues taken up by black
leaders were rail-system construction contracts for minorities and preserving the fifteen-cent fare for ten years.

Also speaking out for black positions on issues relating to MARTA
were the leaders of a black civic organization called the Atlanta Coalition on Current Community Affairs: Marvin Arrington, a city council-
man; Vice Mayor Maynard Jackson; and Leroy Johnson, a longtime
state senator. Speaking to the MARTA board at its July meeting, Maynard Jackson warned that black voters were dissatisfied with various elements of the plan. The referendum, he told the board, "is at this time
headed to a very certain and demoralizing defeat at the hands of the
electorate. We come to assist you in avoiding a repetition of the dis-
heartening defeat of 1968."[31] At its August meeting MARTA responded
to black demands with promises that would satisfy 90 percent of the
core black agenda. It substituted a rail line for the proposed busway to
Perry Homes, endorsed minority contracting, and committed itself to
maintaining a fifteen-cent fare for seven years.[32] In September the
Atlanta Coalition on Current Community Affairs endorsed the amended
plan.

The November 1971 referendum passed in three of the five jurisdictions. It passed by narrow margins in the city and in Fulton and
DeKalb counties, but was overwhelmingly defeated in Gwinnett and
Clayton counties. It passed by 3,358 votes in DeKalb. Initial returns
showed that it passed by 5,943 votes in the city and lost by 3,932 in the
part of Fulton County outside the city. But because the sales tax would
be instituted on a county basis, the city and Fulton County votes were
counted together, resulting in a 2,011-vote positive margin. A recount
reduced the margin to 461 votes for the county as a whole, with the city's
affirmative votes still overcoming the rest of the county's negative votes.

In Gwinnett County only 23 percent voted in favor of the rail plan,
and in Clayton County only 21 percent. Voter turnout was light, with
only 43 percent of registered voters turning out in the city, 43 percent
in Fulton, 45 percent in DeKalb, 40 percent in Gwinnett, and 45 percent in Clayton. This was almost certainly because the referendum was

held in an off year: one year after the gubernatorial election, two years before the next mayoral election, and one year before the presidential election.[33]

There were two reasons that the referendum was so soundly defeated in Gwinnett and Clayton counties. First of all, the MARTA plan would have provided only limited rail service to these counties; each county would get only one of the forty rail stations in the MARTA plan. The second reason was purely racial. There were fears in these predominantly white suburban counties, as there had been earlier in Cobb County, that a rail link with the city would bring in large numbers of African Americans.

White voters in the city were more supportive, though the majority still opposed the plan. The vote among whites was 51 percent against to 49 percent in favor. Among black voters, the margin was 55 percent in favor to 45 percent opposed. Since the positive vote margin in the city had overcome the negative vote margin in Fulton County, black leaders could fairly make the claim that the referendum had passed because a high percentage of African Americans had voted in favor of it.[34] MARTA and its supporters had won because they had run a more politically calculated campaign this time round, and because they had listened to African American leaders, had included them in making their plans, and had been responsive to their concerns.[35]

The Business Community Regains Control

MARTA and the governing coalition had told the public that an extensive rail system would make economic and fiscal sense if there were high-density development near rail stations, and suggested land-use regulations that would generate this kind of development. After the referendum, the Massell administration began taking steps to implement this coordinated land-use and transportation strategy. They hired the consulting firm of Eric Hill and Associates to analyze the rail system's potential effect on land uses and to formulate policies that would channel development into areas around rail stations. The resulting Transit Area Development Studies recommended policies that would generate commercial development around both central-area and selected suburban transit stations, concentrate housing around other suburban stations, and integrate development around the stations with the stations themselves. The city also hired Fred Blair, a nationally known zoning and land-use consultant, to rewrite the city's zoning ordinance so that zoning would reinforce development opportunities created by the rail system. Blair and the city planning staff recommended an ordinance that, like ordinances in San Francisco and Toronto, permitted lower-density development in areas distant from transit stations and reserved the highest densities for the immediate station areas.

In 1976, while the rail system was under construction, the City Council began to consider the new ordinance. But the governing coalition now reversed its earlier position. Forsaking their commitment to nodal development around rail stations, coalition members argued instead for a laissez-faire approach. Central-area businesses and the Atlanta Real Estate Board mounted an intensive and successful campaign to defeat the proposed ordinance. In 1980 the City Council finally passed a watered-down ordinance that permitted high-density development throughout the city's business districts.[36]

As a result of this weaker ordinance being adopted, the rail system has not attracted enough high-density development to increase ridership to a level that would make the system economically efficient. And because the system is not economically efficient, it has required deeper subsidies than were contemplated in the final rail plan. In only one short segment of the rail system have land-use patterns corresponded with what rapid-rail promoters originally proposed. High-density development has clustered around stations along the MARTA line that runs north under Peachtree Street in the CBD and Midtown office districts. This is due primarily to the status of Peachtree Street as an office and commercial location. Peachtree Street addresses in these two areas command land prices two to three times the prices of sites only a block or two away.[37] Plans are currently under way for high-density development around three stations elsewhere in the system.[38] But these plans are taking shape after two decades of unregulated and consequently widely dispersed development, and the plans are purely voluntary. There is still no regulatory assurance that future high-density development will be coordinated with rail lines and stations.

The decision of the city's ruling elite not to organize land-use planning to reinforce the rail system has had serious consequences for the entire metro area. A laissez-faire approach to development has left the city with a rail system that has not significantly changed commuting habits. Low MARTA ridership has meant the continued dominance of automobile commuting, which has meant a continuation of widely dispersed, automobile-based development. As a result, Atlanta now has the longest commuter times in the country. And because automobile emissions have so severely damaged air quality, there has been a federal shutdown of new highway construction in the metro area.

It is important to remember that all this has come about because the city's governing elite broke a promise it made to the voters in the 1971 referendum. In subsequently opposing land-use regulations that would have coordinated development with the rail system, business leaders contradicted the rationale they had used to sell rapid rail to local government officials and the public. It should also be remembered that there is a political reason behind Atlanta's underused, heavily subsidized transportation system: Business leaders used the governmental process to get what they wanted and disregarded rational, realistic planning. The fact that elected officials finally went along with business' wishes has also had a political consequence: It has increased Atlantans' distrust of city government and has generally lowered their level of confidence in political discourse.

Another example—smaller but equally clear—of the excessive power that Atlanta's business interests had is what happened when MARTA built the Peachtree Center station. This station, one of those on the rail line under Peachtree Street in the downtown area, lies beneath Peachtree Center, the high-rise hotel/restaurant/office complex designed and built, and initially owned, by the architect and developer John Portman. The typical way to build a subway is to dig up a street, put in the line, and then cover the street back up. But Portman did not want to lose business while MARTA was building the line and station. In a stunning display of political clout, he got MARTA to work by tunneling, despite the fact that it costs about twice as much as digging up a street. When the Atlanta contingent on the MARTA board presented Portman's proposal, other members, particularly those from DeKalb County, objected to paying the additional costs. They insisted that the increased construction costs be paid for by reducing the size of the Peachtree Center station and the amenities it provided. The board settled on this compromise.

The tunnel MARTA ended up building is quite an engineering feat. Cut through bedrock, it lies 125 feet underground, making it one of the deepest mass-transit tunnels in the world. As originally envisioned in the Central Atlanta Study done in 1971 and in Portman's own original plans, the Peachtree Street station was to have been a street-level mall with the subway immediately beneath it, and with numerous access points to the street from the block-long station. But the smaller station MARTA ended up building has very limited access and requires riders to take four escalators to reach the rail line.

While the downtown subway was being built, other businesses in its path suffered, but none of Portman's clients in Peachtree Center was inconvenienced. As a costly tunnel was being built 125 feet belowground, the pedestrian flow in and out of Peachtree Center was uninterrupted. So was Portman's cash flow.

The Second Phase of Construction: A Broken Promise

Fourteen years after the 1971 referendum approved the MARTA rail system, a second phase of planning began. In December 1985, a month before Mayor Andrew Young's second term began, Charles Loudermilk, chairman of the MARTA board of directors and one of Young's earliest supporters from the business community, proposed that a new branch of the north rail line be extended from Buckhead to the northern suburbs. The concept of a second leg of the north line had strong support from business interests in Buckhead, which wanted increased access to the affluent north side. Business also wanted MARTA to reach the north-central section of the Perimeter Highway, where two new regional shopping centers had stimulated new office development.

Another reason for Loudermilk's proposal was that a final decision had recently been reached to build the Georgia 400 Tollway from I-85 through Buckhead to the Perimeter Highway. The tollway would connect I-85 with the existing non-toll segment of Georgia 400, which traversed the northern suburbs and reached almost to the town of Dahlonega in the Appalachian Mountains, seventy-five miles north of the city. The impending construction of more than six miles of expressway inside the perimeter presented an opportunity to combine highway and rail-line rights-of-way and thus avoid what would have been higher acquisition costs if the projects had been undertaken separately. Furthermore, aligning the rail line with the tollway would allow MARTA to avoid the kind of political opposition it would have encountered if it had tried to build a separate line through an established residential area. The state Department of Transportation had already won this kind of lengthy fight for the tollway, after years of neighborhood resistance.

In promoting a rail line extending to the northern suburbs without corollary land-use regulations, business leaders were doing the same sort of thing they had done in the late '70s, when they had fought against a zoning ordinance that would have concentrated high-density development around rail stations. Once again, they were contradicting the basic rationale they had initially used to gain public support for a rail system. By itself, another north rail line would not concentrate high-density development along the north-central stretch of the Perimeter Highway or restrain the dispersal of office development on the north side. If MARTA went along with what the business community wanted, it would be standing its own public policy on its head. Instead of coordinated rail lines and public policy channeling private development, previous private development would determine where the rail lines would go. Instead of public investment guiding private investment—the original promise made to the public—public investment would follow private investment. Inverting the investment relationships meant that the region's transportation needs would never be met. The situation in Atlanta remains the same today: If private development continues to be effectively unregulated and widely dispersed, public transportation can never hope to catch up.

Deciding whether to build a north rail line involved another important public-policy issue. When Loudermilk recommended that rail service be extended to the mostly white, affluent north side, activists in the African American community pointed out that the 1971 referendum had included a promise to build a line to the Perry Homes housing development. The east-west line was complete and the north-south line was within four years of completion, but the promise to build the west spur to Perry Homes had not been fulfilled. Since the passage of the referendum, the Perry Homes line had been given a low priority by MARTA planners because projections of ridership remained low. There were few other residents living among the landfills and toxic-waste dumps surrounding this low-income housing development. The isolation of Perry Homes, which a rail line was intended to remedy, had become MARTA's reason for opposing the line.

Loudermilk's proposal forced MARTA to confront both a political and a moral issue: Would MARTA honor its fifteen-year-old promise to the black community, or would it abandon its pledge in order to construct a new line to northern white suburbs? Loudermilk claimed that circumstances had greatly changed and that black Atlantans now had a different view of what would best serve their interests: "A lot has changed in 15 years. Years ago the black community felt that the [Georgia] 400 corridor was a way for white people to come into the city, make money and then go home and spend and enjoy it. I think today some people in the black community are saying we need to get the unemployed people in the city's core out to where the jobs are."[39]

But African American political activists insisted that MARTA keep its promise. Joseph Lowery, head of the Southern Christian Leadership Conference and a MARTA board member, reminded everyone that the pledge to build the Perry Homes line had been part of a political bargain that MARTA had struck with the black community to gain its support.[40] Marvin Arrington, president of the City Council, was equally adamant: "We made a promise to those people, and we're going to keep it."[41] Mayor Young offered conciliatory support, but proposed a middle path: a less expensive light-rail connection between Perry Homes and the west line and the business-backed heavy-rail line to the north.

After the state Department of Transportation approved the plan to extend Georgia 400, it gave MARTA four months to decide whether to incorporate the extension of the north rail line into the final plans for the expressway. In January 1986, Loudermilk, with coalition concurrence, formed a Committee of 50 to study MARTA's plans and come up with a (nonbinding) recommendation. He modeled this committee on the Committee of 100 formed by the state Legislature in 1963; the earlier committee had prepared an early version of the mass-transit plan that was eventually offered to voters in the 1971 referendum.

The Committee of 50 was made up of the seventeen-member MARTA board and thirty-three business, government, and civic leaders. Loudermilk appointed David Chesnut, the incoming chairman of MARTA, to head the committee, and named Lowery vice chairman. Mary Sanford, president of the Perry Homes Tenant Association, was the leading representative of the Perry Homes faction. Sam Massell, former mayor of Atlanta and the unelected "Mayor of Buckhead," was the leading representative for Buckhead interests. John Williams, a suburban apartment developer, represented suburban business interests, and Sam Williams, who then ran John Portman's merchandise and furniture marts and who later became president of Central Atlanta Progress and head of the Atlanta Chamber of Commerce, represented central-area business interests.

It soon became apparent that MARTA was determined to build only the north rail line. What happened in the meetings of this committee and between the committee and the MARTA board provides a vivid example of the tactics that a political bloc can use to outmaneuver its opponents. The pro-business faction on the committee displayed a great deal of shrewdness in procedural matters and managed repeatedly to manipulate the meetings to get around the opposition and achieve what it wanted.

The committee had originally been told that it had five months to review MARTA's plans and come up with a recommendation. But at the second meeting, on March 23, 1986, David Chesnut announced that the committee had just two and a half weeks to decide on significant aspects of the north line. He told the committee members that the reason for this abbreviated period of study was that the Atlanta Regional Commission was preparing a regional transportation plan and needed MARTA's recommendations by the middle of April. He also said that if the north line were to qualify for federal funding, it would have to be included in this plan.[42] At its next meeting, in April, the committee voted to include a north rail line of unspecified type in this regional plan. At the same meeting, Mary Sanford and supporters of the Perry Homes line offered a resolution that the Perry Homes line be built concurrently with a rail line in any other area. But the committee ruled that this resolution was premature and did not vote on it. The resolution to build the north line was characterized as a merely procedural matter that did not affect the committee's ability to decide later whether the Perry Homes line should also be built.[43]

In late May, MARTA made its next move. It proposed a busway between Perry Homes and the central business district instead of a rail line with connecting bus routes. It estimated the cost of the busway at $73 million and the rail connection at $124 million and argued that the cheaper alternative made more sense. It estimated the cost of the north rail line at $490 million. It argued that the committee's vote in April to endorse some type of rail for the north line precluded studying busways to the northern suburbs as an alternative, and it concluded that heavy rail was the least expensive option for this line.

MARTA's proposal angered Tom Perdue, the governor's chief administrative officer and a member of the committee. He was upset by the lack of logic in MARTA's argument that a bus route would be cheaper for Perry Homes while heavy rail would be cheaper for north Atlanta.[44] Perdue demanded and received the data MARTA had used to support its conclusions, and state government hired an independent private consultant to review MARTA's technical analysis. The consultants found not only that MARTA's conclusions were weakened by the failure to look at busways as an alternative to the north rail line, but that MARTA had tilted the analysis in favor of heavy rail over light rail by using an "extremely high percentage of transit trips in the [northern] corridor expected to use rapid transit."[45]

At the next committee meeting, on June 4, supporters of a Perry Homes rail line strongly resisted MARTA's proposal for a busway. The first to speak on behalf of a rail line was Reginald Eaves, a Fulton County Commissioner. Eaves had run against Andrew Young in the 1981 mayoral election, and his electoral strength was in Atlanta's poor black neighborhoods. Eaves presented a resolution passed by the Georgia Association of Black Elected Officials threatening to withhold support for the expressway portion of Georgia 400 if a rail line along that route took precedence over the Perry Homes line. After Eaves, several other Perry Homes supporters spoke, and then Mary Sanford reintroduced her April motion that the Perry Homes line be built "concurrently with development of rapid rail in any other area." David Chesnut objected, declaring that the resolution "serves no useful purpose at this time," and he called for a substitute resolution. The resolution then put forward stated that the Perry Homes line would be "given the same consideration that other rail lines has [sic] received in the past and will receive in the future." This substitute motion passed by a single vote, 16 to 15.[46]

Sanford and her allies had fought hard for their position, but they did not have the support they needed from any elected official except Eaves. Almost all black elected officials acknowledged that a promise had been made to the black community and that MARTA had a moral obligation to keep its promise, but acknowledging the obligation did not translate into active political support. Overt support would have meant going against the wishes of prominent business leaders, and no elected black official, except Eaves, was willing to do that.

The legislation permitting the establishment of MARTA required agreement of two of the three participating governments in order to change a plan approved by referendum, and both adding the new north heavy-rail line and downgrading the Perry Homes line from heavy rail to a busway would change the referendum plan. As the first step toward obtaining the approvals, Mayor Young; Michael Lomax, chairman of the Fulton County Commission; and Manuel Maloof, DeKalb executive officer (an elected position) were scheduled to appear at the next Committee of 50 meeting. Maloof appeared; Young and Lomax did not. Maloof argued for expanded rail service in DeKalb County. Statements sent by Young and Lomax straddled the issue, acknowledging the 1971 Perry Homes promise, endorsing the new north heavy-rail line, and urging flexibility regarding the choice of transportation modes on the Perry Homes line.[47] Once the rhetoric had been stripped away, Young and Lomax had endorsed the north-side business community's new rail line and sanctioned building something less than had been promised to Perry Homes.

As the process moved into its final weeks, the MARTA staff made what they expected to be a final recommendation to the committee. They proposed an express busway to Perry Homes, one-station extensions of the east and west lines, and heavy rail in the Georgia 400 corridor. An attempt to mediate an agreement among Perry Homes line supporters, the committee, and MARTA staff led to David Chesnut and senior MARTA staff meeting with Perry Homes residents at the nearby Archer High School in July. The recent revelation of political alignments insured a tense meeting. Residents verbally assailed the visitors, but David Chesnut stopped the show when he pronounced the MARTA staff's plan nonnegotiable, saying, "My honky ass rides the train and your black ass rides the bus."[48] Fortunately, no one was injured.

At a meeting on July 23, the Committee of 50 approved the east and west line extensions, deferred the Perry Homes recommendation to the final meeting, and asked for a review of alternatives to heavy rail for the north line.[49]

At its meeting on August 6—the final scheduled meeting—the committee made recommendations on financing and on the terms and conditions for extending the rail system into counties outside the original MARTA plan, and then it took up the Perry Homes issue. Sanford again presented the April resolution, which had yet to be voted on. After extended debate, the committee voted 17-to-13 to table the motion once again. After the vote was taken, most of the black members and all of the Perry Homes supporters walked out in protest.

The meeting continued after the walkout. The remaining committee members discussed differing estimates of the cost of heavy rail for the north line. Even though available rail manufacturers' estimates showed lower costs for light rail, the committee went along with the estimates MARTA had provided and recommended heavy rail. Because of the walkout, one more meeting was scheduled, for August 13.[50]

During the week the two sides worked out a compromise, and the agreement they reached was formalized at the final meeting. Mary Sanford and the Perry Homes supporters were told that they could have $75 million, which would buy either a busway to Perry Homes or a feeder rail line—a separate 1.4-mile line to a new Bankhead Station. The Bankhead

option would extend rail service by three miles, approximately 40 percent of the way from the Ashby Street station to Perry Homes, but the
Bankhead line would have its own cars and would therefore require a
change of trains at Ashby Street. Existing Perry Homes bus service
would be rerouted to connect with the Bankhead station. The feeder line
was supposed to be a down payment on an eventual Perry Homes line.

Sanford had joined the committee to get a rail line, and she accepted
the offer of part of one. As a part of the offer, Fulton County and city
of Atlanta officials attempted to mollify the supporters of the Perry
Homes line by sweetening the deal. The Atlanta Economic Development Corporation agreed to participate in the development of a strip
shopping center at the site of the Bankhead station. Various local government agencies—most subdivisions of Fulton County—were to rent
office space in the center to make it financially viable. In its final report,
the committee recommended a rail feeder line to Perry Homes—a separate three-mile line with its own cars that would connect with the west
line at Ashby Street. The report also recommended heavy rail for the
north line. The estimated costs were $483 million for the north line,
$77 million for the Perry Homes line, $149 million for the east-line
extension, and $69 million for the west-line extension.[51]

The report included a "Short Range Plan" for construction between
1986 and 1994 and an "Intermediate Range Plan" for construction from
1994 to 1999. In the first part of the plan, the north line was scheduled
to reach the Perimeter Highway. The line would be 9.7 miles long, and
would include a Buckhead Station and a Medical Center Station south
of the perimeter. The plan called for construction of 1.4 miles of the
Perry Homes feeder line to a Bankhead Station, accounting for 40 percent of the entire line. The intermediate plan called for completion of
the Perry Homes line from Bankhead to Perry Homes, and an extension of the north line three miles beyond the perimeter. But the committee refused to be definite about these longer-range plans. It made
this section of the recommendation "subject to revision based on the
availability of federal and new sources of funding as may be determined
by the MARTA Board of Directors."[52]

When the MARTA staff members reviewed the committee report,
they amended the intermediate part of the plan to make it even less

definite, adding five new analytical tests that any new lines would have to pass before MARTA would make a final commitment to build them.[53] When the MARTA board held its September meeting, it found even this too constrictive. The board approved the short-term plan but deferred action on long-range plans until more flexible language could be substituted. Chesnut insisted that MARTA was putting off a decision on long-range plans because of the difficulty of predicting the future: "We don't have a looking glass to see far enough down the line and conditions could change."[54] Fifteen years later, the Perry Homes line has not been built, and MARTA officials state openly that it never will be.

No African American elected officials objected to this postponement. They knew that postponing the Perry Homes line really meant that the line would never be built, but none of them put up a fight. It was now clear that MARTA had never intended to build the line, no matter what the committee decided. MARTA's creation of the Committee of 50 and its apparent attention to the committee's recommendations amounted to nothing more than conflict management. MARTA was too adept politically to ride roughshod over its opponents. Instead, it outmaneuvered them. It gave its opponents a public voice on a committee and pretended to take what they said seriously. Then, when the committee made its recommendation that a Perry Homes line be built, MARTA sidestepped by making its commitment to any future rail lines highly conditional, indefinite, and vague.

MARTA had succeeded in finessing the opposition, but the battle was not quite over. Later in 1986, Michael Lomax, the Fulton County Commission Chair, appeared before the Action Forum to promote the revival of the feeder line to the Bankhead Station and the nearby shopping center. The city of Atlanta and the Atlanta Economic Development Corporation had forgotten their verbal commitments to Perry Homes residents regarding the feeder line, but Michael Lomax remembered his. Lomax was considering a 1989 mayoral bid, but he had an image of aloofness that limited his appeal to low-income voters. He hoped that affiliating himself with an issue that resonated in poor black areas would help broaden his political base. When Lomax made his appeal at this meeting, he was told by Morris Dillard, executive assistant to the MARTA general manager and MARTA's representative to the Action Forum, that the line would be built only if MARTA could be certain of more passengers than were currently projected for the line.[55] Dillard's comments made it clear that MARTA did not feel bound by the agreement reached in the August compromise. Now that the Committee of 50 had approved the north line and had been disbanded, MARTA reverted to its old argument that projections of ridership on the Bankhead line were too low to justify building it.

Lomax accepted MARTA's definition of the problem as a challenge and started pursuing plans to increase ridership on the line. To generate more passengers, he tried to organize the creation of a social-services center adjacent to the proposed location of the Bankhead Station. He negotiated lease commitments with the Fulton County Department of Family and Children's Services, with the food-stamps office, and with Grady Hospital, which would put a health clinic in the center. He also obtained a commitment from the Atlanta-Fulton County Library to open a branch there. With these commitments in hand, Lomax managed to elicit an agreement from H. J. Russell & Company to build the center and to manage it until the end of the lease period, at which point the center would revert to the county.

But Lomax ran into problems. A developer challenged the insider deal Lomax had made with H. J. Russell & Company, and the Fulton County Commission gave the contract to another developer. The library waffled for more than a year on its commitment to a branch, and eventually put in only a kiosk. The center finally opened in 1995, but by then Lomax's political career was over. He had never won the support he needed among low-income blacks and had lost the mayoral elections of 1989 and 1993. With Lomax gone, there was no one willing to step forward and champion the cause of a rail line even partway to Perry Homes.

Due largely to Lomax's efforts to expand ridership on the first leg of the Perry Homes line, MARTA did at last construct a 1.4-mile feeder line from the Ashby Street Station on the west line to a new Bankhead Highway Station. But that's as far as the line will go. By the time the next expansion of the MARTA rail system began to be seriously considered, in the mid-1990s, completion of the Perry Homes line had dropped out of contention. None of the five proposals (extensions of the north, west, and south lines and two new lines serving DeKalb County) included Perry Homes. In spite of the fact that Laura Lawson, a public-housing resident, was elected to successive terms as chairwoman of the MARTA board in 1997 and 1998, extending the Bankhead line to public housing was never considered. In part, this was because Perry Homes was being redeveloped as a smaller community, but a push by established suburban groups seeking rail service was also a factor, as was the fact that the MARTA board, not a more broadly representative committee, was considering the alternatives.

Public interests were also shortchanged by the absence of a requirement for land-use regulations coordinated with the rail project. Reduced congestion, increased accessibility, increased ridership, higher fare-box revenues, and better air quality should have accompanied such a substantial public investment. In the 1968 and 1971 referendums, MARTA's backers could legitimately argue that heavy rail, coupled with density-focusing land-use regulation around stations, would generate or channel the new development that would justify the public investment. The failure to enact the land-use regulations negated the rationale for the system, and the opportunity to shape the growth of the region had been lost. Instead of billions of dollars of public investment leading the way to a more sensibly and healthily organized region, the region's growth has condemned heavy rail to chase new development.

The inversion of the original plan, however, does not mean that linked land-use regulations and transit construction can never again be considered. Cities are dynamic places, and redevelopment often follows development in longer cycles. In the future, extensions of rail should be contingent on both density-focusing redevelopment plans with supporting legislation, and local public-transportation links that can distribute people to the dispersed offices and industries that the present lack of planning has permitted.

The Olympics Era

T he announcement in September 1990 that Atlanta had won
the bid for the 1996 Summer Olympics caused considerable
excitement throughout the city and spurred a major effort to
get ready for the grand event. The Atlanta Committee for
the Olympic Games (ACOG) built several facilities that were
later transformed into permanent features of the city. Two
of these were in the downtown area: the Olympic Stadium
and Centennial Olympic Park, a plaza where corporate sponsors of the Games put on promotional exhibits. After the
Olympics, the Olympic Stadium was converted to a baseball
stadium, and the park became a public square, around which
the city encouraged commercial and residential development
to help revitalize the downtown area.

North of the downtown area, the Georgia Board of
Regents built the Olympic Village, three high-rise buildings
that housed athletes during the Games and were later turned
into student dormitories for Georgia State University.

A number of other Olympics-related projects were undertaken by the city with city, state, and federal funding. These
included converting a public-housing development adjacent
to the Georgia State dorms into a mixed-income community,
the beautification of the downtown area, the improvement
and repair of infrastructure, a traffic-management system
intended to reduce congestion on metro-area freeways, and
the revitalization of a low-income neighborhood.

Positives and Negatives

Observers disagree over whether the Olympics were really good for Atlanta. Supporters have pointed out the obvious, highly visible benefits: a new baseball stadium and various other facilities paid for primarily with Olympics funding, a new downtown plaza, new housing for college students, and all the other improvements and redevelopment projects undertaken by the city. There were also less tangible benefits: Atlanta received worldwide attention, many Atlantans felt a new sense of pride in their city, and the Games themselves were exciting and entertaining.

But other aspects and consequences of the Olympics were not so appealing. First of all, there is the question of fiscal impact. Olympic promoters confidently asserted that Atlanta would make money from the Games. But a careful analysis of exactly how much money federal, state, and local governments actually spent on preparing the city and putting on the Games reveals that the cost to the taxpayers exceeded Olympics-generated government revenues by a wide margin. Atlantans are still being told that the city made money from the Olympics, but an accurate accounting shows otherwise.

Specific parts of Atlanta's Olympics-related redevelopment efforts are also open to criticism. The city spent a substantial amount of money on beautifying the downtown area, but it spent nowhere near enough on upgrading the city's inadequate sewer system and its deteriorating water system. The city spent money on cosmetic enhancements but deferred addressing serious infrastructure problems. Atlanta also spent money unwisely on the highly touted traffic-management system. The system cost almost $50 million, yet it has done very little to reduce chronic traffic congestion on metro-area freeways.

Another dubious feature of the Olympics era was the arrogant disregard displayed by ACOG for those adversely affected by the facilities it built. Those who put together Atlanta's Olympics bid proposed that the Olympic Stadium be built next to the existing baseball stadium and that the older stadium be torn down after the Games. After Atlanta won the Olympics bid, ACOG formed a partnership with the Atlanta Braves and formulated plans with the team for building the new stadium.

But the ACOG/Braves partnership would not allow representatives from the neighborhoods adjacent to the stadium to participate in their planning sessions, and the plan they came up with did very little to limit the damaging effect of the stadium on these low-income black neighborhoods, which had already suffered damage from the existing stadium. ACOG displayed the same attitude when it built Centennial Olympic Park. Almost 100 small businesses were forced to move to make way for the park, yet ACOG and state and local governments gave them no assistance in relocating, so the survival of these businesses was threatened.

Local government did very little to protect stadium-area neighborhoods. Even though some elected officials were critical of the Braves/ACOG stadium plan, the City Council and the Fulton County Commission made only minor changes to the plan. There were several reasons for the lack of resistance. Local government had only a limited role in Olympics planning, and elected officials were under pressure to give Olympics organizers what they wanted. But a third reason was that most elected officials were basically indifferent to the interests of the low-income blacks living in these neighborhoods.

This same indifference to the interests of poor blacks was evident in the redevelopment of the Techwood/Clark Howell public-housing complexes—a project undertaken in conjunction with building the Olympic Village dormitories. The Atlanta Housing Authority (AHA) took several years to formulate a plan for redeveloping these complexes, but the plan that the federal Department of Housing and Urban Development finally approved called for replacing the public housing with a smaller, mixed-income community. This final AHA plan promised the residents of Techwood/Clark Howell that either they would be able to return to the new community or replacement housing would be found for them. But these promises were deceptive. While the housing authority was formulating this plan, it gradually reduced the population of Techwood Homes through attrition and strict enforcement of lease regulations. As the complexes became increasingly empty, other residents began to leave. By the time the final redevelopment plan was approved by HUD, only a few of the residents remained in Techwood. The housing authority did not have to find housing for those who had left. This redevelopment project ended up as yet another instance of forced removal of poor blacks from the downtown area. Furthermore, the AHA still has not replaced all the low-income units that were lost when it replaced the public housing with a smaller, mixed-income community. Once again, just as during the urban renewal of the '60s, the city's stock of low-income housing was reduced.

The city did spend some money during the Olympics preparation period on revitalizing low-income neighborhoods. But the amount of money it invested in poor neighborhoods constituted only a very small percentage of its Olympics-related investment. The city's major endeavor in this regard was its effort to revitalize the stadium-area neighborhood of Summerhill. Summerhill, however, like Techwood/Clark Howell, has been transformed into a mixed-income community, and its gentrification is now forcing out many of its original poor black residents.

For a time, the city intended to make a substantial effort to revitalize a number of poor African American communities. Maynard Jackson's administration commissioned a study to frame recommendations for an extensive series of health, anticrime, education, housing, nutrition, transportation, and other social-service programs, most of which involved strengthening existing community-based organizations and creating new ones. But the business community opted for a corporate-financed, volunteer-based effort that initially eschewed government programs, and this approach supplanted the city's. The Atlanta Project (TAP), led by former President Jimmy Carter, organized a new set of organizations to represent communities, a strategy that aided disorganized neighborhoods but offended existing community organizations. The emphasis on volunteers and the corresponding absence of targeted social-service programs, combined with a time-consuming learning curve and cultural differences between volunteers and residents, limited TAP's early contributions to poor people's lives. Eventually, after the Olympics-induced funding diminished and the bias against social-service programs abated, TAP evolved into a smaller, community-focused institution that made useful contributions, particularly in the area of health care.

Olympics-Era Politics

The person most responsible for bringing the Olympics to Atlanta is Billy Payne, an Atlanta real-estate lawyer. Frederick Allen, in his book *Atlanta Rising*, writes that Payne conceived the notion of the city's submitting an Olympics bid in February 1987. Allen makes it clear that Coca-Cola was at the center of the subsequent effort to organize a bid. Payne, he says, was aware that an Olympics bid had been considered in 1978 but that the idea had been abandoned because of the opposition of Paul Austin, Coca-Cola's CEO. In '87, according to Allen, Payne used a Coca-Cola connection to arrange a meeting with a different CEO, Robert Goizueta. This time Coke was not opposed to the idea.[1]

Around the time that Payne went to Coke with his idea, Mayor Andrew Young adopted the bid as a city project. In March 1987, the city and the Chamber of Commerce dispatched the city coordinator of festival and special events to the initial U.S. Olympic expressions-of-interest seminar.[2] Coca-Cola did not reveal its attitude about the Olympics bid publicly. In private, however, it eventually became an active supporter. In the summer of 1988, Goizueta held a luncheon at Coca-Cola headquarters that raised $1.5 million for the bid project.[3]

In the fall of 1989, Maynard Jackson was once again elected mayor. By the time Jackson took office early in 1990, the process of putting together an Olympics bid was well under way. The group that put the bid together called itself the Atlanta Olympic Committee (AOC). Its members included Billy Payne, Andrew Young, Governor Zell Miller, and representatives of Coca-Cola and the Georgia Institute of Technology. The city's role was minimized because some members of the largely private AOC opposed the group's getting enmeshed in city politics.

When Mayor Young had made the bid effort a city project, he did so without the formal support of the City Council and over the objections of his own advisers.[4] Olympics supporters insisted that the city would make money from the Games, but their claim was greeted with skepticism by some city officials. The city's fiscal resources were limited. It was already heavily in debt, and city officials knew that the majority of the voting public would be opposed to raising taxes to help pay for the

Games. They also worried that the Olympics would interfere with other important projects. In part because of the city's unwillingness to help fund the Olympics, the AOC decided to pay for the Games with a combination of television rights, gate receipts, and large corporate contributions. And because the city played only a limited role in putting together the Olympics bid, the AOC felt free to plan the Games on its own. It effectively made the decisions on what kind of Olympic facilities would be built and where they would be located.

After Atlanta won the Olympics bid, the AOC created the Atlanta Committee for the Olympic Games, the organization that would organize and put on the Games, and elected Billy Payne president and CEO. ACOG set about implementing the plans made by the AOC, and even though the city's participation in formulating these plans had been limited, city officials generally felt compelled to go along with them. Because of the prestige of the Olympics and the pressure of getting ready for them, elected officials found it difficult politically to raise any serious objections to ACOG's wishes.

In many ways, ACOG was a new, formal version of the old downtown business elite. Like downtown business interests, it had so much power and influence that it actually functioned to a great extent as an unelected government. Also, it continued the downtown redevelopment that downtown business leaders had pursued for several decades. ACOG decided to build the Olympic Stadium next to the existing stadium, and when it came up with its Olympic Park idea in 1992, the economic rationale it offered for building this downtown plaza was that after the Games it would stimulate commercial and residential development in adjacent areas. Furthermore, to get the park built ACOG used a political strategy that harked back to a strategy used by the downtown elite. Just as downtown business leaders had allied themselves with state government in the late '40s and early '50s to win approval for the Plan of Improvement, and just as they had used this strategy to secure financing for building the Georgia World Congress Center in the '70s, ACOG allied itself with state government to get the Olympic Park built. ACOG knew that city officials would object to the idea, so no one at ACOG consulted Maynard Jackson or anyone else in city government in planning the park. Olympic planners simply ignored the city and turned to state government for support and financing, and the same state authority that built and administers the Georgia World Congress Center built and administers the Olympic Park.

What the Olympics Actually Cost

To understand fully what the Olympics themselves and the related redevelopment meant to Atlanta, we need to determine how much public money was spent in these areas. More than thirty different sources were consulted to come up with this figure. There were fourteen separate categories of expenditure, provided by various agencies and departments of local, state, and federal government. Table 15 (pp. 150–51) presents a breakdown of expenditures and the sources of government financing. It shows that the total amount spent by all government sources is $1,050,970,000.

This list of Olympics-related expenditures tries to be conservative. Certain projects that were undertaken during the planning and preparation period have not been listed here because they had only a tangential connection to the Games. An example of this is the $23.79 million Phase I of the Truman Parkway in Savannah, where the Olympic sailing competition was held. This highway was eliminated from the Georgia DOT's Olympic Transportation Projects Status Report because the road had been in Savannah's plans for more than a decade and did not affect traffic in areas near the venue sites.[5] Another example is the $304.7 million international concourse at Hartsfield Airport. The extent to which the Olympics were the actual stimulus for the concourse is unclear, and the city bonds sold to finance the project are supposed to be repaid by landing fees, airline fees, building rental, and the revenue from airport concessions.[6]

One expenditure included in the list that does not appear to belong here is the Advanced Traffic Management System. The ATMS includes cameras to monitor traffic on expressways, a computerized system that coordinates traffic signals on arterials, and signals controlling highway ramp access. The camera system improves response to accidents, and messages about traffic conditions can be flashed to motorists on electronic screens. The ATMS does not appear to have any real connection with the Olympics, and the project was under consideration before the city prepared its bid, but the Games were the immediate reason that the project was funded. The ATMS was part of a billion-dollar Olympics wish list that state and local governments presented to the Georgia congressional delegation in early 1992.[7] It was also included in a proposal for Olympics-related redevelopment projects submitted by the city to the International Olympics Committee in the summer of that year.[8] And when the U.S. Department of Transportation announced in 1995 that it was funding 61.9 percent of the ATMS, it issued a briefing paper whose lead paragraph clearly linked the project to the upcoming Olympics: "The Olympic Games in Atlanta present a unique and timely opportunity for the United States to showcase traveler information services and technologies associated with Intelligent Transportation Systems."[9]

Most of the expenditures listed here are capital costs. Short-term, operational, and administrative expenses paid for with public money amounted to $137.47 million. These expenses consisted of $15.80 million for the temporary acquisition of buses from other cities, $0.82 million for funding the Governor's Office of Olympic Coordination, $1.09 million for job-training programs, $12 million in guarantees to ACOG for Games receipts from the cities of Birmingham, Washington, Miami, and Orlando, which were supposed to be reimbursed by ticket sales, and $107.76 million for security.[10]

This list of expenditures also omits services provided by local-government agencies during the Games. The state of Georgia did not seek reimbursement for such expenditures, but the city of Atlanta did. It had a contract for some of the services it provided with ACOG, and it negotiated with ACOG regarding these direct expenses. ACOG ended up paying the city $8 million. This left the city $4 million short of what it needed to cover police overtime, and it had to seek the additional money from the federal government.[11] Other local governments did not have services contracts; they simply asked ACOG to help them cover their expenses.[12] ACOG partly reimbursed the city of Savannah and Fulton and DeKalb counties. Savannah requested $1.2 million and ended up receiving $290,000. Fulton County was paid $790,000 and DeKalb $296,000. But the cities of College Park and Stone Mountain were not paid.[13]

Table 15. Government Expenditures in Support of the 1996 Olympic Games (Figures in Millions of Dollars)[a]

Expenditure Category	Local	State	Federal	Total
Olympic Games and increased airport security[b]	0.36	27.50	79.90	107.76
Metropolitan Atlanta Rapid Transit Authority: leasing 2,000 buses from other cities; upgrading telephone route- and schedule-information system; upgrading system maps; adding handicapped-access buses; removing seats on trains[c]			39.30	39.30
Regional Advanced Traffic Management System[d]				
"Special and Innovative Project" funds and state matching funds		15.53	62.10	77.63
Congestion-mitigation and air-quality funds and state matching funds		10.03	37.71	47.74
Venue access; highway improvements; Olympic signs and landscaping projects; high-occupancy-vehicle lanes; interstate-highway rest stops; visitor centers; Olympic transportation plans[e]	20.37	38.84	155.18	214.39
Olympic-venue construction[f]	30.70	78.34	4.10	113.14
Revenue guarantees, to Atlanta Committee for the Olympic Games; Orlando; Birmingham; Washington, DC; Miami[g]	12.00			12.00
Olympic Village housing[h]		154.20		154.20
Infrastructure improvements: CBD access; Olympic-venue sites; Olympic Village at Georgia Tech; Atlanta University Center[h]	78.66		16.35	95.01
CBD streetscape and park improvements[i,j]	17.15		47.06	64.21
Centennial Olympic Park[k]		5.00		5.00
Post-office renovations[l]			15.00	15.00
Upgrading weather service[m]			1.00	1.00
Job-training program[n]			1.09	1.09
Neighborhood infrastructure improvements[o]	8.35			8.35
Demolition and partial reconstruction of Techwood and Clark Howell Homes[p]	0.50		60.40	60.90
Metropolitan Atlanta Olympic Games Authority–Olympic Neighborhood Development[q]	4.15			4.15
Emergency preparedness[r]			18.50	18.50
Telecommunications, other federal expenditures[r]			11.60	11.60
Total	172.24	329.44	549.29	1,050.97

[a]The General Accounting Office produced a preliminary report in late 1999 that attempted to quantify federal expenditures on the Los Angeles, Atlanta, and Salt Lake City Olympic Games. That report concluded that non-personnel federal expenditures for the Atlanta Games came to $519,354,000. This figure compares with the personnel and non-personnel expenditures figure shown in Table 15 of $549,290,000. Officials from the Atlanta Committee for the Olympic Games and a number of federal agencies made the argument that the federal capital expenditures (approximately $421 million) "would have likely been eventually provided regardless of the Games." In most cases that argument contradicts what both funding agency and ACOG officials were saying at the time the expenditures occurred. See General Accounting

Office, "Olympic Games: Preliminary Information on Federal Funding and Support," report, GAO/GGD-00-44, Dec. 21, 1999.

bCity of Atlanta, Ordinance Number 95-0-0667, May 1, 1995; interview with Terry Gandy, Georgia Office of Planning and Budget, Atlanta, Nov. 29, 1995; Mike Christensen, "Washington's Money Pipeline for '96 Flowing; GA's Delegation Secures $40 Million in Funding," *The Atlanta Journal-Constitution*, Oct. 15, 1994; Alma E. Hill, "FAA Plans to Secure Airspace for the Games," *The Atlanta Journal-Constitution*, Dec. 7, 1995; White House, "Federal Spending on the Olympics: Fact Sheet," May 14, 1996.

c"MARTA Receives $28 Million for Olympic Related Needs," *The MARTA Line 2*, No. 4 (Sept. 1995): 1.

dGeorgia Department of Transportation, *Olympic Transportation Projects Status Report*, Sept. 11, 1995: 1.

eGeorgia Department of Transportation, *Olympic Transportation Projects Status Report*, Sept. 11, 1995: 1–23; Lyle V. Harris, "Taxes: Government Tab: $354 Million," *The Atlanta Journal-Constitution*, April 14, 1995.

fAtlanta Regional Commission, *Olympic Transportation Projects Status List*, Sept. 15, 1995: 9.

gMike Williams, "Orlando Antes Up Financial Backing," *The Atlanta Journal-Constitution*, Nov. 10, 1995.

hHarris, "Taxes: Government Tab: $354 Million"; Ken Foskett, "More Money Is Needed for 2 State Olympic Projects," *The Atlanta Journal-Constitution*, Jan. 6, 1995; Dick Pettys, "State's Olympic Tab Now at $235 Million," Associated Press, Feb. 14, 1996.

iThese improvements captured nearly all $16 million of the first-year Atlanta regional Department of Transportation Intermodal Surface Transportation Enhancement (ISTEA) discretionary funds. They did so on the strength of a vague, one-page application that stated simply that the projects were essential to the Olympics (Interview with Martha Reimann, planner, Georgia Department of Community Affairs, member of Regional ISTEA Project Selection Committee, Atlanta, April 7, 1995); Corporation for Olympic Development in Atlanta, "CODA Infrastructure Projects: Funding Recap," report, June 15, 1995; James A. Hayes, "Fiscal Impacts of the Olympic Games: A Comparative Analysis of 1984 Los Angeles and 1996 Atlanta," master's thesis, Graduate Program in City Planning, Georgia Institute of Technology, May 1995: 110, 112, 113, 130, 138; interview with Danita Brown, Corporation for Olympic Development, Atlanta, July 1, 1996.

jChristensen, "Washington's Money Pipeline for '96 Flowing"; Georgia Department of Transportation, Federal Highway Administration, *A Road to Success: A Guidebook for Sponsors of Transportation Enhancement Activities*, Nov. 1995: 0–1; "Park, Neighborhood Projects Get Grants for Their Greenery," *The Atlanta Journal-Constitution*, Jan. 19, 1995; Kelly Cooney, Interview with Trees Atlanta staff, Atlanta, Nov. 16, 1995; Rebecca Nash, "Renovations To Ready Park For '96," *The Atlanta Journal-Constitution*, April 16, 1994.

kMaria Saporta, "GWCC Giving Olympic Park $2.5 Million," *The Atlanta Journal-Constitution*, Feb. 23, 1996.

lTinah Saunders, "Post Offices To Be Stamped With New Look for '96 Games," *The Atlanta Journal-Constitution*, Sept. 7, 1995.

mNational Weather Service, "National Weather Service to Provide Support for the 1996 Summer Olympic Games," Fort Worth, Texas, May 5, 1995.

nOffice of Information, United States Department of Labor, "Dislocated Workers to be Trained at Olympic Sites," report, Nov. 21, 1995.

oJames A. Hayes, "Fiscal Impacts of the Olympic Games: A Comparative Analysis of 1984 Los Angeles and 1996 Atlanta" (master's thesis, Graduate Program in City Planning, Georgia Institute of Technology, May 1995).

pHousing Authority of the City of Atlanta, "Urban Revitalization Demonstration Implementation Grant Application for Techwood/Clark Howell Homes," May 26, 1993.

qMetropolitan Atlanta Olympic Games Authority, *Olympic Neighborhood Development Project Update* (report, Nov. 1, 1995).

rPress briefing by the Vice President of the United States et al., May 14, 1995.

Another cost not included in the list of expenditures is the indirect cost to local governments of paying employees for working on Olympics projects. This was the largest single operational and administrative Olympics expense paid for with government money. But just how much was spent is not known, because no effective accounting method was put in place. Furthermore, the expenses listed for capital projects include only the "hard" costs of construction. They do not include the necessary "soft," or administrative, costs of planning, writing proposals, political lobbying, intergovernmental negotiations, design, bidding, construction oversight, accounting, and reporting. Millions of hours were spent by government employees in planning, organizing, and carrying through to completion more than $900 million in construction projects. Even if administrative costs are estimated at an unrealistically conservative 15 percent of overall construction costs, administrative expenses would have amounted to $137.03 million.

The Immediate Effect

In an estimate of the economic effect of the Olympics, done for ACOG in 1995, Jeffrey M. Humphreys and Michael K. Plummer, economists at the University of Georgia, estimated that the Games would add $5.14 billion to state's economy between 1991 and 1997.[14] Other economists maintained that this estimate was $1 billion too high because, among other things, it did not pay enough attention to displacement effects: the number of Atlantans who would leave town during the Games, and the number of summer tourists and business travelers who would decide not to visit.[15]

Humphreys' and Plummer's estimate of $5.14 billion is the total of $1.16 billion in direct economic impact, $1.14 billion in out-of-state visitor spending, and $2.83 billion in induced economic impact. Direct economic impact is an estimate of the amount of money ACOG would spend in the state of Georgia actually producing the Games. Induced economic impact is an estimate of the dollars generated by the Games that would be recycled through the local economy in successive rounds of spending.[16]

To understand what $5.14 billion really means to the Georgia economy, some kind of macro measure of the size of the state's economy is needed. We do not have a figure for gross domestic state product, the kind of figure used to estimate the size of a national economy. The best figure available is a measure of the state economy called total personal income (TPI). This is the sum of earnings, dividends, interest, rent, and transfer payments received by Georgia residents.[17] Data from other areas show that the TPI is typically about 10 percent less than the gross domestic state product. Estimates of Georgia's TPI are available for 1991 through 1993. Assuming that there was no growth in the TPI after 1993, the total for 1991 through 1997 would be $906.3 billion.[18]

If this figure is correct—and it is probably too conservative—the $5.14 billion benefit of the 1996 Olympic Games equaled 0.57 per cent of the TPI between 1991 and 1997 period. Weighed against the effort, time, and money that state and local governments devoted to the Olympics, an increase in economic activity of less than 1 percent makes the real economic benefit of the Games seem negligible.

Even so, the Olympics would have been a sensible enterprise economically if state and local governments had ended up making money from the additional tax revenues that the Games generated, as ACOG claimed would be the case. So how large were these revenues?

Humphreys and Plummer calculated that increased economic activity generated by the Games would produce an additional $176.4 million in state revenues. According to their estimates, total receipts from personal income taxes would increase by $65.4 million, receipts from corporate income taxes by $9.3 million, sales-and-use tax revenues by $91 million, and revenues from selective sales taxes (on alcohol, tobacco and the like) by $10.7 million.[19] As for increased tax revenues in the Atlanta metro area, Research Atlanta Inc., a public-policy research organization now affiliated with Georgia State University, analyzed the effect of the Olympics on local sales-tax receipts from 1994 to 1998. It estimated that in the three largest metro-Atlanta counties—Fulton, Cobb, and Gwinnett—the Olympics would bring in an additional $22.72 million. They estimated that Fulton County, including the city of Atlanta, would collect the largest share of this: $17.93 million, or 78.9 percent of the total.[20] The same study calculated that the city of Atlanta would receive an additional $2 million from its hotel/motel sales tax during 1996, a result of higher occupancy rates during the Games.[21]

If we combine all these estimates, the increase in state revenues was $176.4 million and the increase in local revenues $24 million, for a total of $200.4 million. The increase in federal tax revenues has been estimated at $182.7 million. The overall estimated increase in tax revenues on the federal, state, and local levels, therefore, was around $383.1 million. We have already calculated—conservatively—that overall government expenditures on the Olympics should have been $1,050,970,000. So if all the estimates we have used here are accurate, expenses exceeded revenues by a substantial amount. The overall net public cost of the Olympics was $668 million, with local governments paying $148 million, Georgia paying $153 million, and the federal government paying $367 million.

The Jackson administration was skeptical of ACOG's rosy predictions of the Olympics' fiscal impact, and so was the subsequent Bill Campbell administration. In an effort to increase revenues, the Jackson administration in 1993 and the Campbell administration in 1994 asked the state Legislature to allow the city to impose a surcharge on tickets to all events held within the city that would be attended by more than 2,000 people. But ACOG and its supporters opposed this both times, and the measure, which would have returned approximately $7 million to the city annually,[22] never became law. There was nothing unusual about the request. A tax on ticket sales is levied by a majority of American cities, and the organizing committee for the Summer Olympics in Los Angeles in 1984 accepted a similar kind of tax. It was one of three mechanisms used by the city of Los Angeles to pay for the costs of the city services required by the Games.[23]

It should also be pointed out that the Games had some negative economic effects on Atlanta. First, the more than $1 billion in Olympics-related construction projects brought inflation in construction costs. Estimates vary, but the Georgia State University Economic Forecasting Center calculated the increase in construction costs in the metro area at 1 percent to 1.5 percent a month in 1994 and 1995.[24] In Fayette County, the school board's $58 million construction program encountered annual increases of 15 percent. Subcontractors' bids for the

Emory University Conference Center Hotel increased by 30 percent.[25] And the Olympic Village came in at 15 percent over estimates. Since part of the village was converted to dormitories for Georgia State students after the Games, this increase in construction costs caused the State Board of Regents to revise its annual estimate of construction-cost inflation, originally 3 percent to 5 percent, to 20 percent to 25 percent.[26] Because construction costs increased throughout the metro area as the Olympics approached, some projects were postponed until after the Games.[27]

Another inflationary consequence of the Olympics was an increase in rental-housing prices. In July 1995, Intown Properties, a local rental-management company, informed the tenants in its 300 apartments that they had a choice of paying $3,000 a month from May to August of 1996 or vacating the apartments (leaving their furniture behind), so the units could be rented to Olympic visitors. Tenants who chose to vacate were to receive 30 percent of the profit from the Olympic rentals.[28] In August, because of the obvious opportunity for profiteering on the part of landlords, proposals for legislation prohibiting price-gouging were introduced in the Legislature. But even though this proposed legislation was similar to laws the state had already enacted to contain hotel prices, lawmakers declined to act.[29] Then, in the regular winter legislative session, the Senate Judiciary Committee held hearings on a bill that would have limited rent increases to 10 percent. Presentations opposing the bill were made by the Atlanta Apartment Association and four leasing companies. By early February, the bill had died in committee.[30] Price-gouging in the rental-housing market went unchecked. No one knows how many people ended up paying higher rents, the amount by which rents actually increased, or how many renters were forced to move.[31]

The Long-Term Effect

In analyzing the overall economic impact of the Olympics on Atlanta, we should also look at the $913.5 million in capital investments the city made during this period, and evaluate their future usefulness. A truly comprehensive analysis of the eventual value of Olympics-related capital investments for Atlanta-area residents is beyond the scope of this analysis, but we can offer some preliminary observations on some of the larger undertakings, and we can speculate on their future consequences.

Let us look first at the costs and benefits of the new stadium. Olympic planners have claimed that the new stadium was completely paid for with Olympics funding, but this is not entirely accurate. It's true that the $207 million direct cost of building the stadium was paid for with Olympics money. An additional $30 million, however, was needed for related infrastructure improvements and supporting off-site construction, and this was paid for partly by a federal grant and partly by the city. There also exists a public liability for the costs of future construction and maintenance. The current agreement stipulates that this taxpayer liability will be capped at $50 million over twenty years.

There are other indirect costs. Because adequate parking, interstate access, and buffer zones were not provided, neighborhoods adjacent to the stadium continue to suffer noise and traffic problems, and will continue to experience retarded development and depressed property values. Since the tangible benefits of the new stadium are not appreciably greater than the benefits provided by the old stadium, since the new stadium means a twenty-year liability for the city, and since the new stadium has done further damage to surrounding communities, it is questionable whether the city would have agreed to build it had it not been for the pressure to erect an impressive new facility for the Olympics. We should bear in mind that the real beneficiaries of the new stadium are the Atlanta Braves. Public money has been used, and a price is being paid by surrounding neighborhoods, to maintain the revenues of a private business.

The most expensive Olympics-related capital improvement paid for with public money was the modernization of Atlanta's expressway system at a cost of more than $180 million. The project included both the Advanced Traffic Management System, described previously, and the addition of high-occupancy-vehicle lanes. The primary aim of this new traffic-regulation system was to wring more capacity out of the city's expressways. This modernization was a welcome change from the state Department of Transportation's policy in recent years of trying to solve congestion by building more expressway lanes, but Atlanta's continued growth soon overwhelmed this modest improvement in highway capacity. Nearly $200 million seems like a large price for partial and temporary alleviation of the city's growing traffic problems.

The next-largest Olympics-related capital investment was the $154 million spent by the state on building the Olympic Village, the highrise dormitories converted after the Games into housing for students at Georgia State University. This project is supposed to pay for itself: Future rentals from these dorms are supposed to cover the cost of building them. Early Olympics planning had envisioned that after the Games the buildings would be occupied by students from the adjacent Georgia Tech campus. But the State Board of Regents eventually changed this plan. Georgia State is located in the central business district, and Georgia State administrators and various business and civic leaders had long wanted downtown dormitories for Georgia State students. They wanted to change a commuter school into more of an urban university and thus bring more street life to downtown Atlanta at night.

These dormitories are now full, and there is a waiting list, so it seems likely that the buildings eventually will pay for themselves. The rationale for having students from Georgia State occupy dormitories adjacent to Georgia Tech is a dubious one, however. The Georgia Tech campus is located a mile and a half north of the central business district. It seems unlikely that students living in dormitories that far from the CBD will contribute in any significant way to nighttime pedestrian traffic in the downtown area.

Funding for several other Olympics-related capital improvements was included in a bond referendum that city of Atlanta voters approved in July of 1994. The total proposed bond issue was $149 million. Most of the money was to be spent on infrastructure—sewer and water lines, bridges and viaducts, most of which had been built between 1890 and 1930. None of these infrastructure improvements was directly related to the Olympics or directly stimulated by them. Infrastructure problems were long-standing, and in some cases were getting critical. But tucked away in the bond issue were two projects that were clearly tied to the Games. One was an expansion of pedestrian access to Olympic sites in and around the CBD, which would cost $25.1 million. The other was repairing streets and sidewalks in the low-income black neighborhoods adjacent to other venues, which would cost $7.2 million.[32]

The biggest infrastructure problem the city was facing was its substandard storm sewers and water-treatment facilities. Runoff during heavy rainstorms was washing pollutants into streams and eventually into the Chattahoochee River, the source of Atlanta's drinking water. The total cost of improving the entire storm-sewer and water-treatment system was estimated at well over $1 billion.[33] So the bond issue was only a down payment on what would be a long and very expensive effort.

Two incidents brought the problem of the city's aging sewer system to the public's attention and led eventually to the referendum. In June of 1993, an eleven-foot unreinforced-concrete sewer pipe beneath a hotel parking lot collapsed during heavy rain, creating a sinkhole 150 feet long and fifty feet deep and killing two hotel employees.[34] On an unusually cold morning in January 1994, a thirty-six-inch cast-iron water main broke, leaving most of the city without water for several days.[35] City leaders began urging that infrastructure repairs be undertaken, and they put the bond issue on the ballot. The Chamber of Commerce began a $300,000 campaign promoting its passage.

Since nowhere near enough money was being authorized for improving the city's storm-sewer and water-treatment system, it seems frivolous to have been raising money at the same time for what was essentially beautification, intended mainly to impress out-of-town visitors during the Olympics. While the city spent money on cosmetic enhancements, it deferred spending money on a truly serious problem. And not only do these esthetic improvements seem trivial when compared with serious infrastructure needs, they seem trivial in themselves, when viewed as efforts at revitalization. Better streets and sidewalks in poor neighborhoods contribute very little to revitalization. And better sidewalks in the central business district would not make the area attractive enough to businesses to reduce its 25 percent office-vacancy rate.

The Olympics did generate a certain amount of genuine neighborhood revitalization. Much of this was undertaken by the Metropolitan Atlanta Olympic Games Authority (MAOGA). City government created this entity to oversee ACOG's development activities and to exercise the power of eminent domain to acquire land for Olympics-related uses. Along with its primary mission, MAOGA had a legal mandate to promote redevelopment in neighborhoods affected by the Games. MAOGA interpreted that mandate broadly, and used its powers to generate $4.15 million in new housing development in the English Avenue, Mechanicsville, Vine City, Peoplestown, and Atlanta University neighborhoods.[36] But the single largest revitalization project was in the Summerhill neighborhood, just east of the new stadium. Summerhill received a total of $66.4 million in public grants, public loans, and private investment for building new housing. The neighborhood is now in the process of upgrading itself. During the run-up to the Olympics, 189 new units were built in the neighborhood.

This Summerhill revitalization is the most ambitious effort the city has ever made to revitalize a low-income downtown neighborhood. It reverses a long-standing policy of either tearing down such neighborhoods or simply neglecting them. And yet the Summerhill revitalization has not done a great deal for the neighborhood's original residents. Of the 189 units built, 100 are low- to moderate-income ownership units; the other eighty-nine are market-rate ownership units ranging in price from $80,000 to $125,000. In the three years after the Olympics, the market-rate units appreciated to as much as $165,000.[37] After Charis, the nonprofit organization that built the 100 low- to moderate-income units, completed the 100th unit, the neighborhood development corporation overseeing redevelopment told Charis not to build any more. The market-rate units are obviously unaffordable by the neighborhood's poor residents. The revitalization occurring in Summerhill is intentional gentrification: Low-income renters are being supplanted by higher-income homeowners.

The Atlanta Project

One month after the announcement that Atlanta had won the Olympics, Mayor Jackson addressed an Atlanta Bar Association/League of Women Voters luncheon. With his characteristic rhetorical flourish, he defined the city's mission as scaling "the twin peaks of Atlanta's Mount

Olympus." "First peak, we want to stage the best Olympic Games ever. Second peak, we must simultaneously uplift the people of Atlanta and fight poverty in the process." Jackson did not offer a specific antipoverty program, but talked about the need to expand programs for juveniles, drug and alcohol abuse, and mental health.[38]

The administration subsequently hired the Community Design Center of Atlanta to assess human-services needs and to suggest new strategies for addressing poverty. Based on empirical analyses of gaps between present services and needs, and on surveys of community representatives in the six most visible "Olympic Impact Neighborhoods," the CDCA recommended substantially strengthening existing community organizations and spending $16.6 million annually on literacy training; child care and counseling for student parents; dropout prevention; drug-abuse treatment and prevention; employment counseling; after-school programs; home health care; prenatal care; medical care; emergency medical care; outpatient care; day care; adult day care; home-meal delivery and group meals for the elderly; child-protection services; transportation for shopping and medical access; home-chore services; new rental housing; short-term homeless shelters; transitional housing; personal-care housing; and public-safety programs.[39] The CDCA also recommended an extensive community-development strategy to strengthen and expand existing community organizations' contributions. But before these analyses were complete, the governing coalition decided on a nongovernmental strategy for fighting poverty: The Atlanta Project (TAP), a private-sector initiative intended, in Ruth Knack's succint characterization, "not to create a new bureaucracy but to teach people how to deal with existing agencies and to help channel the volunteer spirit of 'rich Atlanta' to reach out to 'poor Atlanta.'"[40]

The decision to focus on a private, volunteer effort followed Jackson's hiring in May 1991 of Joe Martin, president of Central Atlanta Progress, as Olympic coordinator to "bring together a team of experts to formulate a strategy" for the neighborhoods surrounding Olympic venues.[41] In July, Martin characterized the assignment: "It doesn't take a genius to figure out what the story's going to be in 1996. The splendor of the Olympics amid the squalor of Southern poverty. Now we need to address these problems—not to spruce up our image."[42]

In September, at the behest of a "special donor," James Laney, president of Emory University, asked former President Jimmy Carter to lead a campaign to mobilize resources to fight poverty. Carter was an Emory Distinguished Professor at the time, and the Carter Center was a branch of the university. Carter moved quickly, convening meetings with "key Atlanta leaders," and on October 25, 1991, at a meeting with the *Atlanta Journal-Constitution* editorial board, he announced the formation of The Atlanta Project.[43] Dan Sweat, who had preceded Martin as president of CAP, was hired as TAP's executive director in November.

Atlanta shifted the responsibility for pre-Olympic antipoverty efforts to TAP. When the city produced its $1.2 billion Olympic Development Program just before the 1992 Barcelona Olympics, it stated as an objective "to raise the viability, living standards and levels of human service delivery in disadvantaged and aging communities,"[44] but it budgeted no money for human services or community development and cited TAP as the only resource bearing on human-service needs.

TAP raised approximately $33 million in cash and in-kind services over its first five years. The most recent objective assessment of TAP's accomplishments was not released to the public, but a January 1995 evaluation of the first four years concluded that "the overall progress to date appears modest relative to the amount of effort and money expended."[45] TAP's internal list of institutionalized accomplishments cites twenty-nine projects in which it played various roles: initiator, partner, participant, facilitator, consultant, consumer. Among the projects were a new playground in a public-housing community, four school health clinics, and the creation of an immunization database. Along with changes in Medicaid and child health-care programs, TAP contributed to an expansion of health-care services to poor children. According to TAP, the most significant legacy was fostering the involvement of residents.[46]

This is an accurate assessment for some communities outside the city and for several smaller communities within it. But in the much more highly organized neighborhoods surrounding the CBD, citizen participation was not a legacy but a problem. TAP's approach undermined its strategies of empowerment and collaboration by establishing new, autonomous community groups. Organized around public schools with geographies that bisected and trisected established and officially defined neighborhoods, the new "Cluster Committees" directly contradicted twenty-year-old community-based neighborhood organizations and newer community-development corporations. Many existing neighborhood leaders viewed TAP's subdivision of their communities into parts of two or more "clusters," and the assignment of a paid coordinator, as both a political threat and an insult. Because established neighborhood representatives were closely identified with the interests of only parts of the new clusters, and because they were also identified with the interests of areas outside these clusters, they were rarely successful candidates for cluster committee offices. In some cases, former political opponents ascended to those offices, further limiting both empowerment and collaboration.

Because TAP did not initially collaborate with or fund community-development corporations, these groups felt that TAP's raising of $33 million in corporate contributions, the absorption of almost all of that money in administrative and operating expenses, and TAP's policy of not using its substantial resources to fund programs were wasteful, and that TAP's activities diminished the CDC's access to corporate resources. In 1995 most heads of neighborhood planning units and community development corporations were dissatisfied with TAP's progress.[47]

Two other problems plagued TAP's efforts: culture clash and limited perspective. Culture clash, in this case, refers to the substitution of corporate agendas for community-defined agendas. In economic development, for example, when a promised community-driven agenda did not crystallize quickly enough, executives loaned by Atlanta corporations to TAP, who were experts in economic development, substituted their own strategies. The substitutions were well intentioned, but by supplanting a community's responsibility for determining its own priorities, TAP alienated the groups with which it was supposed to be collaborating.[48] Similar dynamics characterized housing and community-development efforts.

The other problem that undermined TAP was limited perspective: a narrow definition of both the geography and the substance of forces affecting poverty. Residents of cluster communities objected to the fact that social class and racially discriminatory land-use regulations, suburban county governments' refusal to participate in mass-transportation systems, discriminatory business and home mortgage lending, and other practices that contributed to poverty and geographic isolation were not within TAP's frame of reference or objects of TAP's activity. Critics argued that the resulting limited conceptions of poverty "blamed" poor people for their condition and refused to accept broader social responsibility.[49]

Eventually TAP recognized the centrality of community engagement, priorities, and agendas, and the reality that community development requires extended commitments of time and resources. The smaller, post-Olympic version of TAP treats neighborhood organizations and community-development corporations and residents with more respect. TAP also narrowed its focus; it now concentrates on early-childhood development programs, after-school programs, and child health and welfare, and it has had successes in these areas.

Substantial amelioration of poverty was a naively ambitious goal, and the substitution of a corporate, volunteer strategy supplanted the more extensive and costly proposals to engage and develop poor communities. Expectations for success deriving from former President Carter's affiliation with the project contributed to the unreasonably high initial expectations. But TAP did organize some previously unorganized communities, and it contributed useful projects to multiple poor communities. Over time, TAP learned to collaborate productively with the communities in which it works.

Downtown Redevelopment
During the Olympics Era

ost of the major redevelopment projects undertaken in and around downtown Atlanta during the Olympics preparation period had problematic, controversial aspects. First of all, the new Olympic/Braves stadium built by the Atlanta Committee for the Olympic Games inflicted further damage on the low-income black neighborhoods that had already suffered from the existing stadium. Neighborhood representatives at first opposed building the new stadium next to the old one, and they called for a participatory planning process to replace the secret agreement on the Olympic stadium. But they eventually recognized that they could not block the stadium or reopen the planning process, so they demanded that specific measures be taken to mitigate the new stadium's damaging effects.

The stadium plan agreed upon by ACOG and the Atlanta Braves and then approved by city and county government included very few of these measures. Even the revitalization of the stadium-area neighborhood of Summerhill had troubling features. ACOG expected area neighborhoods to oppose the site of the new stadium, so in order to undercut unified neighborhood opposition, ACOG promised Summerhill representatives that it would find funding for redeveloping their neighborhood in exchange for Summerhill's support. When the redevelopment took place, it was as a mixed-income community, and gentrification is forcing many low-income residents to move.

Equally troubling is how the Atlanta Housing Authority transformed the Techwood/Clark Howell public-housing complexes into a mixed-income development. There were 70 percent fewer public-housing units in the new community than in the complexes, but the AHA had deliberately reduced the population of Techwood/Clark Howell during redevelopment planning, and thus did not have to find relocation housing for most of those who left. Furthermore, the housing authority still has not replaced all of the public-housing units that were eliminated, despite having promised that it would.

The way ACOG handled the construction of the stadium and the redevelopment of Summerhill, and the way the housing authority transformed Techwood/Clark Howell into a mixed-income community, were reminiscent of Atlanta's urban-renewal efforts thirty years earlier. Once again, those in positions of power ignored the negative effects of redevelopment on low-income African Americans. Furthermore, like urban renewal, turning Summerhill and Techwood/Clark Howell into mixed-income communities was really a way of removing poor blacks from the downtown area. Class and racial prejudice again played important roles in downtown redevelopment.

The Olympic park project also had a number of dubious features. A small business district had to be torn down to make room for the park, and many of the small businesses in the area provided important services to companies and workers. Forcing these businesses to move has damaged a downtown economy that city leaders have been trying to revive. Only one of the businesses that was forced to move received assistance for relocating, and the survival of many of the others was threatened. Finally, residential development that fitted naturally with existing development in the Techwood district was already occurring there. The residential development that is now taking place adjacent to the park is development on cleared land and therefore risks both the sterility of entirely new development and the expense of replacing buildings that could have been rehabitated. Finally, since the city has subsidized the new housing being built in the area of the park, an area that once generated property-tax revenues has become a drain on the city treasury.

The Olympic Stadium

The story of how the Olympic Stadium came to be built begins with the story of the Georgia Dome, Atlanta's pro-football stadium. The Atlanta Falcons of the NFL had been sharing Atlanta/Fulton County Stadium with the Braves for years. In 1986, the team began lobbying state government for its own stadium, and the owners applied leverage by threatening to move the team to Jacksonville. Governor Miller agreed to commission a study of possible sites and configurations for a new stadium, and the governor's Office of Planning and Budget hired two consulting firms to do the study. The consultants delivered their report to Governor Miller in August 1986. Among the alternatives they proposed was one that concluded that the twenty-year-old shared stadium was obsolete for both baseball and football and recommended building both a new football stadium and a new baseball stadium. It proposed that both stadiums be built in the area of the existing stadium.[1]

Negotiations between the Falcons and the state were broadened to include the city of Atlanta and Fulton County. Finally, in June 1989, after two years of negotiations, the city and Fulton County gave final approval to the financing and design for a new stadium. The site agreed upon, however, was not adjacent to the existing stadium but on the west side of the downtown area. Construction on the new facility got under way in October of that year.

The 1986 consultant's study had obliquely revealed that the baseball team, the Atlanta Braves, was lobbying for a new stadium. Subsequently, during the preparation of the Olympic bid, the Atlanta Olympic Committee held secret talks with the Braves, and these negotiations led to an agreement that an Olympic stadium would be built with revenues from the Olympics and that this stadium would be converted after the Games into a new baseball stadium.[2] After the announcement in September 1990 that Atlanta had won its Olympics bid, the AOC made public its overall plan for the Games, including its proposal for a new stadium. The major elements of the stadium proposal were as follows: The new facility would be built south of the existing stadium; it would have a seating capacity of 85,000; it would be used during the Games for the opening and closing ceremonies and for track and field; after the

Games it would be reduced to a facility with a capacity of 45,000 and would serve as the Braves' new stadium; the existing stadium would be demolished.

After Atlanta won the Olympics bid, Olympic planners, the city, and Fulton County began negotiations over the specific plan for the proposed stadium. Meanwhile, residents of the neighborhood south of the stadium, Peoplestown, formed an organization called Atlanta Neighborhoods United for Fairness (A'NUFF) to represent the interests of stadium-area neighborhoods.[3] A'NUFF raised objections to the site of the proposed stadium and to the fact that plans for the stadium had been agreed upon secretly.

In late November 1990, representatives from the AOC and Central Atlanta Progress attended a community meeting with stadium-area residents. A spokesman for the AOC promised that the neighborhoods would be involved in planning the stadium and that a redevelopment plan for the Summerhill neighborhood would minimize the stadium's negative impact on the area.[4] But members of A'NUFF were not satisfied by these promises and decided to make their feelings known through a formal protest. In February 1991 a group of them held a candlelight vigil in front of the home of Billy Payne, head of ACOG.[5]

Opposition to the AOC's stadium plan also came from some members of the Atlanta–Fulton County Recreation Authority, the public body that managed the existing stadium. Among the reasons the Braves wanted a new stadium were that they wanted expanded skybox revenues and that they wanted to manage the stadium themselves. But some of the members of the Atlanta–Fulton County Recreation Authority wanted to preserve the existing facility. They felt that the Braves should continue to play in a publicly owned stadium so that local government would continue to have some degree of management control over the facility. They also wanted to preserve the existing stadium because of the outstanding debt on it. In the summer of 1991, some of the board and staff of the recreation authority and their political allies began a campaign to save the stadium. A'NUFF, meanwhile, was urging all the neighborhood planning units to endorse an open and accessible planning process for the Olympic stadium. In July, the Atlanta Planning Advisory Board, an umbrella organization comprising the presidents of the city's twenty-four neighborhood planning units, issued a draft statement proposing three other sites for the Olympic stadium.

At the end of August, after eleven months of negotiations, ACOG, the city, and Fulton County reached fundamental agreement on a plan for the Olympic stadium. The plan they agreed upon was essentially the same as the AOC plan: A new stadium would be built next to the existing stadium, and the old stadium would be torn down after the Games. ACOG agreed to pay off the $11 million of debt on the old stadium that would still be outstanding in 1996.[6] That same summer, ACOG, the Atlanta Recreation Authority, and the Braves began formal negotiations on the design of the new stadium and how it would be financed.

In September, ACOG took its first formal step toward addressing the concerns of the stadium-area neighborhoods, creating a "neighborhood task force" that included eight neighborhood representatives. But after four meetings over a period of a month and a half, serious disagreements between ACOG and the neighborhood representatives could not be resolved, and ACOG disbanded the task force. The main source of conflict was demands by neighborhood representatives for an environmental-impact statement for the proposed stadium. ACOG and the Braves objected. A full environmental-impact statement would have required them to consider alternatives including other sites, which they were unwilling to do, and would have meant public scrutiny of any private decisions reached. With the stadium-area task force disbanded, the neighborhoods had no effective formal way of influencing the planning negotiations.

In early 1992, A'NUFF changed its basic position on the stadium. The group had received almost no support from elected officials, and negotiations were entering their final stages without community involvement, so A'NUFF abandoned its demands that the planning process be open and that other sites be considered. By dropping their opposition, A'NUFF's members hoped, they could gain a voice in the planning process, limit the damage that the stadium would do to the neighborhood, and perhaps also gain some compensation. They continued to ask for an environmental study of the site and the surrounding area, and in addition they requested an organized plan for parking and traffic flow, a ban on informal parking lots, buffers between the neighborhoods and the stadium, restrictions on late-night fireworks, and adequate security at the stadium and in the neighborhoods. A'NUFF also joined forces with Summerhill representatives and asked that 25 percent of parking revenues be set aside for neighborhood redevelopment, that neighborhood residents be given preference for stadium jobs and vendor contracts, and that a public authority administer the stadium.[7] But A'NUFF's effort to influence stadium planning had no real chance of succeeding. It was entirely up to ACOG, the Braves, and the Atlanta–Fulton County Recreation Authority to decide which neighborhood demands they would respond to. All the neighborhoods could do was make their wishes known and wait to see what happened.

ACOG, the Braves, and the recreation authority reached a preliminary agreement in July 1992. In late October the design agreement for the stadium was released to the public. In November, MAOGA, the government entity established to oversee the construction of Olympic venues, approved the design and the financing agreements. The only part of the plan that had not yet been agreed upon was the amount and location of parking. The negotiators finally reached agreement on these points, and the complete stadium plan was made public on February 8, 1993.

The plan called for a "designer" stadium, a unique structure unlike the circular, generic existing stadium. When converted to the Braves stadium, it would have sixty corporate skyboxes that would generate $3 million a year. The financing agreement stipulated that ACOG would fund construction of the stadium, while the city would use federal funds to repair and replace the infrastructure under the site. The Braves would supplant the Atlanta–Fulton County Recreation Authority as the operating agent for the stadium. The authority would collect $500,000 in annual rent from the team and an additional $1 million in annual contributions for capital costs. The Braves would sign a twenty-year lease with four subsequent five-year options. The team would receive the income from parking and concessions. The plan called for a total of 8,900 parking spaces and included a promise by the city to prohibit informal parking in the stadium area.

The stadium plan did not include most of what the neighborhoods had asked for. It proposed none of the physical buffers they wanted.

It proposed fewer than the 12,500 parking spaces they had counted during sold-out Braves games. So informal parking would continue to be a problem, but the plan included no legal or administrative mechanisms for prohibiting it. Furthermore, if the city were going to be successful in actually eliminating these lots, fans would somehow have to be persuaded to use public transportation, but the plan contained no strategy for doing this. Finally, the plan promised the neighborhoods 8.25 percent of net parking revenues for redevelopment, far less than the 25 percent of gross parking revenues the neighborhoods had wanted.

After the stadium plan was released to the public, disagreement arose between the recreation authority and the Braves over how future capital expenditures and the costs of maintenance would be shared by the Braves and local government. Although the Braves had agreed to pay $500,000 in annual rent and make a $1 million annual contribution to a capital-improvements fund, the proposed contract exposed the public to open-ended capital costs, with only modest adjustments for inflation. Tom Lowe, an engineer, a member of the Fulton County Commission, and a recreation authority board member, estimated the unfunded public liability at up to $214 million.[8] In mid-February the authority began insisting that the capital-costs liability be restructured and that the amounts paid by the Braves be indexed for inflation.[9] The Braves agreed to adjust for inflation starting in the year 2016, when the first of their five-year renewal options would come up. This adjustment was still highly favorable to the Braves, because at that point they would be able to threaten to move once again, and with this strong negotiating position defeat the indexing proposal. But the recreation authority went along anyway, voting 6 to 3 to accept the agreement with this revision.[10]

The stadium agreement now had to be voted on by the City Council. During the week before the vote, the Braves made two new concessions. They agreed to add $10,000 to their annual contribution to the capital-improvements fund, and they agreed to increase their share of the liability should hazardous materials be discovered at the site and have to be removed. Mayor Jackson lobbied behind the scenes for approval. When the council met on March 1 to vote, he appeared before the members and urged them not to reject the agreement in order to

get a more favorable deal from the Braves on the unfunded public liabilities. "This is not poker," he warned. "This is the well-being of
Atlanta. What if the Braves call that bluff? I'm not prepared to lose the
Braves and a $207 million stadium." The council approved the stadium
agreement with the minor lease modifications offered by the Braves in
a 10-to-5 vote.[11]

The final step was a vote on the stadium agreement by the Fulton
County Commission. Tom Lowe was opposed to putting off inflation
indexing until the next century and wanted more protection from
unlimited future capital costs. The Braves made a further concession
and agreed to cap the future liability of the city and the county for
future renovations and improvements at $100 million over the forty-year
lease-and-option period. Michael Lomax, the commission chairman,
was strongly in favor of the stadium agreement. But when the commissioners met on March 3 to vote, a majority wanted more time to
negotiate, and the commission voted to table the final vote for a week.[12]

Immediately after the commission postponed its decision, Billy
Payne put additional pressure on the commissioners by announcing
that ACOG was beginning efforts to identify another site.[13] And the
Braves modified their position once more, agreeing to cap the public
liability for future improvements and renovations to the stadium at $50
million instead of $100 million. ACOG and Braves negotiators also
agreed to increase the size of the community-improvement fund. They
changed the 8.25 percent of net parking revenues proposed in the plan
to 8.25 percent of gross revenues, an improvement but still less than the
percentage of gross revenues the neighborhoods were seeking. The
community fund would not begin receiving revenues until after the
Olympics, so Braves negotiators offered a contribution of $300,000 as a
stopgap. ACOG and the Braves also agreed to eliminate a newly proposed parking lot in Peoplestown. Two agreements unrelated to the stadium were reached as well: ACOG would let the black colleges in the
Atlanta University Center rent out 1,000 rooms during the Olympics,
and ACOG would hire nine black administrators to highly paid positions. On March 19, after all these changes and additions had been
made, the Fulton County Commission voted 6 to 1 in favor of the stadium agreement.[14]

In approving the stadium plan agreed upon by ACOG and the Braves, city and county government largely ignored their obligation to represent the public interest. First of all, in letting ACOG and the Braves decide the site of the new stadium, the city and Fulton County surrendered their responsibility to make this decision themselves. The location of a stadium has wide-ranging effects. It has damaging effects on its surroundings, it requires public infrastructure, and it is the focus of economic activity that can undermine, destroy, or enhance other economic activities in the area. There is a clear necessity on the part of local governments to protect the public's interest by choosing the most intelligent, most beneficial, and least damaging locations for such facilities. The stadium agreement also greatly diminished the role of city and county government in managing a major downtown facility. Whereas the old stadium was a publicly owned facility managed directly by the Atlanta–Fulton County Recreation Authority, the new stadium is managed by the Braves, with the recreation authority having only indirect control.

Elected officials also ignored their obligation to protect the neighborhoods near the stadium. When ACOG and the Braves refused to commission an environmental-impact statement, neither the city nor the county insisted that one be done. They didn't insist on a provision for buffers between the stadium and the neighborhoods, either, and they didn't offer to build these buffers themselves. The number of parking spaces called for in the stadium agreement was inadequate, and the agreement contained no public-transportation plan that would reduce the need for parking, but city and county government made no protest on either issue. The stadium agreement did not include changes to highway and surface-street access to the stadium to control traffic flow through the neighborhoods, but city and county government did not insist on such improvements.

In approving the stadium agreement, not only did city and county government fail to protect the interests of the stadium-area neighborhoods, they failed to protect their own interests. First of all, the city let itself be taken advantage of with regard to infrastructure costs. It was the city, not ACOG or the Braves, that had to find the $10 million to $15 million needed to replace the nearly 100-year-old sewer line underneath the new stadium. Future stadium costs are another example:

Though the city and county gave control of the new stadium to the Braves, they share responsibility with the Braves for future liabilities. Even though the Braves make all the crucial management decisions, if costs for maintenance and repairs exceed a certain amount, they can present the city and county with bills for these costs. So there remains a distinct possibility that the taxpayers will bear a portion of the future costs of a facility that generates revenues for a private business.

The overall stadium plan approved by the city and county was essentially the plan agreed upon by ACOG and the Braves, and it was highly favorable to the Braves. As has happened so often in Atlanta since the '50s, an important decision regarding downtown redevelopment was made by a small group of powerful, influential people, and once again government officials largely went along with what this small group wanted.

Summerhill

The 1986 state-commissioned study of football stadium options examined one alternative that included a new baseball stadium. This alternative suggested that a new baseball stadium be built just east of the existing stadium. This would have meant the demolition of a large part of the Summerhill neighborhood. Summerhill had created a community-development corporation called Summerhill Neighborhood Inc. to redevelop the neighborhood, and when the state study appeared, SNI was in the process of formulating a plan to redevelop the neighborhood as a mixed-income community. The situation changed dramatically when the AOC began preparing an Olympics bid. When Olympic planners decided to build the Olympic stadium next to the existing stadium, they knew they had to do something about the opposition they expected from stadium-area neighborhoods. So they decided to co-opt the opposition and provide themselves with political cover by appointing Doug Dean, head of SNI, along with a representative from a neighborhood not in the stadium area, to the AOC.

Dean and SNI decided early on in the planning process to support the proposed stadium. They calculated that cooperation would give them greater influence on planning and gain them concessions and special consideration. They were right. Olympic planners decided to shift the site of the proposed stadium away from Summerhill to a site south of the existing stadium, on the edge of the Peoplestown neighborhood. They promised SNI that there would be no new stadium parking in its neighborhood, and they promised to help SNI find funding for redevelopment.

Dean's first step in getting support for his redevelopment efforts was to ask Central Atlanta Progress and the city to pay for a comprehensive Summerhill redevelopment plan by the Washington-based Urban Land Institute. CAP and the city raised the $100,000 needed to hire the consultants, and the ULI sent a panel of nationally known planning and redevelopment experts to Atlanta in the spring of 1991. Their report appeared in April. It endorsed much of the redevelopment plan already being formulated by SNI.

Another major element in Summerhill's strategy was to get itself designated as the primary stadium-area neighborhood. SNI felt that if the stadium were considered part of Summerhill, the neighborhood would capture a major share of any redevelopment funding. Summerhill accomplished this by getting the city to change its planning maps to show both the old and the proposed stadiums in Summerhill. In 1973, when the city had established its system of neighborhood planning units, its maps had not shown the existing stadium in any of the three adjacent neighborhoods, identifying it instead as a separate facility between neighborhoods. At the time, none of them had wanted to be identified with a facility that had been the source of so many problems. Once Summerhill had effectively annexed both the old and new stadium sites, not only did the AOC treat Summerhill as the only stadium-area neighborhood, so did the local press. For the first few months after the September 1990 announcement that Atlanta had won the Olympics, all the stories about the proposed new stadium and neighborhood redevelopment focused on Summerhill. No mention was made of Peoplestown to the south of the stadium or Mechanicsville to the west.

Summerhill's preemptive deal with the AOC put Peoplestown and Mechanicsville at a serious disadvantage. Not only would the city's redevelopment efforts be directed primarily at Summerhill, but the AOC's promise that there would be no new parking in Summerhill meant that one or both of the other two neighborhoods would have to give up land for whatever parking the proposed stadium would require. Even more important, Summerhill's compact with the AOC undercut the capacity of the other two neighborhoods to mount effective opposition to the stadium. Two poor, black neighborhoods versus Olympic promoters and the Atlanta Braves was an unequal contest from the outset, especially amid all the enthusiasm surrounding the Olympics. When Summerhill chose to align itself with the Olympic planners, the political leverage of the other two neighborhoods was weakened even further.

Techwood/Clark Howell

The AOC bid plan included proposals that an Olympic swimming and diving facility be built on the Georgia Institute of Technology campus and that the school's three-story dormitory in the adjacent Techwood Homes public-housing complex be replaced by a new dormitory that would house Olympic athletes during the Games. After the announcement that Atlanta would be the site of the Olympics, the Georgia Tech dormitory proposal prompted the Atlanta Housing Authority to propose that all of Techwood Homes and the neighboring Clark Howell Homes be renovated to provide additional housing for Olympic athletes, and that ACOG-organized Olympics rental from these new units pay for the renovation.[15]

The Techwood and Clark Howell complexes were directly across the street from the Georgia Tech campus and adjacent to Coca-Cola's corporate headquarters to the west. Map 7 (p. 177) shows the location of Techwood/Clark Howell relative to surrounding communities. Techwood, the oldest public-housing development in the country, opened in 1935, and Clark Howell opened in 1940. Both complexes were products of the New Deal, both were built as slum-clearance projects,[16] and both were originally all-white. Techwood consisted of thirteen three-story apartment buildings and seven buildings made up of attached houses. Originally there were 604 units in the twenty buildings. Clark Howell comprised fifty-eight two-story buildings containing 630 units. Both complexes were administered by the Atlanta Housing Authority that was established in 1938. In 1966, the AHA replaced a park at the south end of Techwood Homes with a seventeen-story, 250-unit high-rise called the Palmer House, built for elderly residents. In 1973, the

AHA replaced a park on the north end of Techwood with a similar building called Roosevelt House.

Techwood/Clark Howell remained exclusively white until 1968, when they desegregated in response to a presidential executive order ending segregation in public housing. After being integrated, the two developments became increasingly black. By 1975, 60 percent of the residents were black;[17] by 1990, the figure was 96 percent.[18] The racial transition of Techwood/Clark Howell alarmed executives at the neighboring Coca-Cola headquarters. In a 1971 memo to Robert Woodruff, the former president and chairman of the company who remained influential in its direction, Paul Austin, the company's CEO, voiced the fear that when Techwood and Clark Howell became "all black, the felony rate will triple."[19] Austin proposed that both developments be demolished and replaced by a middle-income apartment complex and a shopping mall. He took his proposal to John Portman, the architect and developer, who was then head of Central Atlanta Progress.

Portman agreed that the public housing should be destroyed, but in drawing up his own redevelopment plan he proposed commercial and office development rather than residential development. After Maynard Jackson was elected mayor in 1973, Austin sought Jackson's support for his plan. At first Jackson agreed, but then, fearing the political consequences of backing a redevelopment scheme that would displace poor blacks, he withdrew his support. Portman continued to campaign for commercial and office development, but Jackson resisted him and eventually Portman gave up.[20]

Like Coca-Cola, Georgia Tech wanted the public housing transformed and the area redeveloped. After the announcement that Atlanta would stage the Olympics, a proposal for redeveloping the area was made by a developer named Russell Chandler, a Tech alumnus and the institute's liaison on the AOC.[21] Yet another proposal was made soon afterward by another developer (also a Georgia Tech alumnus).[22]

Mayor Jackson, as he had sixteen years earlier, wanted Techwood/ Clark Howell preserved, but he also wanted the complexes renovated. Raymond Sales, Jackson's chief adviser on housing issues, proposed that the renovation of Techwood/Clark Howell be part of an overall plan that included the redevelopment of Techwood Park, a district of

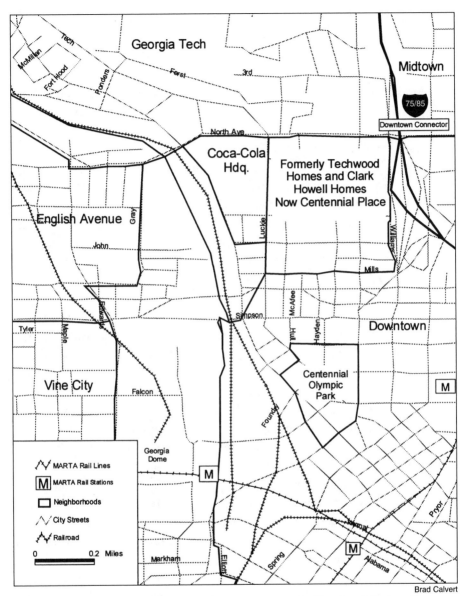

Georgia Tech

Midtown

75/85

Downtown Connector

North Ave

Coca-Cola Hdq.

Formerly Techwood Homes and Clark Howell Homes Now Centennial Place

English Avenue

John

Mills

Simpson

Tyler

Downtown

Vine City

Falcon

Centennial Olympic Park

M

Georgia Dome

/\/ MARTA Rail Lines

M MARTA Rail Stations

☐ Neighborhoods

/\/ City Streets

/\/ Railroad

0   0.2 Miles

Markham

M

Brad Calvert

Map 7.   Techwood/Clark-Howell Homes (Now Centennial Place) and Surrounding Neighborhoods

small businesses and warehouses just south of the public housing and adjacent to the central business district.[23]

Conflict arose among the various interested parties, including the Atlanta Housing Authority, over who would control the redevelopment. In the spring of 1991, to resolve the dispute, Jackson formed the Techwood Advisory Committee to come up with a redevelopment plan. The group included representatives from city government, the AHA, CAP, ACOG, MAOGA, and the Techwood Residents' Association. It also included the presidents of Georgia Tech, Georgia State, and Atlanta University.[24] In July 1991 the committee hired a planning team, using $250,000 provided by (Coca-Cola's) Woodruff family of foundations and the promise of another $250,000 from other Atlanta foundations. The team consisted of three developers, an investment-banking firm, and twelve other consultants, and from the names of the four main members the committee gave the planning team the acronym PATH.[25]

The plan formulated by the PATH team proposed changes for both Techwood/Clark Howell and Techwood Park. The plan called for the redevelopment of Techwood/Clark Howell as a smaller, mixed-income community and the construction of dormitories for Olympic athletes on ten acres of Techwood and Georgia Tech property. Techwood would be renovated and reconfigured, and most of Clark Howell would be demolished. Since public-housing redevelopment plans had to be approved by the federal Department of Housing and Urban Development, and since HUD required that public-housing residents be involved in the planning process, the PATH plan was submitted to residents of Techwood/Clark Howell, Palmer House, and Roosevelt House for a vote on October 1. The plan was approved, 428 to 363.[26]

Federal housing law in effect at the time required that replacement public housing had to be provided for any public housing demolished. It also stated that displaced residents had to be relocated. Replacement housing and relocation housing were not necessarily the same thing. Displaced residents might move into replacement housing or they might move elsewhere. Regardless of where residents relocated, there had to be a one-for-one replacement of any demolished public-housing units. But the PATH plan was extremely vague about both replacement housing and relocation housing. It did not specify the exact number of units to be demolished, the number of units to be renovated, the number of units that would replace the units eliminated, the number of replacement units that would be built elsewhere, or the number of units that would be provided for relocation.[27] Another problem with the plan concerned a program aimed at making it possible for residents to own their units. Only twenty-two of the 1,100 households in residence at Techwood/Clark Howell at the time of the plan earned enough to qualify for this program.[28] The PATH team also misled the residents by having them take part in a survey of their goals and wishes, which was supposed to have driven the redevelopment plan. But the survey was not tabulated or released to the residents until after the plan had been prepared and voted on.[29]

After being approved by the residents, the Techwood-area redevelopment plan was approved by the mayor, the City Council, and the board of the Atlanta Housing Authority. It still needed to be approved by the regional and central offices of HUD, however, and HUD's regional office rejected it on a number of grounds, including a lack of replacement housing, insufficient resident involvement, and inadequate financing.[30] The city and the AHA set about shaping the plan to gain HUD's endorsement.

Meanwhile, PATH planners were trying to come up with an overall plan for the coordinated redevelopment of the entire Techwood area. The total redevelopment cost was estimated at $232 million. PATH expected $90 million from Olympics dormitory rentals and $10 million to $15 million from property taxes. In addition, Coca-Cola had recently purchased a five-acre lot from the Atlanta Housing Authority to build an extension of its corporate headquarters, and the increase in property taxes would underwrite a bond for additional funds. PATH expected $3 million to $6 million from city and state budgets because of the college dormitories and a proposed new elementary school in the area. All this left PATH more than $70 million short, and PATH hoped that HUD would provide these additional funds.[31]

In early January 1992, Mayor Jackson announced the formation of Techwood Park Inc., an agency that would oversee the redevelopment of the Techwood Park business district and devise a property-tax plan for financing part of the redevelopment. Jackson appointed Joe Martin, a former head of CAP, director of the corporation.[32]

On January 30, the PATH financing plan was jeopardized when Coca-Cola announced that it was delaying its decision to build a new office tower.[33] The plan was dealt another blow in February, when the central office of HUD issued an unfavorable review. HUD's review listed thirty-eight objections to the PATH proposal, the major criticisms being that the overall plan was too complex, that too much of the financing plan relied on private loans that were so far uncommitted, that the plan was unclear about who the beneficiaries of the requested federal aid would be, that the residents had not been properly involved, that not enough replacement public housing was proposed, that the location of replacement housing was not identified, and that the relocation plan was unacceptably vague.[34]

When Mayor Jackson read HUD's review, he recognized that the PATH plan was seriously flawed and that an entirely new approach and strong leadership were needed, and he appointed Joe Martin to head a coordinated redevelopment effort for the entire Techwood area.[35] In March, Jackson nominated Earl Phillips to be executive director of the Atlanta Housing Authority and the board approved his nomination. Phillips had held the same position for Houston and Miami's housing authorities, in each case significantly rejuvenating the organization. We can't be sure what Jackson told Phillips his mission was, but one can infer from Phillips's actions that Jackson had decided that a redeveloped Techwood/Clark Howell should remain primarily public housing.

The first step Phillips took as executive director of the AHA was to give the contending factions of residents more direct participation in the planning process than PATH had given them. He formed a planning committee and invited all residents to participate, assigning them to review the PATH plan and decide what changes they wanted. In May, Phillips hired an architect named Richard Bradfield to attend planning-committee meetings, learn what the residents wanted, and come up with a design plan that reflected their wishes. Meanwhile, the conflict between the AHA and Techwood Park Inc. over who would control the redevelopment of Techwood/Clark Howell was growing. At the end of March, Joe Martin, director of Techwood Park Inc., presented a new redevelopment plan to the AHA board.[36] On April 7, reflecting Phillips' insistence that AHA control Techwood/Clark Howell's redevelopment, the board unanimously rejected Martin's proposal.[37] The conflict could not be resolved, and Martin resigned from TPI on May 18.[38]

Meanwhile, Phillips was working on a new financing plan. The AOC bid plan had proposed that new housing for Olympic athletes be converted after the Games into housing for students at Georgia Tech. But Georgia State University, located on the opposite edge of the downtown area, had no student dormitories at all, and university officials felt that Tech, which had a substantial number of dormitories, was scheduled to receive a disproportionate share of Olympics-related capital projects. Discussions were held in the spring among the AHA, Georgia Tech, Georgia State, the State Board of Regents, and ACOG regarding the dormitory issue. Phillips had concluded that the basic PATH plan was unworkable, that integrating Olympic housing with public housing redevelopment was not feasible, and that redeveloping the public housing should be pursued separately. All the parties agreed that a substantially larger dormitory project than the one originally envisioned should be built, and Georgia Tech conceded that after the Games the Olympic dormitories should be converted to housing for Georgia State students. It was agreed that the housing authority would sell 4.5 acres of Techwood to the Board of Regents, to be used for the dorms, and that the proceeds of the sale would be used to help renovate Techwood/Clark Howell. Residents endorsed the sale on May 26. The Board of Regents eventually settled on a price of $2.6 million for the property, and in April of the following year HUD approved the sale.[39]

In October 1992, a new federal program for revitalizing public housing, called HOPE VI, was signed into law as part of a HUD appropriations bill. The AHA had been tracking the bill through Congress, and once it had passed, the AHA applied for $40 million from the program for the Techwood/Clark Howell project. The new redevelopment plan put together by Phillips and Bradfield was submitted to HUD in May 1993 and approved by HUD in August. The plan called for a renovated public-housing community. The major design change that the plan called for was the rehabilitation of parts of Clark Howell instead of demolition. Because part of the Techwood property would be sold to the Board of Regents, and because second- and third-story units would be combined into two-story units under this plan, the rehabilitated community would be somewhat reduced in size. Techwood's 457 units would be reconfigured into 316 units, and 192 of the units at Clark Howell would be reconfigured into 176 units. HUD funding, the sale of the Techwood property, and various unspecified private sources would pay for the renovation.[40]

The HOPE VI program had a ceiling of 500 units, so the remainder of Clark Howell was scheduled for later rehabilitation. But the Phillips/ Bradfield plan would soon be discarded. After Bill Campbell became mayor in 1994, he set about making fundamental changes at the Atlanta Housing Authority. Campbell's views on public housing were radically different from those of Maynard Jackson or Earl Phillips. Campbell shared the increasingly popular view that public-housing developments only exacerbate the problems arising from poverty. He also felt that the Atlanta Housing Authority had degenerated into a bloated, inefficient, self-perpetuating bureaucracy, and he immediately set about gaining control of the AHA. On March 2, less than two months after Campbell's inauguration, Earl Phillips resigned. No explanation was given, but the obvious reason was that Campbell and Phillips differed in their attitudes toward public housing. When, under the AHA board's system of rotating tenure, four seats on the seven-member board fell vacant, Campbell appointed members who shared his views.[41] Campbell then used his influence on the board to have Renee Glover, one of his senior campaign aides and a member of the board, appointed to be Phillips's replacement.

Public-housing politics were changing in Washington as well. The election of Republican majorities in both houses of Congress in November 1994 at first threatened HUD's existence. HUD survived, but as a chastened agency calling for the demolition of some public housing. Since taking over at the AHA, Glover and the other people Campbell has appointed to the board have worked together to transform five of the city's public-housing developments, including Techwood/Clark Howell, into mixed-income communities. They are also in the process of privatizing these redeveloped communities.[42] In addition, CAP has consistently sought expansion of middle- and upper-income housing in and around the CBD and Glover believed that the redevelopment of Techwood/Clark Howell would "have to be a part of the downtown agenda."[43] Glover reshaped the HOPE VI proposal for the Techwood/Clark Howell project and submitted it to HUD on March 17, 1995. Called the Revised Revitalization Plan, it called for replacing the units in the Techwood/Clark Howell development with 900 new units. Only 360 of these new units would be public-housing units. Of the other 540 units, 180 would be moderate-income units financed through tax credits, and 360 would be market-rate units.[44] The plan further proposed that this new, mixed-income community be placed under private management.[45]

The new plan was approved by HUD in 1995, and demolition began on May 12. As of October 1999, 720 of the planned 900 units in the new development, including 300 public-housing units, had been built. The Revised Revitalization Plan pledged that the Atlanta Housing Authority would replace the 1,195 Techwood/Clark Howell units that redevelopment would eliminate. So far, the AHA either has built or is committed to building 590 replacement units, including 360 subsidized units in the new development, which is called Centennial Place.[46] If all 590 units are completed, they will represent 49.4 percent of the 1,195 units demolished. It does not appear likely that the AHA will live up to its commitment to full replacement, and it is no longer under any legal compulsion to do so. As part of the FY 1995 rescission bill, Congress eliminated the long-standing statutory requirement that demolished public housing be replaced on a one-for one basis. The AHA is currently much more interested in transforming public-housing developments into gentrified, mixed-income communities than in maintaining an adequate supply of subsidized, low-income housing.

The most disturbing aspect of the Techwood/Clark Howell redevelopment was the way in which the Atlanta Housing Authority deliberately shrank the population of Techwood during the planning process. Though there is no proof that the AHA deliberately depopulated Techwood, there is clear evidence that points that way. It was the authority's stated policy to reduce the occupancy rate by 20 percent to make the process of redevelopment easier,[47] but the AHA went well beyond that point. In June 1990, 531 of 571 apartments were occupied, an occupancy rate of 92.8 percent. By August 1991, 467 units were occupied, an occupancy rate of 81.8 percent. When Earl Phillips was appointed in March 1992, 408 units were occupied, an occupancy rate of 71.5 percent. By October, only 344 units were occupied, an occupancy rate of 60.2 percent. There were only 457 units remaining after the sale of part of 114 units of Techwood to the Board of Regents in April 1993, and in August of that year, when the AHA was notified by HUD that its HOPE VI application had been approved, only 105 units of these 457 units were occupied, a rate of 22.9 percent.[48] When the residents voted on the final redevelopment plan in February 1995, only twenty-six families remained in Techwood.

The obvious advantage of reducing Techwood's population was reducing the cost of relocation. Fewer residents when Techwood was torn down meant fewer who would have to be provided with alternative housing. The AHA used two administrative strategies to shrink Techwood's population: It did not take in new residents to replace those who left, and it began to enforce lease regulations more strictly than in the past. In none of the plans that the AHA submitted to HUD did it disclose that it was emptying Techwood, but HUD surely must have known what was happening. Eventually, emptying Techwood began to have a snowball effect. The process went so far that some residents left voluntarily because they did not want to live in increasingly empty buildings.

After Renee Glover became executive director, the AHA hired a consulting firm called Integral Partnership to help come up with a redevelopment plan. Integral's Egbert Perry began holding biweekly meetings with Techwood residents in an effort to shape a new proposal. By now so few people were living at Techwood that letting residents participate in planning had become an empty formality. At an important meeting just two weeks before a final vote was held on the new redevelopment plan, only eight residents attended, along with nine AHA staff members and consultants, and some of the residents present were from Palmer and Roosevelt Houses.[49] When the residents voted on the new plan on February 27, 1995, the vote was 66 to 9 in favor.[50]

While Glover and Integral Partnership were putting together their revitalization plan, Techwood residents retained Legal Services, which provides free legal assistance to low-income people, to protect their rights. Legal Services negotiated a contract with the housing authority called the Further Assurances Agreement. The agreement was signed on May 8, 1996, four days before demolition began, and was incorporated into the AHA's contract with HUD. The agreement stipulated that the authority would relocate those still living in the two housing complexes as of August 18, 1994, the date the revised application for HOPE VI funding had been approved, and that these residents would have a preferential right of return to the redeveloped community.

Despite the legal protections provided by this agreement, not all of the households in residence as of the date stipulated have been relocated. Because Clark Howell was not vacated, there were a total of 693 households in residence as of August 18, 1994.[51] As of March 1997, 515 of these had been relocated.[52] This represents 74.3 percent of the households in residence as of the date stipulated in the Further Assurances Agreement. The AHA has been even less effective in implementing the preferential right of return. Of these 693 households, 212 expressed an interest in returning. The housing authority is unable to say how many of the 481 households that did not express interest could not be found, how many were satisfied with their present housing (and therefore, did not return), or how many could not meet the qualifications. Of the 212 households expressing interest in returning, 194 were invited to complete applications. Contact was lost with the other eighteen.[53]

At the end of the process, in 1999, only seventy-eight former resident families had returned.[54] This represents only 11.2 percent of the households in residence as of the date stipulated in the agreement. These figures, however, do not convey the overall impact of replacing Techwood/Clark Howell with a smaller, mixed-income community. The 515 relocated households represent only 45.7 percent of the 1,128 households in residence in both Techwood and Clark Howell when redevelopment planning began in September 1990. And the seventy-eight households that have returned to Centennial Place represent only 6.9 percent of those 1,128 households.

The PATH plan and the Revised Revitalization Plan subordinated the interests of Techwood/Clark Howell residents to other interests. In proposing that the amount of public housing in the area be greatly reduced, both plans gave Coca-Cola, Georgia Tech, and the downtown business community what they wanted. City leaders took advantage of the redevelopment opportunities provided by the Olympics to remove low-income blacks from the downtown area, and they used public funding to do so. This continued a trend started three decades earlier, during the urban-renewal era. The AHA has also repeated the patterns of the past with its inadequate efforts to provide replacement housing and relocation assistance.

Centennial Olympic Park

From the very beginning of redevelopment planning for Techwood/ Clark Howell, the pro-gentrification faction had tried to control the planning process, or least heavily influence it, by insisting that revitalization of the public housing be part of an overall plan to redevelop Techwood Park, an adjacent seventy-acre commercial district to the south. This coordinated redevelopment concept had been resisted by the AHA and the residents. The Techwood redevelopment issue had involved Mayor Jackson in controversy twenty years earlier, so he tried to remain neutral. After HUD rejected the PATH plan in early 1992, Jackson tried to satisfy the AHA/residents faction by appointing Earl Phillips executive director of the AHA, to try to preserve Techwood/ Clark Howell as public housing, and he tried to satisfy the Coca-Cola/ Georgia Tech faction by putting Techwood Park Inc. and its president, Joe Martin, in charge of coordinated redevelopment of the entire Techwood area.

After growing conflict between TPI and the AHA caused Martin to resign, TPI fell dormant and remained so for more than a year. In the summer of 1993, Mayor Jackson revived it. TPI then began preparing a redevelopment study and hired the Community Design Center of Atlanta (CDCA) to analyze the current condition of the Techwood area and to suggest options. On November 17, the TPI board held a meeting to hear the results of the study. The study had a recommendations section, but two days before the meeting, TPI's executive director, Noel Kahlil, instructed the CDCA not to present these recommendations. So there was no discussion of policy options during the meeting.[55]

Two days later, the lead story in *The Atlanta Journal-Constitution* announced that Billy Payne was proposing that the Techwood Park district be redeveloped as a seventy-two-acre gathering place for Olympic celebrations, to be called Centennial Olympic Park. As Payne envisioned it, the park would include a 25,000-seat amphitheater, a hospitality center for Olympic sponsors, pavilions for promoting Southern states, a "European style" circle where the flags of the Olympic participants would fly, and multiple video screens to show action from the Games. The cost of building the facility would be $100 million— $70 million for land acquisition and $30 million for construction. Payne was proposing that the park be privately financed, mainly through corporate contributions. He was also proposing that the project be administered by the Georgia World Congress Authority, the state authority that operated the Georgia World Congress Center, which was located on the southwest side of the proposed park. After the Games, twenty-five acres would remain a state-owned park, and a six-block area adjacent to the Georgia World Congress Center and the CNN Center would be reserved for commercial redevelopment. Disposition of the thirty or so remaining acres had not yet been decided upon.[56]

Before the announcement of the Centennial Olympic Park proposal, Payne had consulted with Robert Goizueta of Coca-Cola and Governor Miller regarding his idea. He had also talked about his plan with Gerald Bartels, president of the Atlanta Chamber of Commerce; Tom Murphy, speaker of the state House of Representatives; and Lieutenant Governor Pierre Howard. There was to be a mayoral runoff election a week later, so once Payne learned that the newspaper was going to break the story, he called the two candidates to inform them about the plan as well.[57] But Payne had not spoken about his park proposal with Mayor Jackson or anyone else at city hall. The announcement in the paper was the first the mayor had heard of Payne's plan.[58] Payne's consultation with Goizueta reveals the extent to which Coca-Cola dominates public policy on issues it considers important. And Payne went to Governor Miller, Tom Murphy, and Pierre Howard because either he or Goizueta wanted the park to be administered by the state. It seems fairly clear that Payne ignored Mayor Jackson and allied himself with state government because he expected opposition to the park from the city. Jackson naturally resented being ignored, but he did not voice his resentment publicly.

ACOG and Coke viewed Techwood Park as an unredeemable slum. But city planners had a different view. They saw the area as a vital part of the downtown economy, and they feared that eliminating the businesses in the area would hurt that economy. They were also afraid that eliminating an area next to the central business district—a site for possible expansion—would constrain the growth and vitality of the downtown area. The city had its own long-range plans for the area; these called for redeveloping it gradually and preserving its character. The city planned to use some of the vacant and underused land in the area for office space and possibly for high-density housing.[59] A study of the area, done by the city in the mid-'80s, called for a series of public subsidies to foster the development of middle- and upper-income housing in the area, and some of these subsidies had already been put in place.[60] The only element of the ACOG park plan that was consistent with the city's plans was the proposed development of middle- and upper-income housing in the area.

The CDCA's analysis of the Techwood Park district had confirmed the wisdom of the city's plans to preserve the essential character of the area. First of all, the district was not a slum. Of the ninety-seven buildings in Techwood Park, only one was dilapidated beyond repair, and only ten were deteriorated. More than seven-eighths of the buildings were in good condition. According to the Urban Design Commission, at least five had historic value.[61] Furthermore, the area did in fact play an important role in the downtown economy. Of the seventy-three businesses in the Techwood area, 40 percent were business-support enterprises, serving businesses and workers in the CBD: small hotels, restaurants, printing firms, machinery-repair services, business-service firms, and parking lots.[62] The area contained more than 2,000 parking spaces on thirty-three parcels of land.[63]

In real-estate terms, the area was a moderately healthy submarket. Vacancies amounted to approximately one-fifth of available space. This was actually better than the vacancy rate for office space in the central business district, which at the time was 25 percent. The Fulton County Tax Commissioner appraised the property in the area at $86,688,000.

The property taxes collected from the area amounted to $1,794,000 annually. Of the 137 parcels in the area, only nine were delinquent in their property-tax payments—a relatively low delinquency rate of 6.6 percent. In other words, investors and property owners were maintaining their financial interests in the area by keeping their tax payments current.[64] Another sign of the vitality of the area was that old loft buildings were being converted to housing and shops. The loft-conversion market in Atlanta began expanding in a significant way in 1992. By 1994, more than 40 properties had been converted, and the city had appointed a task force to reassess its zoning and tax-abatement regulations to encourage more conversions.[65]

All the city's careful, pragmatic, long-range plans for the area were suddenly subverted by Payne's park proposal. But the city did not oppose the park plan. The park was a glamorous concept, it had powerful backing, and Mayor Jackson did not want to appear obstructionistic. All that the public planners could hope to do was to reconcile some of the city's interests with the park idea. The city's main concern was ACOG's plan for future expansion of office space in the area. ACOG was proposing that after the Olympics there be a six-block commercial district on the west side of the park, adjacent to the CNN Center. Public planners felt that this would not generate new development,[66] and wanted the commercial development to be on the east side of the park, adjacent to the CBD.

The city based its view of development possibilities on the history of the area over the previous two decades. The CNN Center had been built in the early 1970s as the Omni, a hotel, office, entertainment, and sports facility adjacent to the World Congress Center. Built by the developer Thomas Cousins, it was expected to attract commercial development along Marietta Street west of the CBD. But while the Omni was being developed, John Portman was building the Peachtree Center office, hotel, and shopping-mall complex on Peachtree Street eight blocks north of Five Points, the historical center of downtown. It soon became clear that Portman had won, as development moved north up Peachtree Street from Five Points to the Peachtree Center and beyond. The only new building on Marietta Street west of the CBD was an ill-fated twenty-five–story tower three blocks east of the Omni: the 101 Marietta Building.

It was sold for $1 in the late '70s real-estate recession. As for the Omni itself, it bounced in and out of bankruptcy and was eventually purchased at a fire-sale price by Ted Turner for his CNN operation. The city's planners feared that these patterns would continue, and that the ACOG plan for commercial development on the west side of the park would lead only to modest projects—or perhaps no projects at all. They also felt that putting a park adjacent to the CBD would eliminate the most likely area for successful new commercial expansion.[67]

After Mayor Jackson had revived Techwood Park Inc. in the summer of 1993, TPI had hired the architecture firm of Rothman and Associates to devise a redevelopment plan for Techwood Park, using the CDCA's analysis of the area. Rothman had just begun working on this plan when ACOG announced its Olympic park proposal. Even though ACOG now had its own redevelopment plan, it agreed to participate in the preparation of the Rothman plan. ACOG wanted to prevent an independent plan from being developed by the city, and it wanted to use this planning process to negotiate at arm's length with representatives of city government.

The Rothman framework plan appeared in January 1994. Instead of considering different redevelopment options for the Techwood district, it accepted the Olympic park as inevitable. However, the plan corresponded with the city's plans for the area in two important ways. First, it recommended that the park be located on the west side of the district and that the east side, contiguous with the CBD, be reserved for future redevelopment. Second, the plan recommended retaining much of the district. It called for preserving valuable and adaptable historic structures, businesses that would encourage future residential development, and as much of the existing infrastructure as possible.[68]

Recommending that the Techwood area be partly preserved made good sense from a professional-planning perspective. One of the lessons that had been learned by cities throughout the country during the urban-renewal era was that retaining part of an existing area provides a physical and commercial base that fosters new development much sooner than completely cleared land does. Another lesson was that preserving part of an area encourages new development that conforms to the existing architectural character, avoiding the sterility, uniformity, and walled isolation that often characterizes residential development in a completely cleared area.

ACOG, however, paid no attention to the Rothman recommendations that did not agree with its own plan. ACOG wanted a plan that was nonbinding, and both city government and TPI went along with ACOG's wishes. The recommendations in the Rothman plan were offered merely as guidelines for redeveloping the area. Once again, the city let ACOG have its way, and the several months of planning that TPI had devoted to the redevelopment of Techwood ended up being wasted effort.

Governor Miller publicly endorsed the Olympic park proposal in January 1994 and announced that he wanted the Georgia World Congress Center Authority to oversee the development and operation of the park.[69] The state Legislature then passed enabling legislation that gave the organization a mandate to purchase land in the Techwood Park area and permitted it to accept private gifts to fund the park project. Governor Miller signed the legislation into law on March 29.[70]

In May of that year, *The Journal-Constitution* reported that ACOG had scaled down the size of the Olympic park from the originally planned seventy-two acres to only thirty acres. ACOG had discovered that it could not raise the $100 million it needed from private contributors, so it had decided to reduce the amount of financing it would seek to $50 million and to eliminate the northernmost eight square blocks from the original plan.[71] (In July, the newspaper reported that Coca-Cola had purchased two of those eight blocks and would be building its own theme park for the Olympics.[72]) During the summer and fall of 1994, ACOG worked on finding the $50 million it would need for the smaller park. The Coca-Cola-related Woodruff Foundation pledged nearly half of the $50 million, other local foundations promised to contribute enough to reach the halfway mark, and the Chamber of Commerce committed itself to raising $10 million from Atlanta businesses. The remaining $15 million was supposed to come from the sale of 750,000 commemorative Olympic bricks, with the purchaser's names on them, that would be used to build walkways in the park.[73]

In the fall of 1995, Central Atlanta Progress began working on a detailed, comprehensive plan for the redevelopment of the Olympic park area after the Games. CAP made the plan public on March 27, 1996, three months before the Olympics. The plan called for 500 to 700 new middle- and upper-income housing units north of the park. A group of foreign investors had been planning to build a hotel on a site southwest of the park near the Georgia World Congress Center, but these plans had fallen through, so CAP proposed an expansion of the Georgia World Congress Center in this area and the relocation of Marietta Street in front of the existing center to accommodate the expansion. The plan further proposed a business park northwest of the Olympic park area, which would capture federally funded Empowerment Zone, state, and local tax subsidies; an entertainment and restaurant district on the east side of the Olympic park; and a new arena for the city's professional basketball team south of the Olympic park, adjacent to the World Congress Center. CAP also announced that it was creating a subsidiary called Centennial Olympic Park Area Inc. (COPA) to oversee the redevelopment.[74]

As a potential catalyst for residential development, the park has dubious features. Land in the Olympic park area is expensive—currently just under $2 million per acre. There are several reasons for this: the park itself, the ease with which Atlanta's zoning is changed, the high densities for office and commercial development permitted under the city's current zoning ordinance and map, and the high price that Coca-Cola paid to acquire the land between its headquarters and the park. Another major reason for the high cost of park-area land is the likelihood that future development in the area will be subsidized. Ironically, because of the high prices and the risk that remains attached to investment in the isolated area, anyone considering residential development adjacent to the park is forced to seek subsidies. The only kind of unsubsidized development economically feasible in the area is high-density office space. But the CBD office market will support only a very modest expansion, and the location of the park prevents office development contiguous to the central area. What is completely unfeasible for developers is the type of lower-density residential development sought by the city's government and business leaders.

There are two ways that residential development can come about in the Olympic park area: The city can either subsidize this development, or it can refuse to provide subsidies for five to ten years and let prices fall to a level that reflects market realities. Because of the political strength of CAP, COPA, and the business leaders who want residential development; because elected officials also want downtown housing; and because Atlanta has a long history of subsidizing privately initiated development projects, the city has begun providing subsidies. Though this may bring about the desired development, it means that a part of the downtown area that used to generate about $1.8 million annually in property-tax revenues will end up costing the city considerable money.

Another problem with residential development in the park area is that it may not have the kind of effect the city is hoping for. The residential development that ACOG proposed as part of its Olympic park plan was supposed to help the city's ongoing effort to bring pedestrian traffic back to the downtown area at night. But whether residential development near the park will do this depends upon the planning and design of the housing. Urban residences connected to streets and sidewalks will encourage pedestrian traffic; this is the kind of integrated residential development that would have occurred had the Rothman plan been followed and had some of the Techwood Park district been preserved. But residential development adjacent to the park will probably take the form of gated communities, such as those built in the Bedford-Pine urban-renewal area east of the CBD. These autonomous communities contribute very little to nighttime pedestrian traffic.

9

Conclusion

ver the past two decades, Atlanta politics has undergone a significant change. No longer is the city's biracial coalition the political force it was in the '60s and '70s. One major reason for this has been a decline in the power and influence of the white downtown business elite. The growth of the north metro area has diminished the importance of downtown as a business center and has created new centers of power in both metro-area and state politics. Just as important, Atlanta's economy has become increasingly national and international in scope, and it is no longer dominated by local business interests. In the present Atlanta economy there are fewer and fewer purely local businesses. Many formerly powerful local businesses now report to headquarters outside Atlanta, and only a handful of local firms are large enough and interested enough to have significant influence on local governance.

But the change is a matter of degree and not a fundamental realignment. A combination of factors make the business-led regime the most potent political force on matters it considers important: History and tradition manifested in established institutions and broadly accepted terms of political engagement, businesses' central role in campaign finance, diminished but still formidable cohesiveness among the business elite, state governments' responsiveness to business initiatives and willingness to act on local issues, interlocking capacities for reciprocal rewards between business and elected officials, active coalition participation by the press, the superior capacity of business to mobilize resources on particular issues, and the corresponding capacity to withhold support for issues not deemed suitable for political consideration.

During the Olympics planning period, downtown business interests asserted their influence in the city's affairs. Coca-Cola and Ted Turner's Atlanta Braves were involved early on in the planning and were major beneficiaries of the Games, and the Olympics brought significant downtown redevelopment. But when the grand event was over, and political attention reverted to the less ephemeral and more basic issues of governance, power was once again dispersed throughout a large, fragmented metropolitan area within an increasingly national and international economy.

Another major reason for the diminished power of the governing coalition is the diminished power of Atlanta city government—primarily a result of the increasingly limited capacity of city government to raise money for expensive undertakings. The deepening poverty of so much of the city's African American population, the growing cost of delivering basic services, overdue bills for maintaining infrastructure, and the debt the city has already incurred for other major projects—all have contributed to the city's fiscal burden and limited its capacity to undertake new projects. Fewer resources have led to a lessened role for city government in economic development. This became especially evident during the period leading up to the Olympics. Black elected officials failed to protect their constituents' interests in planning for the Olympic stadium, and Olympic planners ignored city government entirely in formulating plans for Centennial Olympic Park, instead allying with state government to get the park built.

The metro area has grown so large and diverse, and there are so many conflicting forces at work, that it is unlikely that any public entity or any single interest group could dominate its governance. Fifty years ago the Atlanta Regional Commission, one of the first regional planning bodies in the country, was established. But over the years its attempts to influence regional government have been limited, and its role has remained almost exclusively advisory. The many local governments in the metro area make autonomous decisions regarding transportation systems, land use, and office, commercial, and economic development. Furthermore, the suburban jurisdictions differ substantially from the city proper in their demographics and political interests. Whereas the city is increasingly black, increasingly divided into rich and poor, and predominantly Democratic, the suburbs are overwhelmingly white, frequently middle- and upper-middle-class, and predominantly Republican.

Against this background, the single entity with the most far-reaching power and influence has been the state Department of Transportation. Rapid and largely unplanned growth in the metro region has led to growing traffic congestion throughout the area. The DOT has responded by building new highways and improving and widening existing ones. Its constant expansions of the region's highway system disperse new development and, in conjunction with race and class, largely determine where that development will occur. In a fast-growing metro area where the overwhelming majority of people commute by automobile, the state DOT has influenced regional growth patterns more than any other government organization or any informal group of private interests.

But the DOT's power in transportation and land use may be moderated by an agency created in 1999 by Governor Roy Barnes (who comes from Cobb County) and the state Legislature: the Georgia Regional Transportation Authority. The GRTA has the power to extend mass-transit systems into formerly unserved counties, and it shares responsibility for transportation planning with the DOT. With federal air-quality standards making the state transportation department's nearly exclusive emphasis on highways unfeasible, the GRTA should bring a more thoughtful and publicly responsive direction to transportation policy. But recomposing the region's transportation systems will require substantial investments and considerable time. The DOT's dispersal of the population and the creation of the GRTA as a counterbalance underscore the point that multiple governments and institutions, each with its own political constituency, are now engaged in regional governance.

Atlanta's economy and its politics have changed considerably over the past decade or so, but one thing has not changed: Despite the reduced range of their powers, business interests continue to dominate city government. When Maynard Jackson became Atlanta's first African American mayor in the early '70s, it appeared that black leaders had gained ascendancy over white business interests, and that a new alliance between a unified black electorate and white gentrifiers would govern the city. But this governing alliance was short-lived. The biracial coalition of black political leaders and white business interests was soon reestablished. White business interests regained their dominant position in this reestablished partnership, and they have maintained that dominant position since then.

Clarence Stone wrote that the primary reasons for the continued power of the city's white business elite are its cohesiveness and its capacity to marshal the resources for major projects. Since black elected officials want the political and economic benefits that come from redevelopment, and since they want the perquisites ranging from campaign finance to access to contracts that come from collaboration in the regime, they have either acquiesced in or endorsed the goals of the private sector. Their attitude appears to be that private business interests are, at bottom, the same as the public interest. To a large extent, therefore, capital governs the city and government itself is increasingly irrelevant.

In the '70s, because of pressure from real-estate interests, the city failed to pass land-use regulations that would have concentrated high-density commercial development around MARTA rail lines and stations. Such development would have justified the cost of the rail system, would have helped avert Atlanta's current transportation and air-quality crises, and was the rationale presented to voters for building the system. During the commercial real-estate boom of the '80s, the city once again yielded to pressure from developers and failed to pass land-use regulations that would have restrained new development in the Midtown area and preserved some of the original character of the neighborhood. In the same decade, MARTA responded to demands by Buckhead business interests by committing itself to building an extension of the north rail line from Buckhead to beyond the Perimeter Highway, again without corollary land-use regulations. In doing so, MARTA broke a promise it had made to African American voters: that it would build a rail line to the Perry Homes public-housing community. But MARTA encountered very little resistance from black elected officials.

The subordination of local government was once again evident during the Olympics planning period. The extra-governmental agreement on the new stadium, reached between ACOG and the Atlanta Braves, damaged the poor black neighborhoods around the stadium and contained large potential public liabilities for stadium repair and renovation, yet city and county governments attempted to alter the agreement in only minor ways. Business' long-standing desire to replace Techwood Homes with middle- and upper-income residents was realized without objections from the city, and the city was actually excluded from the initial planning for Centennial Olympic Park.

Even though African American elected officials have generally been compliant junior partners in the governing coalition, they have sometimes been just as eager as downtown business leaders to pursue downtown redevelopment. This was certainly the case when it came to reviving Underground Atlanta. Central Atlanta Progress was the first to promote the idea of a downtown festival marketplace, but the Andrew Young administration enthusiastically embraced the idea and was aggressive and persistent in its efforts to subvert requirements for public referendums to arrange the complicated bond financing. The city financed most of the complex with public money.

Black-run city government has also played an active role in encouraging construction of middle- and upper-income housing in the downtown area. CAP has promoted upscale residential development downtown for more than fifty years, but the Young administration and subsequent administrations have energetically pursued the same goal. Once again, the city encouraged reluctant private investment with substantial subsidies. Black-run city government has also actively promoted the redevelopment of Auburn Avenue, the dilapidated, segregation-era, African American commercial district adjacent to the CBD.

The subsidies for Underground Atlanta, downtown residential development, and the Auburn Avenue revitalization are just three examples of how Atlanta city government has used the public purse to promote private economic development. Furthermore, like other cities, Atlanta has heavily subsidized its professional sports teams. Public money was used to build the first Atlanta Braves stadium, the new football stadium for the Atlanta Falcons, and the new basketball arena for the Atlanta Hawks, and even though the Olympics paid for much of the new baseball stadium, substantial costs were off-loaded to the surrounding poor black neighborhoods, and it's highly likely that taxpayers will end up footing significant bills for future repairs and renovations. All these subsidies are a clear sign of the kind of power that the private sector has wielded over the public sector. Because business interests have been the dominant partner in the governing coalition, they have been able to demand that public money be used to help them achieve their aims.

Another consequence of business' influence on elected officials is the insider government that Atlanta has had since the end of World War II. Corporate penchants for secret negotiations and agreements characterize the style as well as the substance of governance. Almost all the important policy decisions that have guided the city over the past several decades have been made not by government itself, but by small groups of men—sometimes just two men—in private meetings. The basic theme of Floyd Hunter's book on Atlanta politics in the '40s and early '50s and Clarence Stone's book on the city's politics from the '50s through the '80s is that the city has been governed behind the scenes by an extra-governmental ruling elite. From the late '40s through the late '80s, the voting public had very little real awareness of how important decisions were being made. Insider government continued during the period leading up to the Olympics, when early planning was carried on by an inner circle that included members of the Olympics planning committee, Coca-Cola, Ted Turner, Georgia Tech, and Governor Miller.

Not only has the governing process been hidden from the public, but much of it remains inaccessible to researchers and historians. Not only have Atlantans been largely unaware of how decisions were being made at the time, but future generations may never know the full story either. Researchers and historians find it difficult to discover or document the identities of the people who made important policy decisions, what their motives were, and how they reached their decisions. Because of the opacity of the governing process, a completely accurate history of Atlanta politics over the past several decades may never be written.

Even though Atlanta's governing elite has devoted considerable effort and money to downtown redevelopment, most of this work has done very little to revitalize the downtown economy. It is true that the rapid growth of Atlanta's suburbs has made a relatively diminished downtown economy inevitable, but it is also true that city leaders have not been as effective as they could have been in sustaining the economic vigor of the central area. Part of the reason for this is that they have not engaged in publicly accessible, rationally grounded, long-range planning. Pursuit of narrow, immediate interests without the leavening influence of the broader public interest has limited the success of many development projects. None of the three stadiums, two sports arenas, or the civic center the city has built had ever appeared in a city plan before it was constructed. Each of these facilities is so far removed from the CBD that patrons do not combine trips to an event with other activities in the CBD, thus there are no agglomeration economies. The site of the convention center was decided not by a public planning process but by the ability of the business faction to persuade the state Legislature to fund a remote site. The convention center contributes almost nothing to the vitality of the CBD. Nor were there plans for the Olympic park before it was built. In fact, the park superseded plans that city government already had for the area. Each of these multimillion-dollar projects was an almost spontaneous congelation of political energy that ignored many of the likely effects.

What planning the governing elite has engaged in has been ad hoc and superficial. City leaders have generally been reluctant to give careful consideration to the broader effects of their projects, to find less intrusive ways of reaching their goals, or to do genuine cost-benefit analyses. Some of the push to implement without an accessible planning process was intentional in order to mask unspoken aims, as in the urban-renewal projects that removed poor blacks from the neighborhoods around the CBD, but the lack of careful, realistic planning has had unintended adverse consequences as well. Urban renewal and MARTA depopulated downtown streets at night and eventually led to calls for heavily subsidized residential redevelopment in the central area. Locating the World Congress Center on the dormant west periphery of the central business district guaranteed that conventioneers would take cabs between the convention center and their hotels, doing nothing to repopulate the CBD's deserted nighttime streets. (It also required the construction of new streets connecting the hotels with the World Congress Center.) Underground Atlanta was then built, partly to increase downtown pedestrian traffic at night, but the complex's location and its inwardly focused design did very little to accomplish this. So not only has limited planning had unintended negative consequences, but these consequences have required further redevelopment. And further redevelopment has meant additional costs for taxpayers and a heavier debt burden for city government.

Preparing city plans that then have to be adjusted to accommodate the wishes of the current business elite results in a two-tier approach to planning. Residents of poor neighborhoods are told, as they were during the competition for Olympic tie-in money, that their existing plans are insufficient and that they therefore have to prepare new, more thorough, more comprehensive plans. But projects of the business elite are not only exempt from requirements for planning and analytical rigor, they invert the process. Projects contradict existing city plans and require that the plans be reconstituted to adapt to the projects.

This two-tier process, in which powerful interests demand and receive accommodating plan adjustments to narrowly conceived projects while weaker groups spend their far smaller resources on plans that never reach the implementation phase, mocks the idea of planning and alienates residents who are actively trying to redevelop their neighborhoods. Reasoned consideration of proposed major changes might find less intrusive or damaging ways of reaching project goals. The reality of government behind the scenes, coupled with the fact that reasoned assessments might conclude that benefits do not outweigh costs and that projects should not proceed, explains why only superficial analyses, if any, are undertaken.

One of the primary reasons that the governing elite has refused to do practical, long-range planning is that it has been more interested in enhancing Atlanta's image than in genuine economic development. A large part of Ivan Allen Jr.'s motive in building a baseball stadium and persuading the Milwaukee Braves to move to Atlanta was that he wanted to add to Atlanta's prestige. Allen and other city leaders promoted the idea of an extensive rapid-rail system largely because they wanted Atlanta to have a state-of-the-art transportation system. Central Atlanta Progress and the Andrew Young administration pursued the Underground Atlanta project partly because they wanted Atlanta to have the same kind of downtown festival marketplace that other major cities were simultaneously building. All these efforts to add to the city's prestige reached their peak in the city's successful bid for the 1996 Summer Olympics. One of the central themes of Charles Rutheiser's book *Imagineering Atlanta* is that the city has always been highly image-conscious and has always advertised itself as a bustling, thriving, pro-business city. Rutheiser documents how the city's efforts at self-promotion started as far back as the Reconstruction era, and he points out that beginning in the 1970s Atlanta began promoting itself as a cosmopolitan, world-class city.

Part of the reason for all this aggressive image-building is that Atlanta has always been highly self-conscious. Being in the South translates into a sort of inferiority complex, and city leaders have tried to demonstrate to the rest of the country that despite its location, Atlanta is a progressive, enlightened city and therefore an attractive place in which to invest and live. But another reason for the self-promotion concerns the way in which business interests have dominated the city's politics. Private enterprise is highly image-conscious, and two fundamental business strategies are marketing and public relations. These strategies and the attitudes behind them have carried over into the city's business-dominated government. A big reason for that is that Atlanta's major corporate citizen is Coca-Cola. This immensely successful company has been at the center of Atlanta politics for more than seventy years. Much of Coke's worldwide success has come from marketing, and the core of the company is a public-relations operation. It is hardly surprising that city leaders have been heavily influenced by Coke's highly image-conscious corporate culture.

One excellent reason for believing that enhancing Atlanta's image was frequently more important than economic development to city leaders is that the economic reasons offered to the public for certain projects were ill-conceived and unrealistic. Mayor Allen's rationale for building the original stadium where he did was to stimulate the downtown economy by bringing people to the downtown area after working hours. But Allen's plan ignored certain physical realities. Not only was there a three-interstate expressway intersection between the stadium and the downtown area, but state, county, and government office buildings also lay between the stadium and the commercial part of the central business district. The downtown business district was simply not convenient to the stadium: People came to the games and left without lingering in the area. Downtown Atlanta still remained largely unpopulated at night.

City leaders displayed the same lack of realism in their determination to build an extensive rapid-rail system. The city went ahead and built the hugely expensive rail system even though a study by an engineering firm clearly demonstrated that a rail system was not the most efficient transportation solution for a city with Atlanta's low-density, sprawling development. Then, partly at the behest of central-area businesses and over the opposition of city government, the state DOT expanded highway capacity in the rail corridors, undermining the rail system and further dispersing development. So the city now has a rail system that is economically inefficient and that has done very little to solve its transportation problems. The Andrew Young administration and CAP also ignored practical considerations in pursuing the Underground Atlanta project. They financed the construction of the shopping complex even though an earlier version had failed and market research showed that a new version was likely to fail as well.

The city also displayed a lack of practical wisdom during the period leading up to the Olympics. City leaders persuaded a majority of voters to approve a bond referendum in 1994 that included $106.7 million for repairing and replacing deteriorating sewers, bridges, and viaducts, and an additional $32.2 million for widening sidewalks and improving streetscapes in the CBD and in areas adjacent to Olympic venues. The total bill for upgrading the city's infrastructure has been estimated at well over $2 billion. So while the city spent millions on cosmetic enhancements to the downtown area, it spent only a fraction of what was needed to take care of its serious infrastructure needs.

Olympic planners were just as guilty as the city of ignoring practical considerations. When ACOG tore down the Techwood Park business district to make way for Centennial Olympic Park, it eliminated an important economic adjunct to the central business district. Furthermore, ACOG disregarded the potential of the district for residential redevelopment. A study done by a consultant hired by the city before ACOG announced its Olympic park idea had shown that loft conversions taking place in an adjacent area were moving into the Techwood Park area. ACOG touted the Olympic park as a means of stimulating downtown residential development, but it tore down a business district where residential redevelopment was on the verge of taking place spontaneously and unassisted. Since then, the city has responded to private pressure and provided subsidies to encourage private developers to build new housing in the Olympic park area.

An obsession with image, however, does not fully explain why a business-led coalition would have repeatedly pursued redevelopment projects that were ineffective in terms of economic development. A desire to enhance Atlanta's prestige explains why the city's governing elite has found glamorous, high-profile projects so appealing, but it does not explain why the governing elite has consistently ignored practical realities. Oddly, the fundamental reason for this impracticality is that narrowly defined private interests have viewed public investment differently from private investment. The Atlanta business powers have been willing to pursue projects that were poorly conceived from an economic standpoint because these projects either have been paid for directly with taxpayer money or have been indirectly subsidized. City leaders have not felt that a satisfactory return on public investment should guide their actions, as would be the case with private investment. In undertaking expensive redevelopment projects, they have not felt fiscally constrained, and as a consequence have been irresponsible guardians of the public purse.

Another kind of limited vision that has characterized the Atlanta regime is the narrowness of its class structure. Since most members of the governing coalition have been wealthy white businessmen and middle-class black political leaders, the city's white middle class and its low-income blacks have not had a voice in the inner circles of power. As a result, the city's ruling elite has persistently displayed a class bias, generally being either indifferent to or hostile to the interests of these groups.

The coalition displayed its attitude toward the white middle class during the '80s, when white middle-class neighborhoods opposed construction of what is now the Freedom Parkway to the Carter Library on the city's near east side and the extension of the Georgia 400 expressway. In each case the coalition sided with the pro-highway faction. During the same period, the coalition displayed its indifference to the interests of middle-class white residents in the Midtown area. When a battle arose between business interests, which wanted unrestricted commercial development in the area, and residents, who wanted to preserve the small-scale, commercial, and pedestrian character of the neighborhood, the coalition negotiated for a time but eventually agreed to very limited restrictions on development.

The clearest evidence of the attitude of the coalition toward poor African Americans is that a major part of the redevelopment strategy pursued by city leaders has been to remove poor blacks from the city's central area. The downtown portion of the city's highway system was configured to eliminate portions of poor black neighborhoods on the east side of downtown, creating a buffer between the central business district and the remnants of the neighborhoods. When the urban-renewal program tore down even more of these neighborhoods, Mayor Allen chose to build a stadium on the cleared land instead of replacing the housing. The Allen administration also used urban renewal to tear down another poor African American neighborhood, then failed to replace the housing it had demolished. Subsequent administrations neglected to build any housing in the area; finally, some twenty years after the land had been cleared, mostly middle- and upper-income housing was built. As a result of all this redevelopment, poor blacks were pushed out of the downtown area and the city's supply of low-income housing was substantially reduced.

During the '80s, Central Atlanta Progress, the Young administration, and other city leaders decided to focus the city's efforts to revitalize the downtown area on heavily subsidized middle- and upper-income housing. Very little attention was paid to increasing the city's stock of low-income housing. Although Bill Campbell's administration has restored some of the low-income housing subsidies that the Young administration diverted to middle- and upper-income housing, the Campbell administration has also continued the Young/CAP policy of replacing lower-income housing with middle- and upper-income housing near the core. As part of this strategy, the Atlanta Housing Authority demolished the Techwood/Clark Howell public-housing development on the northern fringe of the central area and replaced it with mixed-income housing.

A clear and highly symbolic example of the class bias of city leaders was MARTA's decision in 1986 to build a second branch of the north rail line instead of building a line to the Perry Homes public-housing development, breaking a promise they had made to African American voters. They had relied on votes from the poor black community to get the rail system approved in 1970, and fifteen years later turned their backs on them.

Disregard for poor African Americans was also evident during the Olympics planning period. While designs were being developed for a new stadium, neither ACOG nor black elected officials paid sufficient attention to demands by low-income neighborhoods adjacent to the proposed site that publicly accessible planning precede a decision on where to locate the stadium. The same thing happened to the subsequent requests that measures be taken to limit the effects of the facility on the neighborhoods. It's true that funding was organized to revitalize the Summerhill neighborhood, but this funding was promised to gain Summerhill's support for the stadium and to prevent unified opposition from stadium-area neighborhoods. Furthermore, this funding has been used primarily to build a smaller, gentrified community; the ongoing redevelopment of Summerhill is driving out low-income residents.

One of the most egregious dimensions of the governing coalition's class bias is its consistent willingness to off-load costly elements of development projects onto poor blacks. The urban-renewal and expressway programs destroyed over 10,000 more homes than they replaced. MARTA and Georgia Dome construction paid premium prices to landlords who evicted their poor tenants; their equitable relocation would have cost substantially more. Insufficient parking, a refusal to build protective buffers, and inadequate transportation plans and traffic management at Atlanta–Fulton County Stadium, the Olympic stadium, and the Georgia Dome have weighed heavily on the poor black residents of surrounding neighborhoods in the form of unregulated parking lots, excessive and unregulated noise, retarded redevelopment, and restrictions on residents' mobility during events. The transformation of Techwood and Clark Howell Homes into a mixed-income project brought relocation expenses to fewer than half the residents who were forced to move, and permitted fewer than one in fourteen to return.

The class bias of the black members of the governing coalition since the 1970s has not been driven by the same motives as it was in the '50s and '60s. During the urban-renewal era, black political leaders put up short-lived resistance to the removal of poor blacks from the downtown area. But their failure to defend the interests of poor blacks more aggressively was not simply a matter of bias; it was also a matter of priorities. Both before and during the civil-rights movement, black political leaders had to contend with segregation, a problem that affected all members of the black community. As an electoral minority, they had limited political leverage within the coalition, and they chose to use what leverage they had to try to end systemic segregation. In the '70s, after the brief interlude during which Mayor Jackson broke away from the coalition, black political leaders began to display the same kind of class bias that was characteristic of their white counterparts. Since the reestablishment of the coalition in Jackson's second term, the city's African American elite has grown increasingly similar to the city's white elite. Because they gain political and economic benefits from their partnership with the white elite, they have come to share many of the same goals and values. As a consequence, they have paid very little attention to the problems of the city's poor black population. During the '50s and '60s, faced with hard choices, black political leaders chose to ignore the black underclass on the basis of political priorities, but since then many of them have ignored the black underclass out of their own perceptions of their self-interest.

Self-interest, however, does not entirely account for the behavior of the city's black elected officials over the past two decades. Part of the reason that the Andrew Young administration pursued Underground Atlanta so vigorously, and part of the explanation for how aggressively his and subsequent administrations have encouraged downtown residential development, is that African American leaders see downtown revitalization as a way of bringing white and black Atlantans together. The original version of Underground Atlanta was one of the few public places in the city where blacks and whites mixed socially at night, and one of the motives of the Young administration in reviving the shopping complex was to re-create this type of racial diversity. The efforts the city is making at downtown residential development are explicit attempts to encourage both whites and blacks to live downtown. Atlanta remains a highly segregated city when it comes to residential patterns, and black elected officials view downtown housing as a means of achieving some degree of residential integration. The new Underground Atlanta has failed, but there remains hope that significant numbers of blacks and whites will choose to live in new downtown housing and repopulate the city's center.

Still, pursuit of a less racially divided central city does not fully explain black middle-class elected officials' willingness to purchase diversity at the cost of damage to lower-class blacks. African Americans' subordinate position within the coalition is part of a more complete explanation, but, unfortunately, so is the unavoidable conclusion that the personal and professional perquisites of regime membership outweigh racial solidarity for many black elected officials. What is not clear is whether interclass hostility is partly to blame for the schism. Whether such hostility plays a role, whether the ambitions of middle- and upper-class African Americans produce a rejectionist detachment, whether the myriad disabilities plaguing the lower classes include delusional isolationism—all these questions remain unanswered.

The metropolitan area's growth and the internationalization of the economy have reduced the power that the city's business sector once exercised over regional affairs. At the same time, limited suburban regulation of the area's growth and the lack of attention paid to the fundamental issues of governance by the coalition have produced crises in transportation, air quality, water supply, and sewage treatment. The region's workers now commute greater distances than in any other metropolitan area in the country. These commutes, the congestion they entail, and the weakly regulated public-utility emissions produce air that no longer meets federal air-quality standards for extended periods.

Pollution levels are so high that the federal agencies are in the process of cutting off funding for transportation facilities. This problem could have been greatly reduced by Atlanta's rapid-rail and mass-transit system had the city passed reinforcing land-use regulations. The problem would also be less severe had suburban jurisdictions made more robust efforts to regulate development. But they have only recently started to do this. Given the extent of dispersal and sprawl, solutions to traffic congestion and the restoration of air quality will require decades. The state government, now led by a governor from Atlanta's northern suburbs, is taking steps to restructure metropolitan transportation planning. Combined with federal restrictions and popular recognition that a problem exists, this translates into a political climate supportive of beginning the long process of reshaping the region in more healthful and sustainable ways. Another hopeful sign is that MARTA currently has plans for high-density development near existing rail stations. But whatever measures are taken to alleviate congestion, Atlanta has grown too fast, and existing development in the suburbs is too widely dispersed and too automobile-dependent, for there to be any immediately effective solution to Atlanta's traffic problems.

Water and sewer systems suffer from decades of neglect and the absence of capital-improvement programs to repair and replace aging infrastructure. Estimates to restore both systems to safe levels of performance run to $2 billion. The city has recently built new water-treatment facilities and privatized the water system, but these efforts are insufficient, and the city has done very little to upgrade its sewer system. The failure of city leaders to maintain the city's infrastructure is another striking example of their impracticality. While spending millions of dollars of public money on glamorous, high-profile redevelopment projects, they have neglected essential government responsibilities. But, as with air quality, sprawl, and traffic, more widespread public recognition that there are serious problems holds promise that corrective actions may be devised and the lengthy process of restoration begun.

One of the most serious problems Atlanta faces is black poverty. Atlanta's aggressively expanding economy is increasing, not closing, gaps in income. Partly because a large portion of the city's African

American population is living in poverty, the city has a disturbingly high crime rate. The city also has an inferior public-school system, which is both a consequence and a cause of pervasive black poverty. Misdirected economic development and substandard schools are primary reasons that so much of the city's black population is under-trained and underemployed, and black unemployment, in turn, contributes to the high crime rate. Until very recently, city leaders have done little to improve the city's school system. They have put very little effort and very little money into social-welfare and job-training programs. They have made only minimal efforts to revitalize low-income African American neighborhoods. And they have actually made living conditions worse for African Americans by destroying and failing to replace low-income housing in the downtown area. Economic-development programs have focused primarily on image-enhancing projects, not on the much more serious problems of lower-class underemployment and unemployment. City government run by blacks has been as indifferent to the fundamental interests of poor blacks as was city government run by whites. Because black elected officials rarely advocate the interests of poor blacks, and because middle-class blacks have prospered in Atlanta's expanding economy, poor blacks are increasingly left out, increasingly isolated, and increasingly alienated.

Notes

Chapter One

1. Clarence N. Stone, *Regime Politics: Governing Atlanta, 1946–1988* (Lawrence: University Press of Kansas, 1989), pp. 192–94.

Chapter Two

1. U.S. Bureau of the Census, *1990 Census of Population and Housing* (Washington, DC).

2. Georgia Department of Labor, "Georgia Employment and Wages Averages 1998" and "Georgia Employment and Wages Averages 1980" (Atlanta, 1999 and 1981, respectively).

3. Truman A. Hartshorn and Keith Ihlanfeldt, *The Dynamics of Change: An Analysis of Growth in Metropolitan Atlanta Over the Past Two Decades* (report, Atlanta: Research Atlanta, Inc., 1993), p. 57.

4. Georgia Department of Labor, "Georgia Employment and Wages Averages 1998" and "Georgia Employment and Wages Averages 1980."

5. Guy L. Dorey, *Dorey's Atlanta Office Guide: 1st Quarter, 1999* (report, Atlanta: Dorey Publishing and Information Services, 1999).

6. Class A buildings are defined as competing for premier office users, as being the most prestigious buildings, as having above average rental rates, high quality finishes, and exceptional accessibility. Class B buildings are defined as competing for a wide range of users, having average rents and good to average finishes, and being noncompetitive with Class A buildings.

7. Norman J. Glickman, Michael Lake, and Elvin Wyly, "Distribution of Retail Sales" in *The State of the Nation's Cities: Data Base and Machine Readable File Documentation*, version 1.5A (New Brunswick, NJ: Center for Urban Policy Research, Rutgers University, Aug. 1996); available at www.policy.rutgers.edu/cupr/sonc.htm.

8. Atlanta Regional Commission, *Employment 1998* (report, Nov. 1998), A4, A19, A20, A25–31, A36.

9. H. M. Couly, "Homefinder: Upscale Atlanta," *The Atlanta Journal-Constitution*, Mar. 2, 1997.

10. Sam Massell, ed., *Buckhead Guide Book* (Atlanta: Publication Concepts, Inc., 1998,) pp. 78–81.

11. In 1997, 37 percent of 231 metro-Atlanta business and political leaders considered Buckhead the geographic center of Atlanta's business life. Forty percent named the CBD. The same group predicted that the Galleria/Perimeter would be the "center" in 2010 (David Goldberg, "Northward Ho!" *The Atlanta Journal-Constitution*, Mar. 9, 1997).

12. Claude Werner, national director of Real Estate Research, Deloitte & Touche Realty Consulting Group, Memorandum to author, Atlanta, Sept. 8, 1999.

13. John F. Kain, "Housing Segregation, Negro Unemployment, and Metropolitan Decentralization," *Quarterly Journal of Economics* 82 (May 1968): 175–97.

14. Keith R. Ihlanfeldt and David L. Sjoquist, "The Spatial Mismatch Hypothesis: A Review of Recent Studies and Their Implications for Welfare Reform," *Housing Policy Debate* 9 (4): 849–92.

15. Ibid., p. 881.

16. Gretchen E. MacLachlan, "Atlanta's Employment and Job Skills," in Bob Holmes, ed., *The Status of Black Atlanta, 1993* (Atlanta: Southern Center for Studies in Public Policy, Clark Atlanta University, 1993), p. 49.

17. David M. Smith, *Geography, Inequality and Society* (Cambridge: Cambridge University Press, 1987).

18. Smith provides a thorough treatment of the coefficient of variation in the first chapter of *Geography, Inequality and Society*, pp. 19–21.

Chapter Three

1. Harold M. Martin, *William Berry Hartsfield: Mayor of Atlanta* (Athens: University of Georgia Press, 1978), pp. 50, 51.

2. This is a greatly simplified explanation of the dissimilarity index. It is calculated as follows: Smaller distinct areas that make up a larger area are examined for imbalances. The percentage of people from each group in each smaller area is determined. Then the percentage of people from each group that would have to move to achieve the same percentages that prevail in the entire area is calculated. These percentages are summed up for the entire area, and the overall imbalance for the entire area is expressed as a ratio between the overall percentages and the percentages that would have to move if the different groups were completely separate geographically.

In calculating the dissimilarity indexes for Atlanta that appear in Table 9, census tracts have been used as the smaller areas that make up the larger urban area. The indexes calculated for 1990 show that three-quarters of the black population in both the city and the entire metro area would have had to move into white areas to bring about full integration.

3. Political boundaries for 1940 define the largest areas for which geographically consistent data are available for the past fifty years.

4. Douglas S. Massey and Nancy A. Denton, "Trends in the Residential Segregation of Blacks, Hispanics, and Asians: 1970–1980," *American Sociological Review* 52 (6): 802–25.

5. The eleven metro areas that were more segregated in 1980 were Chicago, Los Angeles, New York, Detroit, Gary/Hammond, Kansas City, Milwaukee, Newark, Paterson-Clifton, Philadelphia, and St. Louis (ibid.).

6. Ibid.

7. Behind Cleveland, Chicago, and Philadelphia. Norman J. Glickman, Michael Lake, and Elvin Wyly, "Cities of the United States Dissimilarity Index: Whites to Blacks" in *The State of the Nation's Cities: Data Base and Machine Readable File Documentation*, version 1.5A (New Brunswick, NJ: Center for Urban Policy Research, Rutgers University, Aug. 1996), available at www.policy.rutgers.edu/cupr/sonc.htm.

8. Lawrence Bobo, Howard Schurman, and Charlotte Steeth, "Changing Attitudes Toward Residential Integration" in John M. Goering, ed., *Housing Discrimination and Federal Policy* (Chapel Hill: University of North Carolina Press, 1986), pp. 152–69; Joe T. Darden, "Choosing Neighbors and Neighborhoods: The Role of Race in Housing Preferences" in Gary A. Tobin, ed., *Divided Neighborhoods: Changing Patterns of Racial Segregation* (Newburg Park, CA: Sage Publications, 1987), pp. 22–27. The most recent research on the attitudes of whites and blacks in Atlanta toward residential integration is included in "The Residential Preferences of Blacks and Whites: A Four-Metropolis Study" (paper presented on May 10, 1996, at the annual meeting of the Population Association of America in New Orleans). The research was done by Reynolds Farley, Elaine Fielding, and Marsha Kryson. The research on Atlanta is inconclusive because the respondents' choices were limited. Forty-two percent of black Atlanta respondents preferred a neighborhood with one in seven (14.3 percent) black residents. Unfortunately, the next hypothetical level of integration was 50 percent white and 50 percent black, whereas other studies have concluded that a majority of black households would prefer a neighborhood that was 20 percent to 30 percent black.

9. Drawn from an anonymous, unpaginated photocopy, "History of Blandtown," obtained from the Blandtown Neighborhood Association in January 1991.

10. The racial purpose behind the annexation plan was clearly stated by Mayor Hartsfield in a letter to civic leaders. Cited in Harold H. Martin, *William Berry Hartsfield: Mayor of Atlanta* (Athens: University of Georgia Press, 1978), p. 42.

11. Community Design Center of Atlanta, *A Redevelopment Plan for Blandtown* (report, Apr. 1991), p. 37.

12. Ibid., p. 18.

13. The industrial district that includes Blandtown had no new construction in 1990. It was one of only two industrial submarkets in the entire region that did not grow. The area is a first-generation industrial area in a market well supplied with better-located, second-generation industrial space. There is very little or no demand for industrial expansion, particularly not for the small, hilly residential lots in Blandtown. Consequently, the industrialists' claims of higher sales prices for industrial land were fraudulent.

14. Rachel Matthews, "An Evaluation of Variables Affecting Black Residential Patterning in Atlanta and Their Application to Black Enclaves" (unpublished master's thesis, Graduate Program in City Planning, Georgia Institute of Technology, 1993), pp. 113–21.

15. William McFarland, "Redevelopment of Johnstown" (unpublished paper, Graduate Program in City Planning, Georgia Institute of Technology, Mar. 1989).

16. Gabriella Boston, "Area Sticks to Its Roots: Small DeKalb Community Resists Inroads of Affluence," *The Atlanta Journal-Constitution*, Oct. 15, 1998, Citylife section.

17. Anthony James Catanese, David Arbeit, and James Crouse, *Planning Barriers to Affordable Housing: The Minimum Floor Area Problem* (Atlanta: Center for Planning and Development, undated), pp. 14, 15.

18. Andrew B. Colbow, "Suburban Fears of Multi-Family Housing" (unpublished paper, Graduate Program in City Planning, Georgia Institute of Technology, June 6, 1997), p. 8.

19. Ibid., p. 7; author's interview with Karl Holley, formerly Cobb County senior planner, Jekyll Island, GA, Oct. 24, 1996.

20. Matt Kempner, "For Developers, Moratoriums Part of Business," *The Atlanta Journal-Constitution*, Jan. 12, 1998.

21. Carlos Campos and Sallye Salter, "Fulton Buys out Developer at $600,000 Premium," *The Atlanta Journal-Constitution*, Nov. 8, 1997.

22. Larry Keating and Maxwell Creighton, *Nonprofit Housing Supply* (Atlanta: Community Design Center of Atlanta, May 1989), pp. 91, 92.

23. U.S. Bureau of the Census, *1990 Census of Population and Housing* (Washington, DC).

24. Bill Dedman, "The Color of Money," *The Atlanta Journal-Constitution*, May 1–4, 1988.

25. Bill Dedman, "Banks to Lend $65 Million at Low Interest," *The Atlanta Journal-Constitution*, May 13, 1988.

26. Larry Keating, "Atlanta: Atlanta Mortgage Consortium," in David Listokin and Elvin Wyly, with Larry Keating, Susan Wachter, Kristopher Rengert, and Barbara Listokin, *Successful Mortgage Lending Strategies for the Underserved* (Washington, DC: Office of Policy Development and Research, Department of Housing and Urban Development, 1998), p. 13.

27. Bill Dedman, "Panel Appointed to Probe Banks' Lending Policies," *The Atlanta Journal-Constitution*, May 5, 1988.

28. Bill Dedman, "City Hall Clout Could Sweeten Home Loan Pot," *The Atlanta Journal-Constitution*, May 4, 1988.

29. Ibid.

30. Ibid.

31. Author interview with Dwight Morris, assistant managing editor for special projects, *The Atlanta Journal-Constitution*, Atlanta, Oct. 3, 1989.

32. Keating, "Atlanta: Atlanta Mortgage Consortium," p. 14.

33. Elvin K. Wyly and Steven R. Holloway, "'The Color of Money' Revisited: Racial Lending Patterns in Atlanta's Neighborhoods," *Housing Policy Debate* 10 (3): 566.

34. Ibid.

35. Susan Harte, "Progress Slow on Mortgages for Minorities," *The Atlanta Journal-Constitution*, June 19, 1999.

36. Margery Auston Turner, Raymond J. Struyk, and John Yinger, *Housing Discrimination Study Synthesis* (report, Washington, DC: The Urban Institute, 1991).

37. Author interview with Joseph Shifalo, Executive Director, Metro Fair Housing, Inc., Atlanta, Sept. 25, 1996.

38. Ibid.

39. David M. Smith, *Geography, Inequality and Society* (Cambridge: Cambridge University Press, 1987), pp. 53–68.

40. Christopher Howard, *The Hidden Welfare State* (Princeton, NJ: Princeton University Press, 1997), pp. 48–63, 93–114.

41. The Federal Home Loan Mortgage Corporation and the Federal National Mortgage Association apply a lower standard for owned housing for the proportion of income devoted to housing (28 percent).

42. Nancy A. Denton and Douglas S. Massey, "Residential Segregation of Blacks, Hispanics and Asians by Socioeconomic Status and Generation," *Social Sciences Quarterly* 69 (Dec. 1988): 811.

43. The example is drawn from Douglas S. Massey and Nancy A. Denton, *American Apartheid: Segregation and the Making of the Underclass* (Cambridge, MA: Harvard University Press, 1993), pp. 118–28. Directly comparable calculations for 1990 are not available, but an approximation of the methodology used by Massey and his colleague Mitchell Eggers indicates that reductions in poverty rates (due in part to economic expansion and in part to an archaic official definition of poverty) have moderated black concentrations by five percentage points at most.

44. Ibid.

Chapter Four

1. Clarence N. Stone, *Regime Politics: Governing Atlanta, 1946–1988* (Lawrence: University Press of Kansas, 1989), pp. 85–98.

2. Robert W. Woodruff was president of Coca-Cola from 1923–38 and in 1945. He was chairman in 1939 and in 1952–54. Although these dates document Woodruff's official and visible roles within the company hierarchy, it is well recognized that he was a figure of central power in running the Coca-Cola Company and in Atlanta politics throughout his lifetime. For further discussion of Woodruff's influence and authority, see Floyd Hunter, *Community Power Structure: A Study of Decision Makers* (Chapel Hill: University of North Carolina Press), 1953, pp. 8–25.

3. Ibid.

4. Ibid., pp. 6–113.

5. Harold H. Martin, *William Berry Hartsfield: Mayor of Atlanta* (Athens: University of Georgia Press, 1978), p. 42.

6. Stone, *Regime Politics*, pp. 219–33.

7. The original version of this civic organization was created in 1941 by downtown business interests as the Central Area Improvement Association. It was later renamed the Central Area Association, and was reorganized in 1966 under its current name.

8. Gary M. Pomerantz, *Where Peachtree Meets Sweet Auburn* (New York: Scribner, 1996), pp. 397–493.

9. This dual dimension of political power has been analyzed by Peter Bachrach and Morton S. Baratz. They contend that when those in power limit the scope of what can be discussed, they create political values and shape institutional processes. Clarence Stone, in an analysis of Floyd Hunter's book, also emphasized this aspect of political power: the power to control the agenda. Stone called it "preemptive" power and saw it as an efficient method used by power elites to avoid conflict. "Instead of expanding resources issue by issue and gaining compliance in that costly fashion," Stone wrote, "elites expend their resources strategically by preventing unfriendly issues from gaining access to the decision making agenda." Peter Bachrach and Morton S. Baratz, "Two Faces of Power," *American Political Science Review* 56 (4): 947–52; Clarence N. Stone, "Preemptive Power: Floyd Hunter's 'Community Power Structure' Reconsidered," *The American Journal of Political Science* 32 (1): 82–104.

10. Pomerantz, *Where Peachtree Meets Sweet Auburn*, p. 457.

11. Ibid., p. 449.

12. Ibid., pp. 458, 459.

13. Author interview with Richard Stogner, Fulton County director of planning and economic development, Atlanta, March 3, 1989.

14. Frederick Allen, *Atlanta Rising: The Invention of an International City, 1946–1996* (Atlanta: Longstreet Press, 1996), p. 180.

15. Stone, *Regime Politics*, pp. 94–96.

16. Allen, *Atlanta Rising*, p. 201.

17. Larry Keating and Maxwell Creighton, "Nonprofit Housing Supply" (Atlanta: Community Design Center of Atlanta, May 1989), pp. 54–67.

18. Pomerantz, *Where Peachtree Meets Sweet Auburn*, pp. 495–98.

19. Charles Rutheiser, *Imagineering Atlanta* (New York: Verso, 1996), p. 4.

20. See the foreword by Andrew Young to Gary Orfield and Carol Ashkinaze's *The Closing Door* (Chicago: University of Chicago Press, 1991), pp. viii–x.

Chapter Five

1. Ivan Allen Jr. with Paul Hemphill, *Mayor: Notes on the Sixties* (New York: Simon & Schuster, 1971), pp. 31–34.

2. Charles Rutheiser, *Imagineering Atlanta* (New York: Verso, 1996), p. 4.

3. Clarence N. Stone, *Regime Politics: Governing Atlanta, 1946–1988* (Lawrence: University Press of Kansas, 1989), pp. 32, 33.

4. Ed Hughes, "Atlanta Must Rebuild 598 Acres," *The Atlanta Journal*, Oct. 3, 1957.

5. When the federal government initiated the urban-renewal program in 1949, it authorized 800,000 units of public housing to meet the need for replacement housing.

6. Leon Eplan, "History of Redevelopment in Atlanta" (lecture. Graduate Program in City Planning, Georgia Institute of Technology, Jan. 19, 1984).

7. Robert A. Thompson, Hylan Lewis, and David McEntire, "Atlanta and Birmingham: A Comparative Study in Negro Housing," in *Studies in Housing and Minority Groups*, ed. Nathan Glazer and Davis McEntire (Berkeley and Los Angeles: University of California Press, 1960), p. 20. Cited in Stone, *Regime Politics*, p. 35.

8. Allen, *Mayor*, p. 156.

9. Ronald H. Bayor, *Race and the Shaping of Twentieth Century Atlanta* (Chapel Hill: University of North Carolina Press, 1996), p. 74.

10. Allen, *Mayor*, p. 158.

11. Bayor, *Race and the Shaping of Twentieth Century Atlanta*, p. 151.

12. Editorial Board, "Grand Plan's Crowning Moment," *The Atlanta Journal-Constitution*, Oct. 30, 1995.

13. Leon Eplan, *Atlanta Stadium Economic and Planning Feasibility Report* (report, Atlanta: Atlanta-Fulton County Recreation Authority, 1964).

14. Community Design Center of Atlanta, *Olympic Impact Neighborhoods* (report, Atlanta: City of Atlanta, 1992), p. 177.

15. Alan M. Voorhees and Associates, *Traffic Impact: Atlanta Model Cities* (report, Atlanta: Model Cities Program, 1970), pp. 1–11.

16. U.S. Bureau of the Census, *1970 U.S. Census of Population* (Washington, DC).

17. Interview with Henry Phipps by Eleanor Hand in "A Re-Viewing of Peoplestown" (unpublished paper, College of Architecture, Georgia Institute of Technology, Spring 1994).

18. *CA Newsletter Supplement* 22 (Aug. 1963). Cited in Clarence N. Stone, *Economic Growth and Neighborhood Discontent: System Bias in the Urban Renewal Program of Atlanta* (Chapel Hill: University of North Carolina Press, 1976), p. 98.

19. Stone, *Economic Growth and Neighborhood Discontent*, p. 101.

20. Ibid., pp. 100, 101.

21. Ibid., p. 102.

22. Ibid., pp. 101–6.

23. Ibid., p. 109.

24. Ibid., p. 110.

25. Douglas E. Wendell, "The Use of Temporary Mobile and Modular Relocation Housing in Urban Renewal Programs," (master's thesis, Graduate Program in City Planning, Georgia Institute of Technology, Aug. 1974), pp. 2, 82.

26. Editorial Board, "Tax to Build Trade Mart Here Rapped," *The Atlanta Constitution*, Jan. 27, 1972.

27. City of Atlanta, Office of Economic Development, *Underground Atlanta Fact Sheet*, circa June 1989.

28. Memorandum from Quintin Tookes, Bureau of Financial Analysis & Auditing, city of Atlanta, to Department of Finance, city of Atlanta, January 18, 1995; Melissa Turner, "Will Underground Survive?" *The Atlanta Journal-Constitution*, Oct. 6, 1997.

29. Interview with Timothy Polk, deputy commissioner, Department of Planning, Development and Neighborhood Conservation, Atlanta, March 30, 1999.

Chapter Six

1. John F. Kain, "Cost-Effective Alternatives to Atlanta's Rail Rapid Transit System," *Journal of Transport Economics and Policy*, 31 (1): 25–49. "If MARTA had pursued alternative policies," Kain concluded, "in particular further improvements in its bus operations and lower fares, it could either have achieved the same levels

of transit for lower cost or far larger increases in ridership with the same real expenditure" (p. 25).

2. Metropolitan Atlanta Rapid Transit Authority, *MARTA Annual Report*, 1973.

3. The city's privately owned bus system, the Atlanta Transit System, published its own transit plan in August 1960. The plan did not capture much public attention. It proposed that fifteen-person cars would distribute passengers throughout the CBD in air-conditioned, transparent plastic tubes one story above the ground. The plan was probably looked on as too weird (Matthew A. Coogan, James H. Landon, James T. Roe, Alan M. Rubin, and Edmund S. Schaffer, *Transportation Politics in Atlanta: The Mass Transit Referendum of November, 1968* [report, Harvard Law School, May 1970], p. 11.)

4. Raleigh Bryans, "Plan Released for Rapid Transit," *The Atlanta Journal*, Aug. 23, 1961.

5. Atlanta Region Metropolitan Planning Commission, *Atlanta Region Comprehensive Plan: Rapid Transit* (report, June 1961), p. 11. Cited in Andrew Marshall Hamer, *The Selling of Rail Rapid Transit* (Lexington, MA: Lexington Books, D.C. Heath & Company, 1976), p. 148.

6. Coogan et al., *Transportation Politics in Atlanta*, p. 49.

7. Ivan Allen Jr. with Paul Hemphill, *Mayor: Notes on the Sixties* (New York: Simon & Schuster, 1971), pp. 68–69.

8. In the city, in unincorporated Fulton County, and in DeKalb and Clayton counties, the amendment received more than 60 percent of the vote. In Gwinnett County, where only 9,408 persons voted, 58.1 percent were in favor. Only in Cobb County was the election close. Out of 28,745 votes, 14,439 favored the amendment, a margin of only 431 votes, or 1.5 percent of the votes cast (Paul Valentine, "Transit Approved; It's Close in Cobb," *The Atlanta Journal*, Nov. 5, 1964).

9. Paul Valentine, "Cobb Alone Says No to Transit Plan," *The Atlanta Journal*, June 17, 1965.

10. Alton Hornsby, Jr., "The Negro in Atlanta Politics, 1961–1973," *Atlanta Historical Society Bulletin* 21 (Spring 1973): 16.

11. Steve Ball Jr., "Negro Unit Voices Transit Condition," *The Atlanta Constitution*, Dec. 11, 1966.

12. Simpson and Curtin, Engineers, *Rapid Busways* (report, June 1967), cited in Hamer, *The Selling of Rail Rapid Transit* (p. 154).

13. The MARTA board opted for bonds issued in MARTA's name. Despite their typically higher interest rates, bonds issued in the name of the authority had the advantage of not counting against local governments' statutory limits for issuing bonds.

14. Coogan et al., *Transportation Politics*, pp. 109, 110.

15. Hamer, *The Selling of Rail Rapid Transit*, p. 162.

16. Ibid., p. 59.

17. Ibid., pp. 61–63.

18. Walker Lundy, "Top Negro Group Opposes Transit," *The Atlanta Constitution*, Nov. 5, 1968.

19. Walker Lundy, "Rapid Transit Fails by Heavy Margin," *The Atlanta Constitution*, Nov. 6, 1968.

20. Coogan et al., *Transportation Politics*, pp. 121, 123.

21. Dick Herbert and Alex Coffin, "Board to Meet Today on Future of MARTA," *The Atlanta Constitution*, Nov. 7, 1968.

22. Hamer, *The Selling of Rail Rapid Transit*, pp. 158–60.

23. Ibid., p. 158.

24. Ibid., pp. 152–54, 158, 159.

25. Cited in Hamer, *The Selling of Rail Rapid Transit*, p. 157. In 1997, CBD employment was 108,716 (Atlanta Regional Commission, *Employment 1997* [report], pp. A–15).

26. Hamer, *The Selling of Rail Rapid Transit*, pp. 158, 159.

27. Cited in ibid., p. 159.

28. M. Dale Henson and James King, "The Atlanta Public-Private Romance: An Abrupt Transformation," in R. Scott Foster and Renee A. Berger, eds., *Public-Private Partnerships in American Cities* (Lexington, MA: Lexington Books, 1982), p. 317.

29. Duane River, "House Approved Tax to Help Rapid Transit," *The Atlanta Journal*, Feb. 24, 1971.

30. Alex Coffin, "Proposed Transit Net Unveiled by MARTA," *The Atlanta Journal*, Apr. 7, 1971.

31. Raleigh Bryans, "26 Black Demands Given to MARTA," *The Atlanta Journal*, July 2, 1971.

32. Alex Coffin, "Rail Line to Perry 15-Cent Fare Given Okay," *The Atlanta Journal*, Aug. 6, 1971.

33. Alex Coffin, "Voters Approve Rapid Transit Plans," *The Atlanta Journal*, Nov. 10, 1971.

34. Phil Gailey and Frank Wells, "MARTA Vote Said Milestone," *The Atlanta Constitution*, Nov. 10, 1971.

35. Clarence N. Stone, *Regime Politics: Governing Atlanta, 1946–1988* (Lawrence: University of Kansas Press, 1989), pp. 99–100.

36. Interview with William Kennedy, former city of Atlanta zoning administrator, Jekyll Island, GA, Oct. 23, 1996.

37. Another reason that office-tower construction in the Midtown area has concentrated along Peachtree Street is that adjoining upper-middle-class neighborhoods in Midtown and Ansley Park have resolutely guarded against any encroachment of commercial development into residential areas.

38. MARTA now has plans for mixed-use development adjacent to the Lindbergh Station between Midtown and Buckhead. And BellSouth has announced plans for office space near the Tenth Street station in Midtown and near the Brookhaven and Lenox Square Stations farther north.

39. Cathy S. Dolman, "MARTA Pondering Whether to Build Perry Homes or Ga. 400 Line First," *The Atlanta Journal-Constitution*, Dec. 10, 1985.

40. Ibid.

41. Durwood McAlister, "14-Year Old Promise Still Hanging Over MARTA," *The Atlanta Journal-Constitution*, Dec. 11, 1985.

42. Gayle White, "New MARTA Panel Given a Deadline," *The Atlanta Journal-Constitution*, Mar. 23, 1986.

43. MARTA, *Study Committee of 50: Report of Findings and Recommendations to the MARTA Board of Directors*, (report, Aug. 1986), appendix.

44. Karen Harris, "Busway to Perry Homes Would Save MARTA $50 Million, Report Says," *The Atlanta Journal-Constitution*, May 22, 1986.

45. Schimpeler, Corradino Associates, "SCA Report" (appendix to MARTA, *Study Committee of 50: Report of Findings*, p. A14.

46. Gayle White, "Northwest Rail Line Loses Vote," *The Atlanta Journal-Constitution*, June 5, 1986; MARTA, *Study Committee of 50: Report of Findings*, appendix.

47. Harvey K. Newman, "A Case Study in Transit Agency-Community Relations" (unpublished paper presented at Urban Affairs Association Conference, Akron, OH, April 1987), pp. 6–8.

48. Author interview with Harvey K. Newman, associate professor, Department of Public Administration and Urban Studies, Georgia State University, Apr. 5, 2000.

49. Karen Harris, "MARTA Seeks Bus Line for Proctor Creek," *The Atlanta Journal-Constitution*, July 24, 1986.

50. Karen Harris, "Blacks On MARTA Panel Walk Out After Proctor Creek," *The Atlanta Journal-Constitution*, Aug. 7, 1986; MARTA: *Study Committee of 50: Report of Findings*, appendix.

51. Karen Harris, "MARTA Panel OKs Rail Service to Perry Homes," *The Atlanta Journal-Constitution*, Aug. 14, 1986; MARTA, *Study Committee of 50: Report of Findings*, p. 1.

52. MARTA, *Study Committee of 50: Report of Findings*, p. 2.

53. This modified report stated that future plans were contingent upon "additional counties joining the Authority, future population and employment patterns, and a detailed evaluation of each segment to determine cost effectiveness, impacts, modes, sequence of construction, and alignments, all as may be determined by the Authority ("Exhibit A: 1986 Amendment to Metropolitan Atlanta Rapid Transit Plan," in "Agenda for the Regular Meeting of the Board of Directors, Metropolitan Atlanta Rapid Transit Authority, Monday, September 22, 1986," p. 5).

54. Karen Harris, "MARTA Board Approves Rail Lines for Georgia 400, Perry Homes," *The Atlanta Journal-Constitution*, Sept. 23, 1986.

55. Interview with John Robinson, deputy director, Fulton County Department of Planning and Economic Development and former executive assistant to the chairman of the Fulton County Board of Commissioners, Atlanta, Apr. 11, 1995.

Chapter Seven

1. Frederick Allen, *Atlanta Rising: The Invention of an International City, 1946–1996* (Atlanta: Longstreet Press, 1996), pp. 24–36.

2. Tom McCollister and L. J. Rosenberg, "Atlanta Interested in Hosting 1996 Olympics," *The Atlanta Journal-Constitution*, Mar. 10, 1987.

3. Melissa Turner, "Coke Chief Played Godfather to Payne's Nascent Dream," *The Atlanta Journal-Constitution*, Jan. 22, 1995.

4. Gary M. Pomerantz, *Where Peachtree Meets Sweet Auburn* (New York: Scribner, 1996), p. 498.

5. Press briefing by Vice President Gore; Mack McLarty; Jamie Gorelick, deputy attorney general, General John Tillelli; Major General Bob Hicks; Mort Downey, deputy secretary of transportation; and Larry Haas, Office of Management and Budget, at the White House briefing room, Washington, DC, May 14, 1996.

6. Douglas A. Blackmon, "Concourse E: Hartsfield's Newest Jewel," *The Atlanta Journal-Constitution*, Sept. 4, 1994.

7. Interview with Leon Eplan, city of Atlanta commissioner of planning and development, Washington, DC, May 8, 1992.

8. City of Atlanta, *Olympic Development Program* (report, July 1992).

9. Atlanta Regional Commission, *Olympic Transportation* (undated report, circa Sept. 1995), p. 9; Office of the Secretary, U.S. Department of Transportation, Joint Program Office for Intelligent Transportation Systems, *Briefing Paper for Atlanta, Georgia*, May 4, 1995, p. 1. Transportation officials in other states also viewed the system as a project inspired by the Olympics. After federal funding for the system was announced, they complained that Atlanta was using the Olympics as a means of unfairly capturing too much of the scarce discretionary federal money available for transportation projects (author interview with Kelly Love, transportation planner, Atlanta Regional Commission, Oct. 15, 1995).

10. The federal government's contribution of $79.9 million to help pay for security at the Games was fought unsuccessfully in Congress by Senator John McCain of Arizona, who argued that either ACOG or Atlanta should pay the full cost (Mike Christensen, "Washington's Money Pipeline for '96 Flowing; GA's Delegation Secures $40 Million in Funding," *The Atlanta Journal-Constitution*, Oct. 15, 1994).

11. Lyle V. Harris, "Deal Reached to Repay City for '96 Costs," *The Atlanta Journal-Constitution*, Oct. 16, 1995; Lyle V. Harris, "Negotiations Went Down to Wire on Final Document," *The Atlanta Journal-Constitution*, Jan. 12, 1996.

12. Lyle V. Harris, "Outside City, Games May Cost Locales," *The Atlanta Journal-Constitution*, Dec. 11, 1995.

13. Kent E. Walker and Shawn Evans Mitchell, "'ACOG Owes Us,' Says Stone Mountain," *The Atlanta Journal-Constitution*, June 17, 1996.

14. Jeffrey M. Humphreys and Michael K. Plummer, *The Economic Impact on the State of Georgia of Hosting the 1996 Olympic Games* (report, University of Georgia, Selig Center for Economic Growth, June 1995), p. 9.

15. Donald Ratajczak, "Impact of Olympics Won't Be Known Until Long After Athletes Leave," *The Atlanta Journal-Constitution*, May 16, 1995.

16. Humphreys and Plummer, *The Economic Impact on the State of Georgia*, p. 57.

17. Gross domestic state product would be a superior measure if it were available, but it is not. Total personal income typically runs approximately 10 percent less than gross domestic state product. It's less because it does not include depreciation, indirect business taxes, retained corporate profits, contributions for social insurance, adjustments for interest income, or business-transfer payments.

18. Suzanne A. Lindsay and Beata D. Kochut, *Economic Yearbook for Georgia's MSA's for 1996* (report, University of Georgia, Selig Center for Economic Growth, Dec. 1995), pp. 78, 83.

19. Humphreys and Plummer, *The Economic Impact on the State of Georgia*, pp. 25, 105–8.

20. David L. Sjoquist, *The 1996 Summer Olympics Sales Tax Revenue: Implications for Government Budgets* (report, Georgia State University, Research Atlanta, and the Policy Research Center, June 1995), p. 2.

21. Ibid., p. 5.

22. Douglas A. Blackmon, "Ticket Tax Nothing New to Big Cities," *The Atlanta Journal-Constitution*, Jan. 17, 1995.

23. Lyle V. Harris, "Shielding Taxpayers from the Games," *The Atlanta Journal-Constitution*, Oct. 2, 1994.

24. Sallye Salter, "Construction Costs Going Up," *The Atlanta Journal-Constitution*, Mar. 23, 1995.

25. Ibid.

26. Sallye Salter, "Metro-Area Building Costs Head Skyward: Olympic Deals Pushing Surge," *The Atlanta Journal-Constitution*, June 22, 1994.

27. Salter, "Construction Costs Going Up."

28. Lyle V. Harris, "Put Rent-Gouging on the Agenda," *The Atlanta Journal-Constitution*, Aug. 13, 1996.

29. Melissa Turner, "Games Gouging Hard to Bear, Official Says," *The Atlanta Journal-Constitution*, Aug. 3, 1995.

30. Shelly Emling, "Anti-Gouging Bill Apparently Dead," *The Atlanta Journal-Constitution*, Feb. 9, 1996.

31. It's known that at least seven transitional-housing facilities emptied their buildings, renovated them, and sought Olympic windfalls (Kelly Cooney, "Supply Side Analysis of Weekly Rentals" [unpublished paper, Graduate Program in City Planning, Georgia Institute of Technology, Mar. 1996]).

32. David Pendered, "Mayor, City Officials Push for Bond Issue: Critics Predict Failure," *The Atlanta Journal-Constitution*, July 7, 1993; Douglas A. Blackmon, "Council Resuscitates Bond Vote for July 19," *The Atlanta Journal-Constitution*, May 17, 1994.

33. Ellen A. Murray, *Stormwater Drainage in Atlanta* (report, Research Atlanta, Sept. 1991); interview with Albert Buckmaster, senior planner, Department of Planning, Development, and Neighborhood Conservation, Atlanta, Feb. 3, 1994; Editorial Board, "Mere Millions Won't Rebuild City," *The Atlanta Journal-Constitution*, Sept. 4, 1993.

34. Douglas A. Blackmon and Bernadette Burden, "Two Killed as Storm Deluges City, Causes Parking Cave-in," *The Atlanta Journal-Constitution*, June 15, 1993.

35. Peter Montius, "Aging Pipe Links River, Reservoir," *The Atlanta Journal-Constitution*, Jan. 20, 1994.

36. Metropolitan Atlanta Olympic Games Authority, *Olympic Neighborhood Development: A Project Update* (undated report, circa Spring 1996).

37. Author interview with Moses Steele Jr., registered appraiser and managing broker, M.S.A. Realty, Atlanta, Aug. 24, 1999.

38. Mark Sherman, "Olympics Seen as Catalyst to Fight Poverty," *The Atlanta Journal-Constitution*, Oct. 24, 1990.

39. Community Design Center of Atlanta, *Olympic Impact Neighborhoods* (report, City of Atlanta, Apr. 1992), pp. 15, 32, 50, 80, 98, 112.

40. Ruth Eckdish Knack, "Empowerment to the People," *Planning* 59 (2): 21.

41. Bert Roughton Jr. and Alma Hill, "A Strategy for Upgrading Olympic Neighborhoods," *The Atlanta Journal-Constitution*, May 24, 1991.

42. Bert Roughton Jr., "'Twin Peaks of Mount Olympus,'" *The Atlanta Journal-Constitution*, July 21, 1991.

43. The Atlanta Project, *TAP: Moving Toward a New Community: A Chronological Summary of The Atlanta Project* (report, Sept. 1, 1999), p. 1.

44. City of Atlanta, *Olympic Development Program* (report, City of Atlanta, July 27, 1992), p. 7.

45. Michael W. Giles, *Evaluation of The Atlanta Project, Part 2: Analysis and Findings* (Atlanta: Carter Collaboration Center, Jan. 6, 1995), p. 63.

46. The Atlanta Project, "Appendix: Community Legacies" in *TAP: Moving Toward a New Community*, pp. A-4–A-10.

47. Giles, *Evaluation of The Atlanta Project*, p. 14.

48. Author interview with Patrick Burke, research associate, data and policy analysis division, The Atlanta Project, Atlanta, Dec. 23, 1999.

49. Ibid.

Chapter Eight

1. Laventhol & Horwath, *Alternative Stadium Options in Metropolitan Atlanta* (report, Georgia Department of Budget and Planning, June 1986).

2. Frederick Allen, *Atlanta Rising: The Invention of an International City, 1946–1996* (Atlanta: Longstreet Press, 1996), p. 237.

3. Bert Roughton Jr., "Olympics Residents Worried," *The Atlanta Journal-Constitution*, Oct. 30, 1990.

4. Bert Roughton Jr., "Fight Vowed Over '96 Stadium," *The Atlanta Journal-Constitution*, Nov. 29, 1990.

5. Susan Laccetti, "Opponents of Stadium Site Hold Vigil at Payne's Dunwoody Home," *The Atlanta Journal-Constitution*, Feb. 4, 1993.

6. Bert Roughton Jr. and Michele Hiskey, "Old Stadium Will Be Razed After Games," *The Atlanta Journal-Constitution*, Aug. 30, 1991.

7. Michele Hiskey, "Residents Demand a Voice," *The Atlanta Journal-Constitution*, Feb. 27, 1992.

8. Tom Lowe, "Braves Win, Taxpayers Lose in Stadium Deal" (letter to the editor), *The Atlanta Journal-Constitution*, Mar. 2, 1993.

9. Bert Roughton Jr. and Michele Hiskey, "11th Hour Demand Leaves Stadium Deal up in Air," *The Atlanta Journal-Constitution*, Feb. 17, 1993.

10. Bert Roughton Jr., "Reluctant Panel OK's Plan to End Stalemate," *The Atlanta Journal-Constitution*, Feb. 25, 1993.

11. Douglas A. Blackmon, "Council Avoids Risk, Supports Stadium," *The Atlanta Journal-Constitution*, Mar. 2, 1993.

12. Ken Foskett, "Lowe Moving to Kill the Pact in the Last Minutes," *The Atlanta Journal-Constitution*, Mar. 3, 1993. Commissioner Lowe, who was also a member of the Atlanta–Fulton County Recreation Authority board, estimated the future unfunded taxpayer liability for the new stadium at $214 million (Lowe, "Braves Win, Taxpayers Lose in Stadium Deal").

13. Bert Roughton Jr., "Search for Alternative Site Begins," *The Atlanta Journal-Constitution*, Mar. 4, 1993.

14. Tom Baxter, "City Saves Face, But Did It Need To?" *The Atlanta Journal-Constitution*, Mar. 11, 1993.

15. Telephone interview with Jane Fortson, Progress and Freedom Foundation, Washington, DC, June 27, 1995. At the time the AHA submitted this proposal to the AOC, Fortson was chairwoman of the AHA board of commissioners.

16. Atlanta Housing Authority, *Techwood Homes: 50 Years of Growth, Hope, and Progress* (report, August 1986), p. 1; Charles F. Palmer, *Adventures of a Slumfighter* (Atlanta: Tupper and Lane, Inc., 1955), p. 10; Howard W. Pollard, "The Effect of Techwood Homes on Urban Development in the United States" (master's thesis, Georgia Institute of Technology, 1968), p. 21; U.S. Public Works Administration, *America Builds* (Washington, DC: U.S. Government Printing Office, 1953), p. 201.

17. J. Michael Gurnee, "An Historic Preservation/Conservation Proposal for Techwood Homes" (unpublished paper, Graduate Program in City Planning, Georgia Institute of Technology, 1975), pp. 4–5.

18. Atlanta Housing Authority, "Resident Characteristics Report." June 1990.

19. Paul Austin, memo to Robert Woodruff, June 11, 1071 (Robert Woodruff Papers, Emory Special Collections, Emory University, Atlanta).

20. Allen, *Atlanta Rising*, p. 186.

21. Mark Silk, "Using Olympics to Help Public Housing Tenants," *The Atlanta Journal-Constitution*, Mar. 21, 1991.

22. Bert Roughton Jr., "Techwood Eyes on Olympics Prize," *The Atlanta Journal-Constitution*, Mar. 17, 1991.

23. Ibid.

24. Darren T. Hamilton, "City's Top Officials Hold Fate of Techwood Homes," *The Atlanta Daily World*, Apr. 11, 1991; Mark Sherman, "Techwood Tenants Agree to 6-month Planning With City," *The Atlanta Journal-Constitution*, Apr. 9, 1991; Editorial Board, "The Chance to Change Techwood," *The Atlanta Journal-Constitution*, Apr 11, 1991.

25. Sallye Salter, "AHA Unanimously Chooses Team to Create Master Plan for Techwood," *The Atlanta Journal-Constitution*, July 19, 1991.

26. Cynthia Durcanin, "Tenants Give Approval," *The Atlanta Journal-Constitution*, Oct. 2, 1991.

27. PATH, "Revitalization Proposal for Techwood/Clark Howell," Sept. 21, 1991.

28. Atlanta Housing Authority, *Resident Characteristics, Head of Household Family Income Report* (May 14, 1995) data current through June 1990.

29. Larry Keating and Carol Flores, "Sixty and Out: Techwood Homes Transformed by Enemies and Friends," *Journal of Urban History*, Mar. 2000.

30. Raymond A. Harris, regional administrator, U.S. Department of Housing and Urban Development, memo to Joseph G. Schiff, assistant secretary for public and Indian housing, U.S. Department of Housing and Urban Development, Washington, DC, n.d.; and Gary Pomerantz, "Feds Rebuke AHA Plan to Revamp Techwood," *The Atlanta Journal-Constitution*, Dec. 25, 1991.

31. PATH, *Proposal for Techwood/Clark Howell Homes* (unpaginated report, Sept. 21, 1991): under "Community Resources and Financing" section; Jane Fortson interview, June 27, 1995.

32. Bert Roughton Jr., "HUD 'Very Supportive' of Techwood Plan," *The Atlanta Journal-Constitution*, Jan. 11, 1991.

33. Sallye Salter and Maria Saporta, "Coca-Cola Backs Off Proposal to Build Office Tower," *The Atlanta Journal-Constitution*, Jan. 31, 1992.

34. Joseph G. Schiff, assistant secretary for public and Indian housing, U.S. Department of Housing and Urban Development, memo to Raymond A. Harris, regional administrator, Washington, DC, Feb. 14, 1991, p. 1.

35. Bert Roughton Jr. and Sallye Salter, "Feds Blast Techwood Games Plan," *The Atlanta Journal-Constitution*, Feb. 22, 1992.

36. Bert Roughton Jr., "Techwood Proposal Shaping Up," *The Atlanta Journal-Constitution*, Mar. 7, 1992.

37. Lyle V. Harris, "AHA Rejects Bid for New Techwood Redevelopment Plan," *The Atlanta Journal-Constitution*, Apr. 8, 1992.

38. Lyle V. Harris, "Martin Bows Out of Techwood Planning," *The Atlanta Journal-Constitution*, May 19, 1992.

39. A. Reid, "AHA to Go Ahead with Sale of Four Techwood Acres," *The Atlanta Journal-Constitution*, Apr. 6, 1993.

40. Atlanta Housing Authority (May 26, 1993), pp. 65–66.

41. Darryl Fears, "Some Say Mayor's Involvement Could Hamper Director Search," *The Atlanta Journal-Constitution*, May 17, 1994.

42. Interview with Renee Glover, executive director, Atlanta Housing Authority, Atlanta, Jan. 13, 1995; interview with John Sweet, chairman, Atlanta Housing Authority Board of Directors, Atlanta, May 8, 1995.

43. Renee Glover, *New Trends in Downtown Housing: Location and Product* (presentation at the Conference on Housing in Downtown Atlanta, Rialto Center for the Performing Arts, Atlanta, May 9, 1997).

44. Atlanta Housing Authority, *Revised Revitalization Plan for the Redevelopment of the Techwood Area* (Mar. 17, 1995), p. 12.

45. Ibid., pp. 29–32.

46. Larry Keating, *Analyses and Recommendations for the City of Atlanta's Year 2000 Consolidated Plan* (draft report, Dec. 22, 1999), p. 15.

47. Jane Fortson interview, June 27, 1995.

48. Atlanta Housing Authority, *Vacancy Prep Status Report, 1990–1993*.

49. Author's notes, meeting of planning task force, Techwood Homes, Atlanta, Feb. 7, 1995.

50. Lyle V. Harris, "Techwood's New Beginning," *The Atlanta Journal-Constitution*, Feb. 28, 1995.

51. Atlanta Housing Authority, *A Report on the Reinvention of the Atlanta Housing Authority: Imagine a Great City* (circa Mar. 1998), Section 10 unpaginated.

52. Atlanta Housing Authority, *HOPE VI/URD* (HUD Quarterly Narrative Performance Report for Jan. 1, 1997 through Mar. 31, 1997), April 30, 1997.

53. Atlanta Housing Authority, *Report on the Reinvention of the Atlanta Housing Authority.*"

54. Keating and Flores, "Sixty and Out," p. 301.

55. Author interview with Noel Kahlil, executive director, Techwood Park Inc., Nov. 15, 1993.

56. Bert Roughton Jr., "Payne Proposes Olympic Legacy," *The Atlanta Journal-Constitution*, Nov. 19, 1993.

57. Melissa Turner, "Billy Payne's Park: How the Pieces Came Together," *The Atlanta Journal-Constitution*, May 29, 1994.

58. In a television documentary broadcast two years after the park proposal had been announced, Jackson was asked how he had learned about the park. He responded, "Well, I found out through the newspaper. Even though I am the city mayor, I found out through the newspaper" (Roger Torta and Kathy Sullivan, *Fences and Neighbors* [PBS documentary, June 6, 1996]).

59. City of Atlanta, *C-5 Central Business Support District Regulation, Atlanta Zoning Ordinance*, Jan. 1992, pp. 16–15.001.

60. Central Atlanta Progress and city of Atlanta, *Executive Summary of Marietta Street Sub-Area Study*, 1985.

61. Larry Keating and Maxwell Creighton, *A Geographic Information System for Techwood Park* (report, Community Design Center of Atlanta, Nov. 1993), pp. 8, 37.

62. Ibid., p. 37.

63. Ibid.

64. Ibid., pp. 15, 17, 18.

65. Cynthia A. Eidson, *Loft Development: An Urban Redevelopment Tool* (thesis option paper, Graduate Program in City Planning, Georgia Institute of Technology, Nov. 1994), pp. 6–45.

66. Interview with Richard Rothman, principal of Richard Rothman and Associates, architects, Atlanta, Sept. 6, 1995.

67. Zewdie Bekele, *The Impact of the Centennial Park on Existing Businesses* (thesis option paper, Graduate Program in City Planning, Georgia Institute of Technology, June 1, 1994), pp. 27–32.

68. Richard Rothman and Associates, *Techwood Park Redevelopment Plan*, Jan. 1994, p. 2.

69. Turner, "Billy Payne's Park."

70. Georgia Legislature, Senate Bill 569, 1994.

71. Sallye Salter and Melissa Turner, "Officials Trim Size of Olympic Park," *The Atlanta Journal-Constitution*, May 12, 1994.

72. Melissa Turner, "Analysis: Coca-Cola Finds a Site to Stage Its Games Fest," *The Atlanta Journal-Constitution*, July 21, 1994.

73. Melissa Turner and Maria Saporta, "Brick by Brick, Centennial Park Closer to Reality," *The Atlanta Journal-Constitution*, Sept. 24, 1994; Melissa Turner, "Olympic Atlanta Takes Shape," *The Atlanta Journal-Constitution*, Sept. 29, 1994; Melissa Turner, "ACOG Expects Windfall From Sale of Centennial Olympic Park Bricks," *The Atlanta Journal-Constitution*, Oct. 13, 1994.

74. Sallye Salter, "Developing Downtown," *The Atlanta Journal-Constitution*, Feb. 28, 1996.

Index

Williams, John, 134
Williams, Sam, 134
Williams, Sam A., 122
Williamson, Q. V., 122
Woodruff, Robert, 71, 79, 176
Woodruff Foundation, 5, 178, 191
Wyly, Elvin, 59

Young, Andrew, 57, 70, 81–82, 84–87, 89, 110–11, 131, 133, 135, 136, 146, 202, 203, 205–6, 207–8

zoning, 46–48, 51–53, 100, 129; back alley dwelling law, 48; class discrimination, 61–67; restrictive, 51–53